The Past Can't Heal Us

In this innovative study, Lea David critically investigates the relationship between human rights and memory, suggesting that, instead of understanding human rights in a normative fashion, human rights should be treated as an ideology. Conceptualising human rights as an ideology gives us useful theoretical and methodological tools to recognise the real impact human rights has on the ground. David traces the rise of the global phenomenon that is the human rights memorialisation agenda, termed 'moral remembrance', and explores what happens once this agenda becomes implemented. Based on evidence from the Western Balkans and Israel/Palestine, she argues that the human rights memorialisation agenda does not lead to a better appreciation of human rights; instead, contrary to what would be expected, it serves to strengthen national sentiments, divisions and animosities along ethnic lines, and leads to the new forms of societal inequalities that are closely connected to different forms of corruptions.

LEA DAVID is Assistant Professor and Ad Astra Fellow at the School of Sociology, University College Dublin. She has held the prestigious Fulbright, Jonathan Shapira and Marie Curie postdoctoral fellowships and established the Critical Thinking on Memory and Human Rights Research Group.

Human Rights in History

Edited by

Stefan-Ludwig Hoffmann, University of California, Berkeley

Samuel Moyn, Yale University, Connecticut

This series showcases new scholarship exploring the backgrounds of human rights today. With an open-ended chronology and international perspective, the series seeks works attentive to the surprises and contingencies in the historical origins and legacies of human rights ideals and interventions. Books in the series will focus not only on the intellectual antecedents and foundations of human rights, but also on the incorporation of the concept by movements, nation-states, international governance, and transnational law.

A full list of titles in the series can be found at:
www.cambridge.org/human-rights-history

The Past Can't Heal Us
The Dangers of Mandating Memory in the Name of Human Rights

Lea David
University College Dublin

CAMBRIDGE
UNIVERSITY PRESS

University Printing House, Cambridge CB2 8BS, United Kingdom

One Liberty Plaza, 20th Floor, New York, NY 10006, USA

477 Williamstown Road, Port Melbourne, VIC 3207, Australia

314-321, 3rd Floor, Plot 3, Splendor Forum, Jasola District Centre, New Delhi - 110025, India

103 Penang Road, #05-06/07, Visioncrest Commercial, Singapore 238467

Cambridge University Press is part of the University of Cambridge.

It furthers the University's mission by disseminating knowledge in the pursuit of education, learning and research at the highest international levels of excellence.

www.cambridge.org
Information on this title: www.cambridge.org/9781108817103
DOI: 10.1017/9781108861311

© Lea David 2020

This publication is in copyright. Subject to statutory exception and to the provisions of relevant collective licensing agreements, no reproduction of any part may take place without the written permission of Cambridge University Press.

First published 2020
First paperback edition 2022

A catalogue record for this publication is available from the British Library

Library of Congress Cataloging in Publication data
Names: David, Lea, 1976– author.
Title: The past can't heal us : the dangers of mandating memory in the name of human rights / Lea David.
Description: Cambridge, United Kingdom ; New York : Cambridge University Press, 2020. | Series: Human rights in history | Includes bibliographical references and index.
Identifiers: LCCN 2020002613 (print) | LCCN 2020002614 (ebook) | ISBN 9781108495189 (hardback) | ISBN 9781108817103 (paperback) | ISBN 9781108861311 (ebook)
Subjects: LCSH: Human rights–Philosophy. | Memorialization. | Collective memory.
Classification: LCC JC571 .D33274 2020 (print) | LCC JC571 (ebook) | DDC 323.01–dc23
LC record available at https://lccn.loc.gov/2020002613
LC ebook record available at https://lccn.loc.gov/2020002614

ISBN   978-1-108-49518-9   Hardback
ISBN   978-1-108-81710-3   Paperback

Cambridge University Press has no responsibility for the persistence or accuracy of URLs for external or third-party internet websites referred to in this publication, and does not guarantee that any content on such websites is, or will remain, accurate or appropriate.

Contents

	Acknowledgements	*page* vi
	List of Abbreviations	ix
1	Introduction	1
2	Human Rights As an Ideology? Obstacles and Benefits	21
3	What Is Moral Remembrance?	41
4	The Institutionalisation of Moral Remembrance: Case Study of Palestine and Israel	66
5	The Institutionalisation of Moral Remembrance: Case Study of the Western Balkans	95
6	Human Rights, Memory and Micro-Solidarity	124
7	Mandating Memory, Mandating Conflicts	186
	Bibliography	214
	Index	240

Acknowledgements

This book is a product of my intellectual growth – from my PhD, when I timidly dared to start developing my own perspective, throughout four postdoctoral fellowships, during which I learned how to dive bravely into the depths of knowledge, without fear and intimidation.

Though I hope this book will contribute to our academic efforts to provoke a meaningful debate on moral remembrance and to disclose the often hidden relationships between ideals and politics and between wishful thinking and real outcomes on the ground, as well as the spectrum of complexities that define those relationships, this book also sheds some light on its author. In a sense, similar to the ways in which anthropology of the body uses scars, bodily deviations or a tooth index to narrate life stories, this book discloses my own, unique path. The imprints I leave here are all a testimony to people who have inspired me, supported me along the way or disputed my approach. My gratitude, my contemplations, my anxieties – all are engraved here in theories and arguments I have used, in particular examples I have showcased and in the voids and silences that appear sporadically in the text.

My biggest and eternal gratitude goes to Siniša Malešević, the world's leading sociologist on nationalism and my Marie Curie Fellowship supervisor (2017–2019) at University College Dublin (UCD), whose intellectual work has had a crucial impact on the ways in which I make sense of the world. I truly doubt that, without his conceptual frameworks and theoretical insights, this book would have had the slightest chance to blossom. His academic impact on my intellectual development, though gargantuan, is nevertheless tiny when compared to the human side of his impact, along with his commitment, evident in his endless support and his willingness to engage in debates, explanations and advice on how to navigate the jungle of knowledge. His kindness, his good intentions and his tenacious encouragement have guided me through the roller coaster of research and writing, and all are imprinted here in this book.

Two other people deserve a special acknowledgement, as my endless conversations with them inspired me, shaped the way I think and left an anthropological footprint on this book. The first is Robert M. Hayden, from the University of Pittsburgh, who was my mentor during my Fulbright Fellowship and who has continued to actively engage with my work – to comment on it, often to tear it apart, to engage with it, to discuss it, to contest it – always pushing me to be courageous and to go against the stream if necessary, even if it is at the expense of being, in an academic sense, not 'popular'. Second, I wish to thank Carol Kidron, who was there for me after I obtained my PhD, when my future looked very bleak and uncertain, and who supervised some of my first independent research. Her work inspired me profoundly, and this book, in many ways, emerged through the cracks she opened for me. She encouraged me to explore them further.

It would be an understatement to say that the many other interactions – long and short – I have had with the people who have influenced my work were 'significant'. Rather, they were decisive, providing me with my intellectual and academic home. My PhD supervisors, Lev Grinberg and Jackie Feldman, gave me both sociological and anthropological foundations in the subjects of memory and nationalism, and the tools to take my first steps independently into research and publishing. In fact, the entire Sociology and Anthropology Department at the Ben Gurion University in the Negev – in particular, Uri Ram, Yulia Lerner, Sara Helman and Nir Avrieli – guided me and supported me in one way or another throughout my PhD and after. At Haifa University, where I held my first postdoctoral fellowship, my research was warmly welcomed and supported by the newly opened and truly inspiring Anthropology Department, in particular by Amalia Saar, and by Arieh Kochavi and Yael Granot-Bein at the Weiss-Livnat International Program in Holocaust Studies. I owe special gratitude to Adriana Kamp from the Sociology and Anthropology Department at Tel Aviv University, who was my adviser but became my friend.

I am endlessly grateful to Malešević for introducing me to the Dubrovnik Divided Societies faculty group, Saša Božić, Niall Ó Dochartaigh, Biljana Kašić, Daphne Winland, Simona Kuti and others. My long conversations with Miguel A. Centeno and Deborah A. Kaple from the Department of Sociology at Princeton University lured me into this endless pit of curiosity that led to a breakthrough in my research. However, my ability to thrive was largely due to my academic home, at UCD's School of Sociology, where I was based during my Marie Curie Fellowship and where I was fortunate enough to be accepted as a permanent faculty member. Small and big talks in the school hallway, guest lectures and day-to-day activities with the faculty members – Andreas Hess, Alice Friedman, Gerard Boucher, Mathew Creighton, Barbara Gornicka,

Thomas Grund, Steven Loyal, Aogán Mulcahy, Sara O'Sullivan, Ruben Flores, Veronica Baker, Deirdre Brophy and others – made me feel welcomed and able to ask, enquire, suggest, propose, discuss or contest freely any ideas that I was struggling with at the time. One person, besides Siniša Malešević, especially made me really feel that this is not a stop on the way to another institutional home –that this IS where I want to be. The Head of the School of Sociology, Iarfhlaith Watson, created an atmosphere of support, appreciation and transparency, without animosity and hostility, but just kindness, which proved to be a true remedy for my soul and body. It felt like a home away from home, a place where the journey could stop and I could just become.

Several conversations about the book brought me in touch with some of the greatest scholars of our times, to whom I am extremely grateful. They were kind enough to listen, open to suggesting and keen to help, and they include Bob Clifford, Omer Bartov and Eric Weitz. My huge thanks go to the editors of the Cambridge University Press series 'Human Rights in History', Samuel Moyn and Stefan-Ludwig Hoffmann, as well as to Michael Watson, the senior commissioning editor, and Emily Sharp, the editorial assistant for History and Area Studies, who helped me go through the process of getting the book manuscript ready.

Many others along the way helped me tie my thoughts together into one solid structure: Gruia Badescu, Taylor MacConnell, Cecile Blaser, Sven Milekić and the entire research network on 'Critical Thinking on Memory and Human Rights' where I discussed my research findings on several occasions. Sporadic conversations with Hannes Baumann, Erika Harris, Orli Fridman, Yossi Harpaz, Filip Ejdus, Jasna Dragović-Soso, Jelena Subotić, Mischa Gabowitsch and many, many others helped me tremendously in shaping my research. I also want to thank Gary Branigan, who has been there closely editing my work since its very inception, and my sister Mia David, who had to suffer my endless talks on my desires, aspirations and disappointments on how the book cover should look.

Finally, it was my family who had the best and the worst of me during this entire process. My husband Nery, my twin daughters Aya and Zoe, our late dog Riva and our new dog Sushi – at the end of the day, they were my anchor, my tribe. Thank you for moving continents, changing culture, weather and landscape for me, and pushing me to dare against all the odds!

This project has received funding from the European Union's Horizon 2020 research and innovation programme under the Marie Skłodowska-Curie grant agreement No 745922.

Abbreviations

AAA	American Anthropological Association
ASA	American Sociological Association
BADIL	Resource Centre for Palestinian Residency and Refugee Rights NGO
BDS	Boycott Divestment and Sanctions movement
BiH	Bosnia and Herzegovina
CFP	Combatants for Peace
CNA	Centre for Nonviolent Action
CSF	Civil Society Facility
EIDHR	European Instrument for Democracy and Human Rights
ENP	European Neighbourhood Policy
EP	European Parliament
EU	European Union
FBiH	Federation of Bosnia and Herzegovina
FGD	focus group discussion
FGYO	Southeast Europe Initiative of the French–German Youth Office
ICC	International Criminal Court
ICCPR	International Covenant on Civil and Political Rights
ICESCR	International Covenant on Economic, Social and Cultural Rights
ICTR	International Criminal Tribunal for Rwanda
ICTY	International Criminal Tribunal for Yugoslavia
IDF	Israeli Defense Forces
IDP	internally displaced persons
IFI	international financial institution
IHRA	International Holocaust Remembrance Alliance
IMTFE	International Military Tribunal for the Far East
INGO	international non-governmental organisation
IPA	Instrument for Pre-accession Assistance
IPCRI	Israel–Palestine Center for Research and Information

IPSOS	Ipsos Group S.A., a global market research and consulting firm
IPTF	International Police Task Force
ISA	International Sociological Association
IW	Impunity Watch
JAT	Yugoslav Airlines Transportation
JNA	Yugoslav People's Army
LGBTI	lesbian, gay, bisexual, transgender and intersex community
MECA	Middle East Children's Alliance
NANSEN	NANSEN Dialogue Centre
NATO	North Atlantic Treaty Organization
NGO	non-governmental organisation
NORAD	Norwegian Directorate for Development Cooperation
NSSP	Neveh Shalom/Wahat el Salam School for Peace
ODIHR	Office for Democratic Institutions and Human Rights
OHCHR	United Nations Office of the High Commissioner for Human Rights
OHR	Office of the High Representative
OPT	occupied Palestinian territory
OSCE	Organization for Security and Co-operation in Europe
P2P	People 2 People Programme
PA	Palestinian Authority
PCFF	Parents Circle–Families Forum
PLO	Palestinian Liberation Organization
PLU	person like us
PNA	Palestinian National Authority
PRIME	Peace Research Institute in the Middle East
R2P	Responsibility to Protect
RECOM	Regional Commission Tasked with Establishing the Facts about All Victims of War Crimes and Other Serious Human Rights Violations Committed on the Territory of the Former Yugoslavia from 1 January 1991 to 31 December 2001
RS	Republika Srpska
RYCO	Regional Youth Cooperation Office
SFRJ	Socialist Federal Republic of Yugoslavia
SIDA	Swedish International Development Agency
SUBNOR	Association of Fighters of the National Liberation War
TRC	Truth and Reconciliation Commissions
UDHT	Universal Declaration of Human Rights

UN	United Nations
UNRWA	United Nations Relief and Works Agency
USAID	United States Agency for International Development
USHMM	United States Holocaust Memorial Museum
VLJI	Van Leer Jerusalem Institute
YIHR	Youth Initiative for Human Rights

1 Introduction

On December 7, 1970, German Chancellor Willy Brandt laid down a wreath at the memorial of the Jewish ghetto in Warsaw. He stepped back, and fell to his knees in front of the memorial, remaining completely still for half a minute on the wet stone floor. This small and spontaneous, yet powerful gesture was a changing moment in world history, seemingly opening up new possibilities for post-conflict reconciliation. Yet, 35 years later, on 11 July 2015, on the twentieth anniversary of the Srebrenica mass killing of 8,000 Bosnian Muslim men and boys, when Serbian Prime Minister Aleksandar Vučić came to pay respect to the Srebrenica survivors, instead of manifesting a moment of catharsis, he was forced to flee the memorial after being stoned by an angry Bosniak mob. They pelted him with stones, shoes and bottles as he arrived at the mass burial held to mark the atrocities. Prime Minister Vučić had been explicitly and heavily pressured by the international community, weeks prior to the event, to publicly apologise for the genocide committed in 1995.[1] But instead of finding the dignity accorded to the 'Brandt moment', a rock was thrown that struck him in the face, breaking his glasses. Why did those two events of public apology have such completely different outcomes? Why did the international community pressure Serbian Prime Minister Vučić into apologising in the name of the Serbian people? Most importantly, how did this gesture affect realities on the ground?

This book is about the rise of a new phenomenon worldwide – termed here *moral remembrance*. Moral remembrance prescribes standards for a 'proper way of remembrance' with which states are expected to comply when dealing with legacies of mass human rights abuses. It refers to a standardised, isomorphic set of norms, and is based on normative worldviews of human rights that promote 'facing the past', 'duty to remember' and 'justice for victims' as its pillars. Moral remembrance points to the current preference, worldwide, for memory standardisation, institutional

---

[1] See all three Srebrenica Genocide Resolutions adopted on 7 July 2005, 15 January 2009 and 7 July 2015.

homogenisation and norm imitation. It provides a technocratic-like set of policies and a tool kit of practices that aim to advance a human rights vision of memorialisation processes to promote democratic human rights values across the globe.

This book brings into question one of the most basic, deeply embedded assumptions in human rights and transitional justice: that 'proper' memorialisation is a crucial step in establishing moral responsibility for past atrocities and, consequently, human rights values in conflict and post-conflict settings. This study questions whether such standardisation is useful in achieving 'reconciliation' through close analysis of the actual effects – in real-life settings – of attempts to mandate history in, and after, ethnic conflict; it sees such standardisation as being generally ineffective at best and counterproductive at worst. The book argues that the human rights memorialisation agenda is constructed and adopted as a result of experiences based on historically grounded events that, once transformed into policy-oriented memorialisation efforts, translate into an oppressive force. Along the way, those de-contextualised memorialisation efforts produce a long list of false premises that, for the reasons elaborated in the book, in the long run end up enforcing divisions on the ground.

Standardisation of Memory at the World Polity Level

Since the late eighteenth century, national memory has been largely regarded as an internal matter for nation-states. However, in the course of the past several decades, we have witnessed a growing global trend that promotes the idea that societies, just like individuals, inevitably need to face and deal with their troubled past to prevent a recurrence of violence and to promote democratic and human rights values. This notion argues that memorialisation has become 'a critical element in current struggles for human rights and democracy' (Brett et. al. 2007: 1). The term 'memorialisation' covers a range of initiatives that aim 'to preserve the memory of past abuses for present and future generations, by such means as monuments, museums, commemorative ceremonies, and rituals' (Blustein 2012: 19). Attempts, at the world polity level, to find and implement proper policies and modes of memorialisation for societies involved in massive human rights abuses, starting from World War II onwards, gave birth to myriad approaches and methods that promise to secure a sustainable peace and a gradual transition to democracy. The global memorialisation agenda, promoted through various institutions, polices, discourses and practices, is closely connected with, and gains its power and legitimacy from, the transnational human rights regime. Approaches such as peacebuilding, transitional justice and conflict transformation, management, resolution and reconciliation are, broadly speaking, offspring of the presumption, advanced by the human rights agenda (or regime), that the implementation of human rights values and norms is a condition for the proper memorialisation of atrocities. They are used and implemented under the assumption that a proper, morally driven memorialisation can transform and direct nationalist realities in conflict and post-conflict societies towards a non-violent course, simultaneously placing them on a safe path to a brighter democratic future. Memorialisation efforts have become core issues in the quest for post-conflict justice, peace and reconciliation, gaining significance and relevance and becoming an inseparable part of any human rights agenda. The overwhelming presence of memorialisation efforts and their ongoing embeddedness into organisations and institutions are phenomena of global proportions. The United Nations, Amnesty International, Human Rights Watch, the Organisation for Security and Co-operation in Europe (OSCE) and, in fact, every single non-governmental organisation (NGO) or human rights institution that deals with conflict areas, one way or the other, promotes an agenda grounded in the assumption that a 'proper memorialisation' is essential for 'healing' societies with a difficult past and moving beyond trauma and violence. Universities teach courses and have entire programs dedicated to peacebuilding, conflict resolution/management/transformation and transitional justice, feeding the need for dedicated professions that can fill numerous positions in the NGO sector, human rights institutions, international and domestic criminal tribunals and courts, local and international human rights campaigns, and even state-sponsored memorialisation efforts. All of those trained professionals, as well as enthusiasts and activists, irrespective of the sometimes substantial differences between their approaches and methods, are on the same mission: to direct and advocate for the parties involved to achieve a particular vision of the future by embracing certain ways in which they are supposed to frame, remember and commemorate their troubled past. This desired vision of remembering atrocities in a very particular way – atrocities committed by different parties in wars or under totalitarian regimes – is based on the assumption that a 'proper' framing of remembrance represents an effective means for promoting universalist human rights values in conflict and post-conflict settings (David 2017a). In other words, human rights advocates operate under an unquestionable assumption: that a proper memorialisation of a difficult past is essential for both democracy and human rights.

The pressure to engage in particular forms of memorialisation after mass human rights abuses started to emerge in the 1980s, by which time a human rights vision of memorialisation as a process of remembering the wrongs of the past and honouring the victims had developed, together with the idea that public and official recognition of crimes is essential for preventing further violence in divided or post-conflict societies. In 2014, the United Nations (UN) adopted *memorialisation standards,* promoting Western memorial models as a template for the representation of past tragedies or mass crimes and, in so doing, requiring states with difficult pasts to adhere to prescribed *standards of memory* (UN General Assembly 2014). According to these standards, memorialisation may include sites such as 'concentration camps, former torture and detention centres, sites of mass killings and graves and emblematic monuments of repressive regimes; symbolic sites such as permanent or ephemeral monuments carrying the names of victims, renamed streets, buildings or infrastructure, virtual memorials on the Internet, and museums of history/memory; and activities such as public apologies, reburials, walking tours, parades and temporary exhibits' (UN General Assembly 2014: 5). These commemorations are mandated based on the assertion that 'ensuring public recognition of past crimes is indispensable to the victims, essential for preventing further violence and necessary for redefining national unity' (UN General Assembly 2014: 5).

Yet, how compelling are these claims? How sound is the causal logic? How valid are the theoretical and factual assumptions on which they are based? Can there be universally correct ways of remembering past atrocities? Most importantly, what are the possible negative side effects of the demands envisioned, regulated and imposed by the human rights regime upon conflict and post-conflict states for them to engage with their contested pasts in a particular manner and to compel standardised memorialisation practices? Can that bring human rights values? This book challenges those assumptions. It shows that the advancement of *moral remembrance* – the standardised set of norms, promoted through human rights infrastructures at the world polity level, in which societies are supposed to deal with the legacies of mass human rights abuses – does not stand up to its expectations. On the contrary, it often destabilises post and in-conflict realities, enforces animosities and strengthens ethnically based nationalism.

Hence, we need to understand how this massive promotion of moral remembrance became a top priority on the human rights agenda. How did we come to see moral remembrance with its unified discourses, with its same language phrases and practices, spreading around the world (albeit unevenly), even to the most remote conflict areas? The reason for this memorialisation madness, I claim, lays in the fact that systematic, historical–sociological, comparative research has never been carried out that probes the fundamental assumption in which is grounded all the activism, advocating, policy-making and research that claims the inevitable causality between 'proper memorialisation' and human rights and democratic values.

The Intersection between Memory and Human Rights

Despite the fact that memory studies have been one of the most popular areas of research in recent years, memory as a subject of social inquiry had been greatly neglected until relatively recently. There are several reasons for this omission. Not long ago, memory as a subject wasn't perceived as a sociological issue. It had been pushed aside and often treated as a 'soft' issue, something that did not have a significant impact on societal organisations and structure. In 1925, one of Émile Durkheim's students, Maurice Halbwachs (Coser 1992), coined the term 'collective memory', asserting that individuals are incapable of remembering in a coherent manner outside the connections and constraints of their group and, therefore, it is society that determines and fashions their memories. This term only gained momentum in the 1980s. Durkheim himself, in *The Elementary Forms of Religious Life* (1976 [1915]), addressed memory only briefly in relation to commemorative rituals. Historians, anthropologists and psychologists addressed this subject separately, placing their focus on different aspects of memory. The anthropologist E. E. Evans-Pritchard (1940) developed the notion of 'structural amnesia' in his famous study of the Nuer. Frederic Bartlett (1932) was amongst the first modern psychologists to attend to the social dimensions of memory, attributing decisive importance to group dynamics in individual remembering. Historians, for their part, have their own long-standing history–memory division, in which memory has often been reduced to a complementary methodological tool, introduced through 'oral histories and severely influenced by the role of historiography and its rise within nation states. John Gillis (1994) rightly pointed out that history had taken celebratory, sacralising functions previously assigned to memory.

Within the discipline of history, the history–memory nexus gained attention due to the 'history of mentalities' that has dominated French historiography since the 1960s. Historians like Philippe Ariès (1974) and Maurice Agulhon (1981) began to study the history of commemorative practices, which they saw as mechanisms of political power, thus shifting historiographical interest from ideology to imagery and from meaning to manipulation. Later on, historians such as Assmann Aleida, Pierre Nora, David Lowenthal, Patrick Hutton and many others wrote extensively on the rift between history and memory. Barry Schwartz (1996) ascribes this increased interest in the social construction of the past to three historical processes. First, he claims, it has to do with identifying historiography as a source of cultural domination; second, it's due to the postmodernists' attack on linear historicity – thereby linking history with memory and power; and third, it reflects the production of a class-based account of the politics of memory, that highlighted memory contestation and the instrumentalisation of the past.

It was actually one of the greatest sociologists of the twentieth century, Theodor Adorno, who paved the way for an uncritical adoption of the assumption that societies need to honour the memory of those who died, since a 'duty to remember' is an insurance policy against the repetition of massive human rights abuses (David 2017a). Adorno (1986 [1959]), in his famous article 'What Does Coming to Terms with the Past Mean?', elaborated in length about how post-conflict societies need to readdress their difficult past, arguing that a culture of forgetting threatens democracy because real democracy requires a self-critical working through of the past. Adorno's approach was backed up both by the famous and publicly well-mediated historian debate (*Historikerstreit*) which took place in media outlets in West Germany (focusing on a process of returning remembrance into public awareness) and by the discussions of human rights activists in Latin America that explored how to deal with former right-wing regimes. Adorno, however, wrote his article not as a sociologist but as an engaged intellectual and philosopher, aiming to promote a desired vision of social reality, which was also strongly influenced by a wave of growing popularity for psychoanalysis.

It is important to stress that the social approach to memory developed in parallel to the development of the human rights memorialisation agenda and became deeply influenced by, and embedded in, the same agenda, becoming overwhelmingly burdened by the normative approach and enthusiastic support for human rights. The vast majority of researchers within the field of memory studies are conducting their research not from a standpoint of critical thinking, wherein they try to untangle often-hidden relationships between power, societal structures and agency, but rather as devoted activists who tend to promote a certain desired (in this case, human rights) vision of social reality. Indeed, it is a great challenge in the field of memory studies to resist sliding down the slippery slope of 'the world as it should be', with all its normative baggage (even when morally speaking, this seems the right thing to do), instead of critically engaging with 'the world as it is', without any attempt to fit the research to a certain political agenda.²

On the one hand, the intersection between memory and human rights is often perceived as detached from any historical roots and widely seen as apolitical, morally superior (Talal 2000) and even 'natural, self-evident, and essential' (Elliott 2014: 408). It takes for granted notions that, in fact, have very particular historical and political roots, such as the alleged imperative to 'face the past', assuming a very particular framing of the past based on purified categories of victims, perpetrators and bystanders. This omnipresent approach suggests that society as a whole, like individuals, needs to face its troubled past and remember it in a particular way. However, to start with, viewed through sociological instead of ideological lenses, individuals and societies are nothing alike. 'Facing the past', though perhaps useful to individuals, is hardly applicable for entire communities or societies. The reasons for that distinction are numerous, as Brandon Hamber and Richard Wilson (2002: 35) have shown. They convincingly demonstrated that nations are not like individuals in that they do not have collective psyches, that nation-building discourses on reconciliation often neglect individual needs, and that individual and collective processes of healing work on different timelines. What we today perceive as a 'logical' and 'natural' way to deal with past atrocities is actually historically rooted and contextualised in the post–World War II experience, better known as the 'German model' (Gabowitsch 2017). This model, through the institutionalisation of discourses, practices and policies, became a backbone agenda for the human rights regime. Historically bounded ideas, borrowed from psychological (psychoanalytical, in particular) and intellectual discourses, were uncritically translated into the human rights activist sphere, which gradually gained organisational power. In the process of ascribing morality to memorialisation practices and processes, what was lost was their deeply historical, cultural and societal context. Moreover, the three main guiding principles of moral remembrance – 'facing the past', 'duty to remember' and the 'justice for victims' approach – all have their own historical roots that need to be properly understood, conceptualised and contextualised (David 2017a).

On the other hand, human rights promoters are interested not only in justice and punishment, but, more importantly, in the transformation of values. This transformation is based on human rights moral views, as

---

² That is not to say that social sciences are ideology-free, or even that such a state is entirely possible to achieve, but that the conclusion we reach must be grounded in a theoretical and methodological framework instead of an ideological one.

sketched in the UN Charter (1945) and the Universal Declaration on Human Rights (1948), wherein human rights are a peculiar sort of rights with special moral weight. Despite the fact that different people hold different concepts of human rights (Dembour 2010), these rights are generally understood as universal and moral principles or norms, embedded in the idea that certain rights are inherent to all human beings, regardless of nationality, place of residence, sex, national or ethnic origin, colour, religion, language or any other status, and they should be protected as legal rights in municipal and international law. Though rights are individual, they can only be appreciated in a collective setting where those rights are recognised communally. Thus, the argument is not (only) about individuals who are obliged to face and remember their misconducts, but about entire communities and societies. Cementing human rights values in remembering past human rights abuses turns memorialisation into a pivotal process in achieving a human rights vision of the world.

The assumption that transformative acts exist, which human rights advocates believe are accomplished through the processes of 'proper memorialisation', gradually became the force majeure in policing memory around the globe. To understand those macro processes at the world polity level and their impact on different political settings, one must question how social structures, which many regard as natural, are shaped by complex social processes in the long run. This book is precisely about the impact that the accumulative process of worldwide institutionalising of standardised and isomorphic forms of memorialisation, along with its naturalisation (that has been transformed from an isolated, contextually and historically bounded idea into taken-for-granted standardised memorialisation policies and practices), have on the ways in which in-conflict and post-conflict societies comprehend their difficult past.

Moral Remembrance: The Three Processes of Ideologisation

To understand the emergence of moral remembrance and its impact on the ground, I analyse the human rights memorialisation agenda through three separate but interrelated processes, conceptualising it not in a normative fashion, but as an ideological force. Opposite to the lay understanding of human rights, where the agenda is presented as apolitical or above politics, universal and morally superior (often endorsed as such by human rights activists), I analyse and treat human rights as an ideology.

Human rights, just as any other ideology, tend to homogenise and monopolise the vision of the world as it should be. All ideologies, including that of human rights, 'seek to establish their hegemony by presenting themselves as the only right way to look at social reality' (Malešević 1999: 580). The success of human rights as an ideology can be measured exactly by the degree to which certain meanings and practices are almost universally seen as innocent, natural, clear and apparent.

Borrowing from the sociology of ideologies, in particular from the vast literature on nationalism, I follow (1) the institutionalisation of its organisational power that grows through human rights institutions, discourses and practices; (2) the institutionalisation of its dogmatic (ideological) power that relates to the particular content and reasoning that has shaped moral remembrance at the world polity level; and finally, (3) the forging of attachments of solidarity between group members that can push them into a moral action based on the ideological reception. In other words, both organisational and ideological power are necessary but not sufficient preconditions to make human rights an emotionally recruiting ideology. It is vital to understand that the persistence and the success of any ideology lie in its capacity to ideologically and organisationally penetrate people's feelings of attachment and mutual solidarity and link them into a relatively coherent and potentially recruiting ideological meta-narrative (Malešević 2013b). Hence, once the discourses, practices and logic of moral remembrance hit the ground, the question becomes: do people internalise human rights values in the long run?

In this book, I explore the ways in which human rights gained organisational and ideological power over the years, enabling it to promote a particular, historically contextualised, memorialisation agenda across the world in general and in conflict and post-conflict settings in particular. In other words, the focus in this book are questions that, in today's ideological turmoil, bear much political, moral and policy-making weight: Can the promotion of particular memorialisation standardised norms in conflict and post-conflict settings ensure the adoption of human rights? Can it defeat or at least dissolve nationalist-driven conflicts and bring a lasting change?

Based on accounts from Serbia, Croatia, Bosnia and Herzegovina (BiH), Israel and Palestine, I demonstrate here that the outcome of such external mandating of memorialisation standards has quite disturbing results – it rarely has transformative power on the ground. In fact, very often, the forging of feelings of solidarities in small groups, a key to the ideological implementation of human rights, is harvested back by the nation-state to promote nationalist, ethnically based agendas. The comparison between Israel and the Palestinian National Authority[3] and Serbia, Croatia and BiH[4] is not random. For Israel and Palestine, the centrality of the Holocaust legacy serves as a diversion from Palestinian suffering, a fundamental issue in their already seven-decades-long conflict. For Serbia, Croatia and BiH, contested memories from different historical layers affect the region in every possible sense, putting it a spark away from yet another conflict. In both settings, attempts to mandate the remembrance of past human rights abuses, through the global human rights infrastructure, actually end up perpetuating their conflicts, rather than promoting human rights.

Major Claims

Let me make clear at the outset that I do not claim that human rights fail to produce significant changes for many around the globe. Nor do I reject human rights as an ideal. On the contrary, it is, by far, the best ideal to strive for. However, human rights also produce undesired outcomes that are too often discredited and overlooked, that stay either completely ignored or are treated as minor setbacks.

I do not seek to undermine the unprecedented achievements of human rights that have made a real difference on the ground – from social equality issues to gender, political and cultural rights. However, I engage here critically in one particular area of human rights – where advocates of human rights attempt to coerce a 'proper' way of remembrance, which has tremendous and far-reaching consequences on the ground. Hence, my focus in this book is not primarily on the fact that human rights are often a tool for powerful states to enforce their political goals (Chomsky 1999; Herman and Peterson 2010; Žižek 2005). Nor does my critique deal, per se, with the 'paradox of empty promises' wherein governments often adopt human rights norms of behaviours as a matter of window dressing, radically decoupling policy from practice and, at times, exacerbating negative human rights practices (Hafner-Burton and Tsutsui 2005).

---

[3] Palestine is certainly not a state in a narrow sense, since it has neither a well-defined territory nor internationally recognised sovereignty. However, since Palestine does have a recognised government, it is still useful to work with the assumption that Palestine is a state, especially since the diplomatic practice seems to be the most important argument for viewing Palestine as a state.

[4] Bosnia is a unique case: there is no single state actor and no single official history accepted in Bosnia, but rather narratives divided across ethnonational lines – Serbian, Croatian and Bosniak.

Part of my argument relates to the coercive power of the human rights memorialisation project, which is often perceived as being implemented at the expense of autochthony and which results in a resurgence of nationalist, ethnically narrow sentiments. But this outcome, I show, has more to do with the inability of human rights to push people into internalising human rights values. Hence, this book is less about general attitudes towards the external human rights memorialisation agenda (though those do have an impact on the ground), and more about small face-to-face encounters in which human rights ideology is spread and disseminated in an attempt to determine whether, if and when human rights ideology can push people into moral actions in the long run.

Though the claims I present in this book are unfashionable, I am hardly a lone voice and far from the first to pursue this sort of critique. Others have made the case for the damaging effect of the human rights memorialisation agenda, such as Natan Sznaider, Alejandro Baer and Carol Kidron, to mention a few. All of these scholars have demonstrated the troubling impacts of this agenda on the ground. In this book, I go further and challenge a deeply embedded idea, continuously promoted globally by human rights advocates, that the human rights memorialisation agenda implements human rights norms and values. For the sake of clarity, I lay out my explanation up-front, in the form of six general theses.

Understanding Human Rights As an Ideology

I promote here an idea that, instead of conceptualising human rights in a normative fashion, as a desirable set of values, the adoption of which will inevitably bring a liberal peace, we should conceptualise it as an ideology. The theoretical model on the potency of nationalism developed by Siniša Malešević (2010, 2012a, 2012b, 2013a, 2017) is, I suggest, well equipped to help us understand how and why a particular memorialisation has been mandated in the name of human rights. Understanding human rights in methodological and theoretical terms as an ideology helps us distinguish three crucial processes that determine the successes and failures of the ways in which people on the ground interact, internalise and/or reject human rights values: (1) the institutionalisation of the organisational power of human rights; (2) the institutionalisation of its ideological power; and (3) the creation of micro-solidarity bonds based on human rights values in local communities. In other words, we need to understand the rise of institutions and organisations (organisational power) that promote certain content (ideological power) and to analyse whether organisational and ideological powers are capable of producing feelings of attachment and solidarity that push people into internalising human rights in the long run.

Understanding human rights as an ideology is beneficial, as it shifts the focus from a normative framing of rights and the desired realities on the ground and opens up a new avenue for evaluating how human rights beliefs and values generate change and affect societal structures that are shaped by historical, political and cultural processes. Understanding the ways in which human rights ideology perpetuates, promotes and diffuses coercive and cumulative organisational and doctrinal power may help us shed new light on whether human rights ideology is capable of producing solidarity at the micro level, to the extent that it mobilises social actors into human rights–based actions. Viewing human rights through the lens of ideology can bring some ground-breaking and fruitful insights, in particular in areas that are under-researched due to the current focus on rights and wrongs. Questions such as whether human rights ideology produces new forms of inequalities, when it perpetuates violence, and which mechanisms are used for sustaining human rights ideology on the ground are just some questions, I suggest, that can benefit tremendously from this approach.

The Emergence of Moral Remembrance at the World Polity Level

To shed light on the impact that standardisation of memory has on conflict and post-conflict settings, it is necessary, I argue, to understand how the human rights promotion of memorialisation processes became institutionalised and consequently a strong and influencing factor in the world polity system, here defined as 'the system of creating value through the collective conferral of authority' (Meyer 1987: 44). Meyer and Rowan (1977), DiMaggio and Powell (1983), Mayer (1987), Powell and DiMaggio (1991), and others have argued that the social structures of the world polity provide a sociological institutionalist reflection of global relations, which prescribe actions and goals and provide a set of cultural norms or directions. This is important because states tend to conform, adapt to, and comply with the external standards of world-polity isomorphism for the sake of gaining legitimacy in international arenas.

Whereas world polity theory has been heavily criticised for its overtly cultural approach, it treats the human rights memorialisation agenda as a universal and undisputable moral code, one that has obscured and blurred its political and historical contexts, and enabled its standardisation and gradual adoption worldwide. Human rights have acquired and accumulated organisational and ideological power in the world polity, starting from the end of World War II, but particularly since the 1970s (Moyn 2012). In this context, the human rights promotion of memorialisation processes became a strong and influencing factor of the world polity system, providing a set of cultural norms or directions, labelled here as *moral remembrance*. Three main principles have crystallised over the years and become pillars of the human rights memorialisation agenda: (1) the 'facing the past' principle; (2) the 'duty to remember' principle and (3) the 'justice for victims' principle. These three principles have become so deeply rooted within human rights memorialisation practices and norms that their historical–political context has been whitewashed and misinterpreted as being apolitical, natural and the only proper way to remember the past. Thus, moral remembrance refers to the standardised set of norms, promoted through human rights infrastructures at the world polity, further adopted and filtered through nation-states, in which societies are supposed to deal with the legacies of mass human rights abuses.

Moral Remembrance Clashes with the State-Sponsored Memorialisation Agenda

Moral remembrance, as an agenda promoted (unevenly) through centres of power at the world polity level, often enters national arenas through peace agreements – either through the front door (as in the case of the Dayton Agreement in the Western Balkans, where all parties had to commit to facing their mass human rights abuses) or through the back door (as in the case of the Oslo Accords in Israel and Palestine, where the human rights memorialisation agenda was introduced via a peacebuilding framework). In reality, this means that the human rights memorialisation agenda (1) has often been regarded as coercive and oppressive and (2) has clashed with various sectorial political agendas as well as with official historical narratives and the ways in which people in local communities narrated their past. Whereas the process of standardising moral remembrance and its adoption at the world polity level de-contextualised, de-historicised and de-politicised the core content of the human rights memorialisation ideas, pushing this agenda through peace agreements further deformed and mutated its idealistic premises. States, pressured in various ways, guided by the agendas of their political elites, further distorted and instrumentalised the human rights memorialisation agenda to fit their own, often narrow nationalist needs.

Moral Remembrance Strengthens the Categories of Nation and Ethnicity

At the macro-state level, the human rights memorialisation agenda is particularly subject to clashes between the believed truth of the past, which is sponsored by the state, and the truth mandated in the name of human rights. To be clear, the human rights memorialisation agenda always lands onto particular historical settings. Hence, the way in which it will be accepted, rejected (fully or partially) or modified is inevitably a subject of an already deeply developed and deep-rooted relationship with certain segments of national past and current political needs. Human rights, with the centre of their power being in the world polity, are always unavoidably filtered through the needs of a state. This means that some states will pretend to comply with world polity norms while, in reality, they welcome some rights but reject others, perceiving the latter as damaging to their own interests.

Further, the human rights memorialisation agenda – which frames personal and collective experience through the prism of 'duty to remember', 'facing the past' and a 'victim-centred agenda' – assumes a particular moral order in which there is no dispute regarding what is morally right or wrong. This assumption effectively enforces the idea that human rights norms must trump cultural norms and heritage. Hence, the human rights memorialisation agenda is always understood (at least partially) as oppressive and coercive, a threat to a seemingly homogenous body of the nation. If Serbs, or Germans, or Hutu are asked to comply with the norm set in moral remembrance by publicly apologising, this, in fact, homogenises people with different political views and from different classes and backgrounds into one categorical order through which the category of belonging to a certain nation (or ethnic or religious group) gains additional value. Thus, contrary to a desired, mandating memory in the name of human rights, it re-establishes boundaries, not dissolves them.

Moral Remembrance Produces New Social Inequalities

At the mezzo-state level, individuals and groups who suffered the consequences of the wars may find themselves trapped between, on the one hand, the advocates and NGOs that promote human rights notions of morality and, on the other hand, the state political elite. Victim groups oscillate between the slow and controversial processes of limited justice and widespread denial by the other side of the conflict. In their constant pursuit of justice, victim groups are crucified between two opposing poles.

At one end of the spectrum, such groups make efforts to have their suffering (fully or partially) recognised by human rights promoters, both locally and globally. Human rights promoters target victim groups by offering them not only much needed (financial or psychological) support that is denied by the state (for all sorts of reasons), but also a framework through which the victims can frame their sufferings and their memories and consequently their rights. This recognition plays an important role in their individual and communal recovery. However, it often lacks any institutional long-term support.

At the other end of the spectrum, the problem is that victim groups' inclusion and recognition into infrastructures of their own nation-states is not guaranteed and comes with a great cost. In practice, this means that, for both human rights groups and political elites, the suffering party can gain status only through the position of victims, which needs to be constantly reaffirmed. It is precisely here, in the day-to-day politics of victimhood, that new social inequalities are produced. The process of reaffirming victim status has two direct implications. First, the need for the ideal-type victim means that victim groups inevitably (and often very consciously) engage in homogenising their group members. One side effect of such a homogenisation process is attempts to sanction any complexities or messiness that might jeopardise their victim position in the power struggle between two opposing camps – that of the human rights and nationalist-centred ideologies. Second, and even more importantly, the homogenising and pushing of the victim group into this framework of 'ideal victim' means that other victim groups become understood as rivals and opponents in the struggle for scarce resources. In reality, this means that both the nationalist and human rights–centred ideological outlooks are often used to form new class divisions, based on differential access to state power and bureaucratic apparatus as well as to external funding.

Moral Remembrance Does Not Make People More Appreciative of Human Rights Values

Finally, at the micro-state level, based on prolonged human rights–sponsored 'facing the past' dialogue encounters in Israel and Palestine, and in Serbia, Croatia and Bosnia-Herzegovina, we have little evidence to suggest that people become more appreciative of human rights values, and even less evidence that they become willing to carry out any moral action that transcends their narrow interests. While we see a significant short-term impact, in the long run the perceptions of their national histories become more significant; hence those feelings are destined either to be hijacked by the state or to crumble and fall apart. This happens for two main reasons. First, human rights are not capable of competing with nation-state memorialisation infrastructures (such as state-sponsored commemorations, monuments, national calendars, history textbooks or national museums) and their impact is limited in terms of their power to transform nationally bounded sentiments into global and universal human rights values. Second, human rights in general, and the human rights memorialisation agenda in particular, do not offer any real alternative to a narrow and limited nationalist, religious or ethnically marked collectiveness. This is because the experience of attachment and solidarity in small group encounters is not instinctive, but rather a function of the interpretation of symbols, situational context and history. Hence, instead of harvesting strong emotions and a sense of loyalty from people in local communities that might become an ideological cement of human rights norms and values, the framework produced through moral remembrance is likely either to disappear or to be harnessed by the state, potentially destabilising and adding fuel to the very same nationalist fires that it is supposed to extinguish.

The Layout of the Book

Chapter 2 of this book focuses on two main issues. First, I discuss why it is beneficial to understand human rights as an ideology. I explain why ideology in general, and nationalism in particular, can add to our understanding of the impact that human rights have on the ground. I introduce Malešević's theory on the organisational and ideological power of nationalism and its relationship to the ideological perception and forging of solidarity attachments for people on the ground. This is important because, though the distinction between the promotion of human rights as opposed to the promotion of nationalist-centred memory is allegedly apparent, what is lacking both in the scholarly literature and in practice are theoretical tools to assess their impact in the long run. The lack of a suitable theoretical paradigm reduces our ability to grasp the complex meaning-making processes that are crucial and inseparable from the process of memorialising the past. Second, I show the historical obstacles to conceptualising, in a systematic way, human rights as an ideology, exploring how disciplinary baggage has downgraded our ability to assess human rights and value production across the globe.

In Chapter 3, I trace the rise of moral remembrance. In this chapter, I deal with the gradual emergence of memorialisation standards and policy-oriented attempts to engage transitional societies in developing and adopting specific normative forms of remembrance. This perspective of globalised and standardised cultures of memory has been heavily embedded and dispersed through an accumulative process of institutionalisation and ideologisation of human rights. Thus, moral concerns are promoted through agendas of 'justice for victims', 'duty to remember' and 'facing the past' that are supposed to prevent a recurrence of violent conflicts, gaining their power and legitimacy from the world polity level. I discuss the transitional justice paradigm that, from the late 1980s, brought to the fore primarily legal mechanisms to deal with past human rights abuses; I then address the reality that, since the year 2000, memorialisation has become seen as central to the processes of democratisation and regional integration. In practice, this shift in perception has brought a tremendous change in the ways of understanding memorialisation processes, moving the paradigm from simply a 'duty to remember' to specific, policy-oriented 'memorialisation standards'.

Implications of moral remembrance are far-reaching. Plenty of memorialisation-policy papers have been issued by a variety of governmental organisations, as well as international and regional NGOs, such as the UN and the US Institute for Peace, Open Society Institute, Impunity Watch, the Van Leer Institute and RECOM, among others. These policy-oriented reports provide memorialisation guidelines and recommendations not only in general but also for particular countries such as Burundi, Bosnia and Herzegovina, South Africa, Guatemala, Cambodia, Kosovo, Burma, Indonesia, Sri Lanka, Nepal, Thailand, Timor Leste, Egypt, Argentina and Chile. I intersect those with major historical developments that have impacted knowledge production, discourses, practices and policy-making, providing evidence for (1) the institutionalisation of a particular memory agenda; (2) the generative growth of the human rights agenda, through expansion of infrastructures, discourses and practices into a mainstream human rights agenda; and (3) the adoption of the 'facing the past', 'duty to remember' and 'victim-centred' principles.

Whereas in Chapter 3 I deal with the expansion, embeddedness and promotion of the human rights memorialisation agenda globally, in the next two chapters I analyse specific case studies, seeking to disclose the localised versions of moral remembrance. In the Balkan cases, the international community has played a significant role in pressuring Serbia, Croatia and BiH to shape their national histories in accordance with the mandates of a specific human rights regime. In contrast, Israel and Palestine offer different dynamics. In Chapter 4, I show that, whereas the European Balkan states faced financial conditionalities during the various steps of the EU accession process, Israel and Palestine were much less pressured by the international community to exhibit an even nominal acceptance of a cosmopolitan history, through which global concerns and values become part of local experiences. Having said that, the Oslo Accords, signed in 1993 and in 1995, that projected the independent state of Palestine in 1999, were of great importance for bringing new memorialisation agendas, never discussed per se in any of legal documents but indirectly promoted in multiple ways. Surprisingly, even in 2000, when it became clear that the Oslo Accords had failed, memorialisation practices, promoted by human rights institutions and funds, continued to blossom. Chapter 4 deals with the ways in which the memorialisation agenda was promoted in Israel and Palestine and how specific historical and political conditions affected it.

In Chapter 5, I show how, in the Western Balkans, and more specifically in Serbia, Croatia and BiH, the pressure imposed by the international community (the EU in particular) was a given from the very beginning: following the wars of the 1990s, they all formally committed to the Europeanisation process. Each state's entrance into the EU was supposedly conditioned upon, among other things, facing its criminal past of human rights abuses. The main request posed to Croatia, Serbia and BiH by the EU was cooperation with the International Criminal Tribunal for Yugoslavia (ICTY). In the cases of Croatia, Serbia and BiH, the post-conflict institutionalisation of human rights, as defined and enforced by EU bodies and institutions, created several mechanisms, different in their purpose and efficiency, to implement and impact memorialisation processes and practices. In Chapter 5, the memorialisation agenda for the Western Balkans is disclosed and analysed.

While in Chapters 4 and 5 I place the institutionalisation of the human rights memorialisation agenda into the specific historical, political, cultural and economic contexts of the Western Balkans and Israel and Palestine, in Chapter 6 I try to understand how moral remembrance resonates for the people in local communities. As it is a necessary condition for an ideology to be emotionally recruiting, I turn my attention to micro-group solidarity. I briefly theorise the concept of solidarity as understood so far, placing particular focus on Randall Collins' theory of interaction ritual chains and emotional energy. Central to his 'interaction ritual theory' is the notion that people in face-to-face encounters produce mutual rituals that are sustained through an emotional energy that results in a feeling of membership and in a desire for action that is considered a morally 'proper' path. This is crucial because, in dialogue groups sponsored by the human rights memorialisation agenda of moral remembrance, interaction rituals that produce and sustain emotional energy are based on the contested representations of a shared past.

Drawing on numerous human rights projects and memorialisation initiatives in both the Western Balkans and in Israel/Palestine, I analyse the myriad of 'facing the past' dialogue groups that bring people together based on either a categorical order (e.g., as victims or perpetrators), their ethnic positionality (e.g., in dialogue groups) or both. 'Facing the past' encounters ritualise historical narratives and generate strong emotions, such as anger, fear, excitement and pain, together with a particular vocabulary of sentiments, which, I show, end up strengthening ethnic homogenisation, essentialisation and group polarisation. I demonstrate that, while being in those face-to-face groups is often described as a 'life-changing' experience – and even produces real feelings of solidarity among the group members – in the long run, this solidarity, which allegedly overcomes narrow ethno-nationalist solidarity bonds, does not translate transnational solidarity into human rights values. In other words, moral remembrance does not offer a real alternative to sustaining those emotions and transforming them into solid, long-lasting human rights values. In fact, I argue that moral remembrance does not offer sufficient infrastructures to compete with the narrow, ethnically based nationalist perceptions of collective memory. Moral remembrance is not capable of sustaining transnational solidarity; instead, doing so requires permanent affirmation and reinforcement among millions of people across the globe. Based on theoretical and empirical evidence, I discuss the impact that human rights memorialisation isomorphism had on nationalist realities on the ground. I elaborate what is lost in translation once a proper way of remembrance, with its particular, historically bounded logic, is introduced and advanced through human rights instruments, showing how and why instead of cementing a human rights vision of the world, it actually ends up reproducing nationalist discourses and practices.

In the concluding Chapter 7, I engage in a more speculative debate, while offering several explanations of moral remembrance's global impact. I broaden the discussion to speculate about the significance and possible dangers of this new global moral remembrance regime. Three questions are being asked that define the impact that moral remembrance has on the ground. The first question deals with the tension between moral remembrance, promoted through the morality of human rights memorialisation and the nation-state–sponsored memorialisation agenda. I discuss differences and similarities in the ways in which human rights and nationalist-centred ideologies understand, conceptualise and advance memorialisation processes and practices. The basic difference between human rights and nationalism is that human rights stand for worldwide inclusion of all people into one moral community, whereas nationalism presumes nationally bounded collectives. Nevertheless, moral remembrance, as a grand global memory regime, is always filtered through the needs of a state, which significantly reduces and cripples the fundamental ideas and values embedded in the human rights memorialisation agenda.

The second question deals with the under-researched and neglected impact that the human rights memorialisation agenda produces on the ground – namely, the production of new social inequalities. Here, the tension between, on the one hand, moral remembrance as an ideal and the back-stage politics of its organisation, structures and politics, and, on the other hand, the political interests of various groups behind nation-states and nationalism, results in very particular and often tangible trade-offs between groups affected by wars, national political elites and various human rights organisations. Such negotiations, trade-offs, transactions of real or symbolic benefit and the political struggle over scarce resources lead to new social inequalities and the marginalising of those who cannot afford (for various reasons) to participate in those mnemonic battles.

In the third question, I ask whether moral remembrance has the potential to transform individuals in local communities into believers in human rights values and motivate them into moral action based on those values. Moral remembrance, which frames personal and collective experiences through the lenses of 'duty to remember', 'facing the past' and the 'victim-centred' agenda, assumes a particular moral order in which there are no disputes over what is morally right or wrong. This is troubling because every individual and every local community are shaped in profound ways by symbols and by what is perceived to be their shared history. Hence, moral remembrance, as an all-inclusive ideology, is not able to offer a sustainable and emotionally engaging alternative to an exclusive collectiveness understood in terms of ethnicity, nationality, religion or any other reductionist category, in the long run.

Finally, I conclude the book by posing questions about the legitimacy and usefulness of moral remembrance in creating democracies and the implementation of human rights values and norms, arguing that mandating memorialisation standards not only fails to bring stabilisation and peacebuilding, but actually strengthens animosities and nationalist ideologies along ethnic lines.

2 Human Rights As an Ideology?
Obstacles and Benefits

Introduction

Are human rights an ideology? In this chapter, I will not try to persuade my readers why human rights qualify as an ideology, but instead will demonstrate why it is important to conceptualise them as an ideology. It is my intent to show why doing so is beneficial and may better our understanding of the ways in which human rights impact an array of social phenomena on the ground – from the production of new inequalities, class systems, economic disputes and power relationships to the alterations of value systems, micro- and macro-solidarities, ethnic hostilities and much more. I will not engage with most of those issues per se, but rather seek to present a theoretical model that can be further applied to those research areas. My main interest in this chapter is to advance a theoretical model, borrowed from research on ideology in general and nationalism in particular, through which we can analyse human rights. Research on ideologies has been a prominent field in social sciences for decades; hence, the question is, why has it never been applied in a systematic manner to the study of human rights? Why does bringing together human rights and ideology sound to many as blasphemy? To that end, I present obstacles that have caused delays and impeded research in what I consider to be a very worthwhile direction. In the chapters to come, I will apply this three-legged model to one particular area – the human rights perception and promotion of memorialisation processes worldwide.

The aims of this chapter are twofold. I propose understanding human rights as an ideology, arguing that applying models of research in the area of ideology to human rights may have the advantage of overcoming the blind spots that arise from narrowly defining human rights as a struggle over rights. In this exercise in historiography, I provide a meta-narrative of the ways in which social scientists' relationship to human rights has developed over the years, showing the long-standing refusal within the discipline to address human rights as an ideology.

First, I wish to address two historical locks that have discouraged and caused serious delay within social sciences in its grasping – theoretically and methodologically – of human rights as an ideology. The first baggage comes from the Marxist understanding of ideology. From the nineteenth century onwards, ideologies have provoked an emotional reaction and have been almost exclusively understood in a negative light. The second impediment has to do with two long-lasting and ongoing debates in social science in general, and in sociology in particular, focused on universalism versus cultural relativism arguments and on value-neutral versus normative advocacy claims that have largely contributed to confusion and disagreements in research of human rights.

Second, I wish to make the case why understanding human rights as an ideology can bring fruitful and novel explanations and significantly advance our knowledge on the ways in which human rights norms are being adopted and glocalised on the ground. Instead of conceptualising human rights in a normative fashion, as a desirable set of values designed to bring a liberal peace, I will conceptualise it as an ideology that, through its institutionalisation, produces coercive organisational and ideological power. The organisational power of human rights – defined as an ongoing historical process that grows through discourse, knowledge and institutions, through those institutions' bureaucratic apparatus – draws from the constant increase of its organisational capability for coercion (Malešević 2013a, 2013c). From this coercive foundation, the organisational power of human rights attempts to institutionalise and mandate normative standards – ideological or doctrinal power; in turn, this tendency to monopolise and homogenise places human rights in line with other ideologies. However, as I will show in this book, both the organisational and ideological power of human rights may remain alienated if they cannot produce effective emotional attachments and solidarity in small groups that can affect the worldview in the long run.

In the second part of the chapter, I conceptualise human rights as an ideology, which like any other ideology, can be traced through three long-term historical processes: (1) institutionalisation of its cumulative organisational power; (2) institutionalisation of its cumulative doctrinal power and (3) its ability to effectively bond people on the ground and produce attachments of solidarity. However, the real benefit of conceptualising human rights as an ideology relates to the question of whether the organisational and doctrinal power of human rights produces effective emotional attachments and solidarity in small groups and whether those attachments can be sustained in the long run. In other words, to unlock social problems at the large-scale level, we need to understand how (and if) the organisational and doctrinal power of human rights is capable of creating solidarity in micro-structure encounters. The main purpose of this chapter is to propose new avenues of inquiry for pushing boundaries and expanding our knowledge of the impact of human rights on the ground.

Ideology

Are human rights an ideology? This question bears much weight, not only because it may define how we perceive human rights, but most importantly because it can define our methodological and theoretical approach towards human rights. Interestingly, human rights have rarely been addressed and analysed through the theoretical lens of ideology. This 'omission' is associated with the development and understanding of both human rights and ideologies within the discipline. On the one hand, until recently sociology was reluctant to deal with human rights but was heavily invested in research on ideologies. On the other hand, while human rights have been extensively researched by legal scholars and political scientists, this scrutiny has rarely taken place through the prism of ideology.

The literature on ideology has been long fragmented and compartmentalised. I will not try to review the entire history of the concept, but instead refer readers to the excellent sketch available in Heywood (2003). Here, I highlight the points that are most useful for situating ideology and human rights within the field of social sciences. The notion of 'ideology' as a separate area of research concerned with ideas was developed in nineteenth-century France. The term was actually first used in public in the eighteenth century (1796) by the French–Scottish philosopher Antoine Destutt de Tracy, who was interested in the 'ideological' as opposed to 'psychological' sides of humanity. His universal, technical and value-neutral meaning of ideology was gradually turned into its opposite.

The conceptualisation of 'ideology' as a key political term comes from its use in the writings of Karl Marx. Marx was the first – and, to date, the most important – social and political thinker to historicise the notion of ideology. Consequently, the prominence that ideology enjoys in modern social and political thought in general, and Marx's understanding of the term in particular, can largely be explained in terms of the later generations of Marxist thinkers. For many decades, sociologists were among the most enthusiastic users of the concept of ideology, whether as advocates, critics or simply commentators. However, social sciences in general, and sociology in particular, was burdened with – and in many respects still suffers from – the Marxist understanding of ideology, adopted from Engels' notion of 'false consciousness', which is understood as a set of false ideas that help to legitimate a dominant political power. For Marx and his followers, ideology was primarily about delusion and mystification. According to Marx, ideology is tied to different economic systems and the dominant modes of production and is seen as a form of social pathology – the product of false consciousness. Following in his footsteps, social scientists predominantly understood ideology as a manifestation of power.

Despite the fact that the Marxist notion of ideology can be understood only in terms of the connected notions of alienation, mystification and reification (Birnbaum 1960), many continued analysing ideology as a form of power domination and class stratification. Antonio Gramsci (1971 [1948]), an Italian Marxist and social theorist, used cultural hegemony to explain why the working classes have a false ideological conception of their best interests. Building on some of Gramsci's ideas, Louis Althusser (1971: 162), a French Marxist philosopher, tried to shift the emphasis further from the repressive machinery of the state and towards what he termed 'ideological state apparatus', saying that ideology is a 'representation' of the imaginary relationship of individuals to their real conditions of existence. Hannah Arendt, a political theorist, thought that ideology is the ruthless logical working-out in the real world of the implications of a single, simplistic premise. According to this usage, ideologies are secular religions, which, by claiming a monopoly of truth, refuse to tolerate opposing ideas and rival beliefs; they possess a 'totalising' character and serve as instruments of social control, ensuring compliance and subordination (Arendt 1951). The works of Adorno, Horkheimer, Benjamin, Lukác, Fromm and other Frankfurt School theorists; the works of Goldman, Levi-Strauss and Althusser – these were the names and texts that dominated discussion, all deeply inspired by the Marxist conceptualisation of ideology. Indeed, a massive sociological literature exists on the subject, especially in the period from the 1950s to the early 1980s.

Karl Mannheim, a Hungarian sociologist and founder of the sociology of knowledge field, was one of the earliest sociologists to attempt to construct a non-Marxist concept of ideology, by substituting intellectuals for the proletariat (Kumar 2006). As opposed to the Marxist reading of ideology, in *Ideology and Utopia* (1968 [1936]), Mannheim described ideologies as thought systems that serve to defend a particular social order, and that broadly express the interests of its dominant or ruling group. Later, Clifford Geertz, one of the most influential American anthropologists, together with his followers, developed a symbolic theory of ideology that shifted the attention from the neo-Marxist focus on the function of ideology towards the content of ideological messages.

In opposition to the Marxist way of understanding ideology, the so-called anti-foundationalists, such as Michel Foucault, Gilles Deleuze and Ernesto Laclau, take truth claims to be always contingent, discursive and motivated by power and control. Despite their differences, they all share the view that 'discourse analysis, with its emphasis on language use and construction, reveals more about the structuring of the social order than any ideology critique does' (Malešević 2011b: 337). The cognitivist approach tries to overcome relativism, and claims that all truths are equal and incommensurable (Freeden 1996; Mann 2004b). One way of dealing with this problem, following the path laid by Michael Freeden (1996), is to highlight the morphology of an ideology in terms of its key concepts. Each ideology is therefore characterised by a cluster of core, adjacent and peripheral concepts, not all of which need be present for a theory or a doctrine to be recognised as belonging to that ideology. However, recent innovative strands of post-Marxism, in the hands of initially Lacan and later Žižek and Laclau, have attempted to revitalise thinking about ideology by welding psychoanalysis to notions of semantic social control and distortion. In so doing, they have discovered that those two components doubly disable it from conversing fruitfully with analytical political philosophy (Freeden 2006).

Despite the significant distance traversed by the social sciences since Marx, the heart of the study of ideology remains the distinction between appearance and reality, between error and 'truth', and between a necessarily distorted subjective consciousness and an objective world (Kumar 2006: 171). This serpentine road taken by the research of ideology in the past century has been heavily burdened by the prevailingly negative connotations of the term 'ideology'. These, coupled with the moral imperatives of human rights, have thwarted any significant research into human rights as an ideology. Simplistically put, mixing the negative connotations of ideology with the positive and highly moral intentions of human rights feels like, and is often perceived as, blasphemy. Here, the stress is on 'feels': one of the biggest obstacles for researchers in social sciences when approaching human rights and analysing them through the prism of ideology is the researchers' emotional and moral stakes. The portrayal of human rights as an ideology often resonates as if it implies that human rights are yet another trickery of *false consciousness*. This 'polluting' of human rights with the notion of ideology is viewed as not just an immediate critique of human rights, but in fact goes against the very humanity, against the very purpose, of social science itself.

Sociology and Human Rights

The history of social sciences testifies to the study of ideology being filled with negative and emotionally engaging connotations. When it comes to human rights within the discipline of sociology, the problem is further magnified. In sociology, there has been a lasting debate as to whether human rights are to be considered a part of the sociological field and, if so, what the proper way is to articulate a theoretical framework that will make sociological sense out of current human rights discourse and practice. The matter of human rights has been the focus of extended discussion and debate within the emerging world community for well over half a century. Two major debates within the field of sociology have caused delays and distortions in the ways in which sociologists have dealt with human rights. The first issue has to do with the ongoing debate on universalism versus cultural particularity in human rights; the second relates to the age-old issue of the relationship between morals and social inquiry.

The universalism versus cultural relativism dialectic stands as one of the most debated issues in the theory of human rights, echoing loudly across the social sciences. Simply put, universalism refers to the notion that human rights are universal and should apply to every human being, while cultural relativism is a set of doctrines that imbue cultural relativity with prescriptive force. However, from the very beginning, the stated core principle of human rights – as being universal regardless of geography, culture, race, nation, ethnicity, religion or gender – was uncomfortable for sociologists (and even more so for anthropologists). The critique of the idea of universal rights was prominent in the works of Marx, Durkheim and Weber, and by the time human rights started gaining momentum, the rejection of universalism was already well embedded in sociological thinking. In his 1844 article *On the Jewish Question*, Marx attacked proponents of the universal rights of man, arguing that the rights of man exemplify individualism, whereas individuals are still bound to material constraints on freedom by economic inequality and the wider social class relations of capitalism. In mainstream sociology, both Durkheim and Weber also emphasised the specificity of laws and morality in relation to particular societies, leading to a critical attitude towards universal rights claims. In fact, in 1947, the Executive Board of the American Anthropological Association (AAA), under the guiding influence of Melville Herskovits, formulated a 'Statement on Human Rights' that was sent to the United Nations Commission on Human Rights, which was then drafting the Universal Declaration of Human Rights. This statement rejected the validity of a universal declaration of human rights on both empirical and ethical grounds (Goodale 2006). Similar to Durkheim's discussion of comparative ethics, the anthropologists pointed out that normative humanism assumes the assertion of a single dominant ethical principle, which tends toward a kind of moral imperialism when the disciplinary power of human rights discourse is employed in the service of transnational capitalist relations of production (Goodale 2005). In their 'Statement on Human Rights', the anthropologists, while acknowledging certain cultural universals, championed the principle that each culture must be understood (and respected) on its own terms and, in a way, set the tone for sociologists as well.

Cultural relativists, and anthropologists in particular, stand firm behind the AAA statement of 1947 that 'standards and values are relative to the culture from which they derive so that any attempt to formulate postulates that grow out of the beliefs or moral codes of one culture must to that extent detract from the applicability of any Declaration of Human Rights to mankind as a whole' (AAA 1947). Universalists are often accused of neo-imperialism through the global enforcement of Western de-historicised and de-contextualised values (David 2017a). For their part, universalists blame cultural relativists for being essentialist and for approaching culture as if it is static and homogeneous, whereas culture is actually a range of deeply contested symbols, practices and meanings over, and with, which members of a society constantly negotiate and struggle. Further, it has been argued that cultural relativists ignore or misplace politics and that, in their attempt to defend different cultures, they often end up romanticising and glorifying a past that – if it ever truly existed – is no more.

Having said that, as a result of the ongoing debate, serious efforts have been invested in finding a way to bridge the gap between the binary positions of universalism and cultural relativism. Some distinguished anthropologists, such as Clyde Kluckhohn and Ralph Linton, have attempted to isolate universal moral principles. More recently, a group of anthropologists directly addressed the nature of universal human rights (Sjoberg, Gill and Williams 2001). Nagengast and Turner (1997), for example, tried to bridge the gap between individual and collective rights and public and private spaces, arguing for a culturally mediated universalism. Handwerker (1997) positioned 'freedom from violence' as a universal human right, saying that it generates 'a distinctive syndrome of self-destructive emotions and behaviour which accounts for an extraordinary proportion of national health care budgets, pulls money out of health care and into criminal justice systems, and constrains economic productivity and growth and that all people, everywhere, evaluate specific experiences with essentially the same criteria'. Jack Donnelly, a highly respected political scientist, offers a conception of human rights that is shared by a large number of scholars in this arena. Donnelly (1984) insists on what he calls the 'relative universality' of human rights, arguing that, if universal human rights are properly understood, they leave considerable space for national, regional and cultural particularity and other forms of diversity and relativity. While placing much emphasis on universal human dignity, Donnelly (2007) promotes the idea that human rights norms and practices arose not from any deep Western cultural roots, but rather from the social, economic and political transformations of modernity. Thus, they have relevance wherever those transformations have occurred, irrespective of the pre-existing culture of the place (Donnelly 2007).

Amongst sociologists, Bryan Turner (1993) was the first to take the lead in conceptualising the nature of human rights. To do so, he emphasised 'human frailty' and the precariousness of the institutions that cope with frailty, an argument that he later developed into the notion of 'universal ontological insecurity' (Turner 2011) to ground human rights without appealing to traditional natural law theory. Turner envisages human frailty as a modern surrogate for the older conception of natural rights, in that the former provides a justification for why human rights are an essential basis for the contemporary social and cultural order. In his ground-breaking article 'Outline of a Theory of Human Rights', Turner (1993) critiqued the key founding theorists of sociology – Durkheim, Weber and Marx – calling for the destruction of natural law theory and for a normative recognition of human rights as a universal need for protection and empathy for others in relation to citizenship rights. Turner's contribution to sociology has first and foremost been opening up the subject of human rights to sociological inquiry.

However, research on human rights was inhibited not just by the universalist–cultural relativist debate; that is, it was also delayed by the lack of interest in morality as a subject of sociological inquiry, with morality becoming a popular topic for study by sociologists only in the 1990s. Frezzo (2011: 204) describes sociology departments in the 1980s and 1990s as being torn by 'the thorny debates on humanism and antihumanism, modernity and post-modernity, the meaning of scientific progress, the contradictory legacy of Enlightenment thought, the successes and failures of the project of human emancipation, the persistence of Eurocentrism, and the possibility of espousing a genuine universalism'. This tone, however, had already been set by the classics of sociology. Although recognising that moral issues may enter into the formulation of a sociological problem, the Weberians contend that the scientist's worldview should call for value neutrality in the actual investigation of social and cultural orders. In a similar vein, Durkheim believed that there is no universal morality for humanity, since each society creates its own set of moral rules over time, which can vary dramatically from one society to another. Indeed, value neutrality and opposition to any normative and engaged claims lie at the very heart of any social science research. The theoretical and empirical import of human rights is a topic that, with rare exceptions, has been skirted around by sociologists, being regarded and dismissed as a moral system. Bryan Turner emphasised above all that sociology's neglect of human rights could be attributed to its lack of engagement with normative theories, and that sociology thus required a normative grounding for human rights to endorse human rights while studying them. Turner was convinced that, in opposition to the prevailing sociological tradition, sociologists need to find a universal normative foundation for their approach (Sjoberg, Gill and Williams 2001). Thus, it took quite some time for human rights laws, language, values, discourses, principles and practices to gather momentum, from garnering sporadic interest by sociologists to attracting the sustained attention that led to its development into a more extensive field of study. Not surprisingly, greater interest generally arose in regions where overt conflict was under way and the language of human rights had a political immediacy, such as in Latin America, the Balkans and the Middle East.

The field of the sociology of human rights has only recently been established, dating back to when the British Sociological Association Study Group in the Sociology of Rights held its first workshop in 2009. Subsequently, in 2010, the XVII International Sociological Association (ISA) Annual Conference dedicated a section to the sociology of rights. Modules that bring the study of human rights into sociology programmes and degrees have been proliferating in the United Kingdom, Europe, Asia and the Americas, along with the sociology of rights, leading to the emergence of the distinct field known as the 'sociology of human rights'. However, from the beginning, the ISA and the American Sociological Association (ASA) defined the sociology of human rights as a twofold endeavour: to analyse the construction, diffusion, contestation, and transformation of rights by a variety of social actors, and to *advocate* for human rights. Some of the most prominent sociologists, such as Judith Blau (Blau and Moncada 2007) and Michael Burawoy, called for *public* sociology, arguing that 'the purpose of sociology is not only to analyse social inequalities, but also to *advocate* remedies for social inequalities' (Frezzo 2011: 208). Those views correspond with Zygmunt Bauman's (1998) notions of morality, which claim that responsibility is the core of morality and the necessary condition to think sociologically about morality. This shift from value neutrality to advocacy and activism brought to the fore gaps in the ways in which sociologists grapple to overcome the tension between the analysis of, and advocacy for, human rights. The moral demand to act so as to lessen the suffering of distant social actors emerged as a focus of sociological engagement from the 1990s onwards, which became possible only in the intersection between 'humanitarianism' and the emergence of liberal society, with its distinctive features of capitalism (the market) and democracy (civic equality and citizenship) (Sznaider 1998: 118).

This blurring of the boundaries between analysis and activism often made sociologists of human rights concerned with not only developing principles, methodologies and empirical findings, but also, and primarily, promoting the human rights agenda, identifying solutions and actively engaging with the public to promote change. Most sociologists of human rights see duty, rather than harm, in such engagements and are often blind to the slippery slope of activism which frames research in normative terms of achieving a particular worldview. The transition from value-neutral to normatively engaged sociology remains highly disputed. Hynes et al. (2010) rightly pointed out that sociological research 'should not be confused with normative commitment but be grounded in theoretical and methodological rigour'. Yet most of the current sociological research on human rights is designed to promote the human rights worldview, even if that aim is not explicitly stated. This goal, though noble in itself, often comes at the expense of understanding social reality as it is, and not as we would like it to be. Ideological participants do not perform a good analysis of their movement because they analyse it through the categories promulgated by that movement. Only by viewing the entire historical process with greater detachment does it become possible to make a sound sociological contribution.

Human Rights As an Ideology

This short history of the obstacles faced by the sociology of human rights has been presented to show why researchers in sociology find the notion of binding human rights with ideology hard to process. Carrying legacies of the Marxist understanding of ideology as a false consciousness, together with the universalism versus cultural relativism debate and the value-neutral analysis versus normative activism debate, shaped the sociology of human rights as a highly contested field of research.

The negative connotations of conceptualising human rights as an ideology are evident and well embedded in the sociology of human rights. In fact, those who bring together human rights and ideology are seen as 'radical sociologists' (Hynes et al. 2010). 'Radical sociologists', such as Immanuel Wallerstein (2004), who conceptualised a 'world-system' with US hegemony, regard human rights as part of an ideology which obfuscates underlying capitalist economic relationships shaped by colonialism. This line of critique is followed by other 'radical' thinkers such as Chomsky, Herman, Peterson and Žižek. Chomsky, Herman and Peterson understood human rights as politics, with the 'political economy of human rights' (Herman and Peterson 2010) being a conspiracy-like theory in which powerful states, first and foremost the United States, use human rights ideology for personal gains (Goodale 2006). Although taking different approaches, all of these scholars questioned whether the West, via human rights, is seeking to impose its categories onto the rest of the world. The term 'ideology' as a foundation for a critique used by 'radical' thinkers is often employed in its derogatory meaning as a form of bashing, but *not* as a theoretical model.

Several other attempts have sought to link human rights and ideology. Alain Pellet, Professor of International Law at the Université de Paris Ouest–Nanterre La Défense, in 1989 coined the term 'human-rightism'; this label has been sporadically used since then, provoking adverse reactions within the community of human rights advocates. With the notion of human-rightism, Pellet (2000) tried to warn of the costs and dangers of the slippery slope of activism within the arena of international human rights law. 'Human-rightism' was immediately ascribed pejorative meanings and used to express different forms of critique when it came to human rights. For example, in 2012, Vaclav Klaus, the Czech president, warned against the dangers of human-rightism, claiming that human rights are, in fact, a revolutionary denial of civil rights. Similar to Arendt's arguments, developed several decades ago, he claimed that by denying civil rights, human-rightism calls for the destruction of the sovereignty of individual countries, arguing that human-rights ideology has nothing in common with practical issues relating to individual freedoms and free political discourse, but rather deals with entitlements.

As opposed to previous thinkers who often equated ideology with dogma, Louis Henkin (2000), a director of the Human Rights Institute at the Law School at Columbia University, adopted a more neutral approach to ideology, claiming that human rights became a political ideology on the American continent and in France towards the end of the eighteenth century. Samuel Moyn (2012), a Yale professor of law and history, took a different approach, arguing that the blossoming of human rights since the 1970s should be explained and understood against the backdrop of the global realisation that ideology had actually died.

However, Makau Wa Mutua (1996), a Kenyan American professor of law, was among the first to grasp – both theoretically and empirically – the interconnectedness between ideology and human rights, developing the proposition that human rights and Western liberal democracy are virtually tautological. Kabasakal Arat (2008), a political scientist, has promoted the same idea that human rights should be understood in terms of a distinct ideology which is embedded in the International Bill of Rights. This assessment is made by analysing the extent to which human rights ideology is able to oppose the concentration of political, economic and social power that is defined in relation to the positions taken on the state, property and discrimination to promote equality in dignity. To date, this has probably been the most serious effort to prove that 'human rights' qualifies as an ideology.

Human Rights As an Ideology: The Importance of the Model

So, are human rights an ideology? In his article 'The Elements of the Concept of Ideology', Malcolm Hamilton (1987) identified twenty-seven different components in definitions of ideology. Probably the most basic, and yet profound, difference regarding how researchers define ideology is in understanding ideology as a belief system, as opposed to viewing it as a form of discourse (Schull 1992). To avoid dispute, I choose to use here Andrew Heywood's (2003) definition precisely because it is neither original nor novel and is entirely in line with the social-scientific usage of the term. Following Heywood's definition of ideology, human rights are an ideology because (1) they offer an account of the existing order, a worldview, meaning they offer (relatively) clear moral boundaries of the world as it should be; (2) they advance a model of a desired future, a vision of 'good society'; and most importantly (3) they explain how political change can and should be brought about.

In other words, this definition suggests that organisational power needs to be in place – meaning institutions that promote and legitimise certain doctrinal power, a normative system of beliefs to advance a particular worldview. As with other ideologies, human rights offer a set of ideas that provide the basis for organised political action, which may be intended to preserve, modify or overthrow the existing system of power. However, what is omitted in Haywood's definition is how those organisational and doctrinal powers are translated, understood and internalised in small-group encounters that are essential to push for any moral action. Those three levels are interconnected, and the impact human rights have on the ground cannot be understood properly when looking at those levels separately. This is important since, I argue, it is exactly how human rights ideology operates.

Regardless of how we understand human rights on the spectrum of Mannheim's (1936) 'particular' or 'total' conceptions of ideology, Seliger's (1976) 'fundamental' or 'operative' levels of ideology or Freeden's (1996) 'fully fledged' or 'thick' ideologies, the real question is *why it matters* whether we understand human rights as an ideology. I argue here that it matters greatly, because understanding human rights as an ideology offers us the analytical tools to systematically evaluate the evolution of the Western-led global institutionalisation of values and norms. What is even more important is that viewing human rights through the prism of the institutionalisation of organisational and doctrinal power may advance our understanding of how human rights are internalised across different socio-political strata.

Over the course of the past several decades, human rights became heavily institutionalised or, to use Durkheim's term, 'a social fact'. Evidence for this gradual but massive institutionalisation of human rights is abundant and well researched. The widely diffused human rights infrastructure became increasingly embedded in a set of regional, international and global linkages. Human rights norms shaped a new global legalism that challenged conventional assumptions of nation-state sovereignty and claimed to confer legitimacy upon international and domestic politics (Teitel 2003). On the global scale, human rights ideology, with its founding document, the Universal Declaration on Human Rights, served as the foundation for the creation of an entire framework of international and transnational human rights discourses, within which the most important human rights instruments, non-governmental organisations, and international publications were established, developed and grew in power and influence (Goodale 2006).

Human rights ideology gradually started to dictate norms and behaviours at the world polity level, and many states started adopting human rights principles. It has been generally recognised (Donnelly 1999; Falk 2000; Forsythe 2018) that the power of human rights discourse stems from what Elliott (2014: 410) called 'the triumph of the individual' and a 'belief in the inherent dignity and equality of each individual person'. This foundation can be further translated into an ability to constitute social events by interpreting grievances and defining them as violations that should not, and need not, be tolerated.

Human rights form a significant part of the normative setting of world polity and are embedded in a whole variety of international regimes and organisations. Thus, they have increasingly defined 'civilised states' that belong to the shared community of the world polity (Risse 1999).

The power and the potency of human rights lie in the world polity, where human rights are promoted and maintained through global linkages by powerful nation-states vis-à-vis other nation-states. Human rights ideology draws its power and legitimacy from the macro level of a world polity system.

One way to understand the institutionalisation of the organisational and doctrinal powers of human rights is to see it from a neo-institutional perspective. Neo-institutionalists understand the world polity as a global system capable of creating values and norms through the collective conferral of authority (Boli and Thomas 1997; Meyer 1987). According to them, human rights ideology operates as 'a single global social system' (Berkovich 1999) in the world polity, meaning that states adopt human rights (often as window dressing) to comply with norms, ideas and practices at the world polity level. For example, by tracing the widespread institutionalisation of human rights since the mid-nineteenth century, Elliot (2014) showed that an important component of the expansion of human rights is the rise of the universal, egalitarian individual as the primary entity of social organisation in world society. In a similar fashion, Koo and Ramirez (2009) analysed the adoption rate of human rights institutions from 1966 to 2004 at the national level, convincingly demonstrating that the enactment of the human-rights–affirming nation-state model parallels a global trend of increasing numbers of human rights organisations and treaties worldwide.

Under the assumption that 'the widespread dissemination of a human rights discourse enables oppressed groups to translate events and policies into rights discourse and to appeal to courts, politicians and the media in order to seek remedies for their grievances' (Gordon and Berkovich 2007: 244), political sciences and political sociologists such as Finnemore (1993, 1996), Risse (1999), Sikkink (1993) and Ancelovici and Jenson (2013), among others, studied – and continue to study – processes of institutionalisation regarding human rights and the impact that human rights norms and ideas have on international and domestic politics. These actors tend to comply with external standards and structures; consequently, the diffusion of this structure has led to a phenomenon described as 'isomorphism' (McNeely 2012). Isomorphism points to the ongoing process of worldwide patterns of standardisation, institutional homogenisation and norm imitation, wherein 'models and norms that are institutionalized at the world level acquire taken-for-granted status over time' (Levy and Sznaider 2006). According to DiMaggio and Powel (1983), three processes – coercive, mimetic and normative – lead to the isomorphic outcome. This conclusion should be applied with great caution, however, because evidence shows that, at times, those isomorphic mechanisms support processes of divergence (Beckert 2010) and, once glocalised, produce various results on the ground.

Furthermore, the institutionalisation of human rights should not be misunderstood as being a linear process. In addition, it would be incorrect to ignore the historical and political dimension of human rights, as powerfully described in Joas' (2013) *Sacredness of Person* or Moyn's (2012) *The Last Utopia*. A wide range of scholarship demonstrates the importance of the role of non-state actors, such as voluntary civic associations, faith-based organisations, non-governmental organisations, community-based organisations, professional organisations, corporations, universities and transnational advocacy networks, that have pushed for certain agendas to be included in the human rights ideological framework. However, their work would hardly be possible – or at least would be more fragmented in its success – without the legitimacy that human rights as an ideology has gained at the world polity level. In other words, the power of the human rights ideology as a moral system results from its position in the formal hierarchy within international arenas (Donnelly 2007). This is significant, as the source of power can tell us a lot about the dynamic of organisational and doctrinal dispersion and the ways in which ideology is being institutionalised. For example, in nationalist-centred ideology, the nation-state is the main source of power and legitimacy. Siniša Malešević, a sociologist of nationalism, notes that, over the last three centuries, mass ideological doctrines have played a crucial role in justifying the existence of some of the most powerful organisations, such as the nation-state. He claims, furthermore, that ideological messages transmitting the potency of nationalism are generated by centrifugal ideologisation. Centrifugal ideologisation refers to

... an organizationally generated, mass scale process whereby specific ideological doctrines gradually start to permeate diverse social strata in different societies. The ultimate outcome of this process is a greater ideological unity among disparate individuals inhabiting the same social or political space. This historically contingent, uneven and contested process is expressed in the way that different social strata became highly receptive, not only to ideological justification of particular forms of social action, but also for ideological mobilization in the pursuit of such action. (Malešević 2013c: 26)

Instead of talking about centrifugal ideological power, when it comes to human rights, the term 'fractal doctrinal power' seems more appropriate. Doctrinal power is duplicated across macro, mezzo and micro levels, forming a never-ending pattern of diffusion of human rights. The term 'fractal' is used here as a metaphor, but it has qualities that help us understand the ways in which human rights' organisational and doctrinal power grow. Human rights ideology aims at duplicating and multiplying itself like fractals, infinitely complex components, yet these components are marked by self-similarity across different scales. Though human rights ideologies are positioned differently in historical and geographical terms, just like fractals they are created by a simple repetition process. In the case of human rights, this process occurs via discourses, practices and infrastructures, repeated over and over again in an ongoing feedback loop – a claim of universal human rights. In a way, just like natural fractals such as trees, rivers, clouds, mountains or coastlines, human rights aim at being perceived as natural and above politics, a one-for-all universal fit. The fractal nature of human rights points to an illusion through which one can understand the Mannheim paradox of ideology that is also well embedded in the field of sociology of human rights: one cannot maintain a position that all worldviews are ideological without simultaneously accepting that one's own position is ideological, too. I suggest that understanding the generative and accumulative force behind the organisational and doctrinal power of human rights and their ability to replicate and perpetuate moral forms and norms across diverse cultural and societal settings is essential for research of human rights.

However, both organisational and doctrinal penetration are necessary but not sufficient preconditions to transform any ideology from a poster ideology to a mobilising one. The persistence and success of any ideology require organisation (Collins 2008) and lie in its capacity to ideologically and organisationally bind together and translate micro-solidarity into a recruiting ideological action. It is vital to understand the impact of the processes of meaning-making at the micro-solidarity level and 'their capacity to ideologically and organisationally penetrate the micro-world and to link disparate pockets of micro-solidarity into a relatively coherent, all embracing, macro-narrative of ideological unity' (Malešević 2013c: 30). As a micro-level phenomenon, solidarity has been conceptualised as pro-social behaviour across different situations, avoiding breaches in situations of trust, and moral repair when violations have taken place. Starting from Durkheim (1964) onwards, sociologists have posited social solidarity as a universal, trans-historical and, for the most part, uniform phenomenon. Most forms of genuine durable solidarity entail a substantial degree of interpersonal contact and face-to-face interaction. Micro-solidarity matters greatly because it ultimately shows how certain values, ideas and norms recruit people into a moral, value-based action.

Benefits of Understanding Human Rights As an Ideology

The potential of stripping away our normative lenses and recognising human rights as an ideology brings to the fore questions that were not previously introduced and researched under the sociology of rights. Since Bryan Turner, a great number of sociologists have invested significant efforts in recognising the interconnectedness that exists between the sociology of rights and the sociology of human rights. These sociologists are increasingly conceptualising poverty; global economic inequality; social inequalities of race, class, gender, age and sexual orientation; and even memory not as social problems, but rather as human rights abuses. Though many of their studies have made a significant impact and expanded our knowledge base on human rights abuses, they all tend to understand human rights in a normative fashion, as a desirable societal outcome. Furthermore, although it seems implausible to openly deny that the human rights corpus is the construction of a political ideology, the discourse's major authors present it as non-ideological (Matua 1996). Hence, the focus on human rights abuses shrinks sociological research by omitting, blurring and covering up important sociological questions.

Omitting the conceptualisation of human rights as an ideology inevitably leads to ignoring the fact that human rights, just like any other ideology, tend to homogenise and monopolise the vision of the world as it should be. In that sense, the 'success' of human rights as an ideology can be measured precisely by the degree to which certain meanings and practices are almost universally seen as innocent, natural, clear and apparent. Having said that, and contrary to Ritzer's (1996) 'McDonaldization Thesis', those processes of homogenisation produce multiple overlapping but also significantly different results on the ground that often lead to greater inequality and social stratification. It is wrongly assumed that 'more human rights' improves equality; therefore, it is crucial to bind organisational and doctrinal power together with micro-solidarity to establish whether, how and when people and groups internalise and act upon human rights norms and values.

Hence, using this three-dimensional model of organisational power, doctrinal power and micro-solidarity as an analytical tool can help us bring together largely separate bodies of work to better understand how those levels interconnect and what mechanisms are in place that push social actors into change. When, for example, can the routinisation of organisational power within civil society serve as an important source of power? What is the impact of a decrease in the organisational power of human rights, as in the case of the United States' withdrawal from the Human Rights Council? Why is certain content included versus excluded from human rights ideology – for example, which political and societal processes lead to the adoption of a 'facing the past' agenda as a core pillar of human rights memorialisation (David 2017a)? What are the consequences of the partial inclusion of the 'right to self-determination' for the globalisation of justice and the ways in which human rights ideology mobilises social movements (Omer 2009)?

For research into human rights, it is of utmost significance to assess the organisational and ideological (dogmatic) power of human rights as that of an ideology encompassing an emancipatory potential, which is instinctively attractive to subjugated people – yet some important features of this process have remained largely unrecognised (and ignored) within the research of human rights. How and under what conditions do human rights produce inequalities? For example, how does human rights ideology shape inequalities through the hierarchies of victimhood in post-conflict settings (David 2017b)? How does it push people to overlook their health priorities and deeper racial and class inequalities (Hochschild 2016)? Why were economic rights excluded from its doctrinal power (Moyn 2018)? How can the politics of human rights (Bob 2005; Perugini and Gordon 2015) explain generative sociological processes in the long run, and the link between post-nationalist solidarity and democracy (Misztal 2010)? I suggest that, once human rights are conceptualised as an ideology, we may be able to comprehend issues surrounding human rights in a new light, through timely and exigent questions such as whether, if and when human rights ideology is capable of mobilising masses into violent action, when it serves to obscure political realities on the ground, and under what circumstances human rights ideology deepens poverty and racial inequality.

Finally, whereas organisational and doctrinal power relate to the structure and content of the cumulative and coercive power of human rights ideology, at the end what matters is the experience of solidarity in small groups and how it builds on interpersonal ties. Here, the rich scholarship on human rights as a practice, such as in the works of Mark Goodale and Selly Engle Merry, James Griffin and Fuyuki Kurasawa, brings to the fore a bottom-up approach to examine how individuals internalise human rights, and can shed new light on this topic once we understand the interconnectedness of organisational power, doctrinal power and micro-solidarity. How are human rights understood in face-to-face and mediated interactions? How and when do they create symbols, mark boundaries and exert pressure towards conformity? Why do they sometimes bring distant people together, yet other times just fade into indifference? In other words, the actual recruiting power of an ideology in the long run is always reflected in small-scale societal groups.

Extensive research, such as that of Michal Mann, Omer Bartov, Randall Collins, David Laitin, Siniša Malešević, Rogers Brubaker and Danny Caplan, shows the importance of micro-social attachment and individual motivation to ideological mobilisation. It is precisely in those small societal pockets that the might of ideology to effectively promote values can be captured. While we have some idea why, for example, soldiers fight in wars and how small-group attachments may produce terrorists, we have little idea why some people are motivated to help on some occasions yet stay indifferent in other situations. More strikingly, we lack any significant research on how those whose lives are heavily impacted by human rights infrastructures and values, such as refugees, internally displaced persons (IDPs) and victims of violence, understand human rights. Do they internalise human rights in the long run? How will their experiences of solidarity, filtered through a particular interpretation of symbols and history, impact their social attachments? Do those who become a subject of human rights interventions become more supportive of human rights? Are human rights capable of forging solidarity across different societal pockets in the long run? These are crucial questions, and any light their answers may shed may be of tremendous benefit, possibly altering the ways in which we understand human rights. Conceptualising human rights as an ideology matters because it can help us understand and assess if and why human rights values are being successfully embedded in microsolidarity groups and whether such human rights-centred solidarity is capable of mobilising masses into social action.

Conclusion

Understanding human rights as an ideology shifts the focus from the normative framing of rights and the desired realities on the ground and opens up a new avenue for evaluating how human rights beliefs and values generate change and affect societal structures that are shaped by historical, political and cultural processes. The model of human rights ideology that can be traced through a process of institutionalisation of human rights ideology – perpetuated, promoted, sustained and diffused through coercive and cumulative organisational and doctrinal power – may help us determine whether human rights ideology is capable of producing solidarity at the micro level to the extent of mobilising social actors into human rights–based actions. Finally, I argue that understanding human rights through ideology can bring some ground-breaking and fruitful insights, especially in areas that are under-researched because of the current focus on rights and wrongs instead of the potency of human rights as an ideology.

To further demonstrate the benefits of such an approach, I will analyse in the coming chapters one particular area of human rights – its memorialisation agenda. Using the previously elaborated three-legged model of ideology, I will describe a gradual historical–sociological process of the institutionalisation of organisational power, in terms of institutions and organisations that have enabled the promotion of the human rights memorialisation agenda, and as a result of that, the institutionalisation and rise of its ideological power. The adoption of particular content – ideological power – as a foundation for the human rights memorialisation agenda reveals its political and historically specific character, which later became obscured and concealed. Finally, I will demonstrate what happens when the human rights memorialisation agenda lands on conflict and post-conflict realities, showing the troubling effects it produces on the ground.

3 What Is Moral Remembrance?

Introduction

Barbara Misztal (2003: 147) rightly points out that coming to terms with the past (a specific version of it) has emerged as the grand narrative of our times. Memorialisation carries the burden of being a magic panacea. The UN report 'Memorialization Processes' (UN General Assembly 2014: 6) states that 'memorialization should be a means of combating injustice and promoting reconciliation', and that memorialisation gears itself 'not only towards the past (recalling events, recognizing and honoring victims, and enabling stories to be related), but equally to the present (healing processes and rebuilding trust between communities) and the future (preventing further violence through education and awareness-raising)'. In this chapter, I trace the emergence of a new global phenomenon called *moral remembrance*. This refers to the standardised ways, promoted through the human rights infrastructures of world polity, in which societies are supposed to deal with legacies of mass human rights abuses. It is based on three grounded principles: 'facing the past', 'duty to remember' and 'justice for victims'. These three principles have become deeply rooted in human rights memorialisation practices and norms. Collectively, they form a toolkit that offers a variety of memorialisation practices, including public expressions of emotions such as guilt, shame and remorse; performative actions such as public apologies, models of reconciliation and the erection of monuments and museums; and legal, penal or financial measures such as reparations, restitution, truth telling, international domestic and hybrid courts and memory laws, in addition to educational and artistic projects, dialogue groups, memory activism, historical justice claims and peacebuilding memorialisation activities. Although the list is endless because these practices replicate, fractal-like, over spatial and temporal dimensions, all are grounded in the same logic. It is this replication and growing of the cumulative organisational and ideological power of the isomorphic human rights memorialisation framework that has proliferated and, over the years, has coerced states into adapting to prescribed memorialisation standards. The guiding principle has been to force states to face, and become accountable for, past human rights abuses. States are expected[1] to conform to the international human rights norms of facing their criminal past and becoming accountable for massive, past human rights abuses. However, although states often (pretend to) willingly adopt human rights memorialisation norms, memorialisation agendas are almost exclusively enforced though different forms of international pressure.[2] This relationship arises because nation-states see their 'natural' (and exclusive) right in promoting memorialisation agendas as a means to formalise, codify and objectify systems that monopolise not only legitimate physical force, but also legitimate symbolic force. Hence, the main question I pose here is: once adopted (in some shape or form), is moral remembrance capable of producing and sustaining human rights values on the ground in the long run?

This chapter proceeds in four parts. First, I position, briefly, the notion of moral remembrance within world polity theory. Second, I employ a longue-durée historical–sociological perspective to address how the organisational power of the gradual process of memory standardisation became institutionalised and, in turn, how its establishment led to the emergence of moral remembrance. This standardisation of memory refers to a historical process through which the human rights understanding of memorialisation processes became institutionalised and gained organisational and ideological power. The process refers to a gradual, accumulative development from 'duty to remember' as an awareness-oriented approach to a contested past, to the policy-oriented 'proper memorialisation' standards understood and promoted as an insurance policy against the repetition of massive human rights abuses (David 2017a). This shift is grounded in the assumption that 'proper memorialisation' is essential for 'healing' societies with a difficult past and moving beyond trauma and violence. The organisational power of human rights, defined as an ongoing historical process that grows through discourse, knowledge and institutions, through their bureaucratic apparatus, involves the continual growth of an organisational capability for coercion. Organisational power points to the imprint in societal structure.

The third part of this chapter traces the emergence of the content of moral remembrance. Through its coercive foundation, the organisational power of human rights attempts to institutionalise and mandate content – normative standards understood here as ideological or doctrinal power. The more the organisational power institutionalises a structure, the

---

[1] By no means equally or evenly, but in relation to their position in the world polity.
[2] Never constant in its intensity, sustainability and reliability.

stronger and more coercive the content promoted through ideological power becomes. I bring to the fore the envelopment of what have become the pillars of the human rights memorialisation process: 'facing the past', 'duty to remember' and 'justice for victims'. All three are understood and promoted as an insurance policy meant to prevent the recurrence of violent conflicts.

In the fourth and final part of the chapter, I show how numerous false assumptions become institutionalised once concrete historical contexts become transformed into abstract memorialisation standards and look at some results of such processes.

Moral Remembrance and the World Polity

Ernest Gellner (1997), one of the first and most influential theoreticians on nationalism, claimed that 'the clue to understanding nationalism is its weakness at least as much as its strength'. The same caveat, I would argue, applies to human rights. Human rights are generally understood as moral principles or norms that describe certain standards of human behaviour. According to the Office of the UN High Commissioner for Human Rights: 'Human rights are rights inherent to all human beings, whatever our nationality, place of residence, sex, national or ethnic origin, colour, religion, language, or any other status. We are all equally entitled to our human rights without discrimination. These rights are all interrelated, interdependent and indivisible'.[3] According to *Encyclopedia Britannica* online:

Human rights are rights that belong to an individual or group of individuals simply for being human, or as a consequence of inherent human vulnerability, or because they are requisite to the possibility of a just society. Whatever their theoretical justification, human rights refer to a wide continuum of values or capabilities thought to enhance human agency or protect human interests and declared to be universal in character, in some sense equally claimed for all human beings, present and future. (Burns 2019)

Starting from Enlightenment philosophy as well as the French and American revolutions, as a collection of not yet well-grounded ideas, via the Universal Declaration of Human Rights, and up to the establishment of human rights institutions such as the United Nations (1945) and Amnesty International (1961), human rights gradually acquired and accumulated organisational and ideological power in the world polity,

---

[3] United Nations High Commissioner for Human Rights. What are human rights? Available at www.ohchr.org/en/issues/pages/whatarehumanrights.aspx

leading to a discursive shift from the 1970s onwards. The strength of human rights, understood as moral principles or norms that describe certain standards of human behaviour, lies in their universalism and globalism; that is, they assume a set of universal human needs across the globe regardless of historical, political, national or cultural context. Human rights stand for the worldwide inclusion of all people into one moral community, as opposed to nationalism, for example, which presumes nationally organised collectives.

The institutionalisation of human rights in global governance, and its impact on the nation-state in general, has been heavily documented and discussed. However, since the late 1970s, the Stanford School brought to the fore a new approach to explain how global world polity ideas become implemented through global actors. This is important because, unlike nationalism, for example, human rights ideology draws its power and legitimacy from the macro level of the world polity system. To understand how the organisational and ideological powers of human rights became institutionalised is to recognise the capability of the world polity as a global system that creates values and norms through the collective conferral of authority (Boli and Thomas, 1997; Mayer 1987). The intensification of universalistic conceptions of politics and morality in the post–World War II period coincides with the growth of a global human rights–oriented civil society sector (Anheier, Glasius and Kaldor 2001; Boli and Thomas 1999; Sikkink and Smith 2002). Therefore, the enactment of the 'human rights affirming nation-state' model (Koo and Ramirez 2009) is facilitated through the organisational power of human rights ideology, defined here as the ability of the organisational structure to utilise all mandatory resources in favour of its ideological development. These actors tend to comply with external standards and structures.

Within this setting of global polity, in which human rights became adopted as desired moral and cultural norms, moral remembrance emerged. Moral remembrance refers to the standardised ways, promoted through the human rights infrastructures of the world polity, in which societies are expected to deal with legacies of mass human rights abuses. Moral remembrance is grounded in one of the core assumptions of human rights – that coming to terms with the past is crucial for the implementation of democracy and the principles of human rights. In the past four decades, memory construction has become a crucial category through which the human rights regime enforces moral responsibilities for past atrocities. The human rights memorialisation agenda advances abstraction for the sake of universalism: every person is endowed with the same set of basic rights. Emerging from this observation, the suffering of others – no matter where or who they are – becomes 'our' moral and political concern. Moral remembrance refers to a gradual, accumulative development from 'duty to remember' as an awareness-oriented approach to the contested past, to policy-oriented proper memorialisation standards, understood and promoted as an insurance policy against the repetition of massive human rights abuses. This shift is grounded in the assumption that 'proper memorialisation' is essential for 'healing' societies with a difficult past and moving beyond trauma and violence. The process through which moral remembrance gradually developed can be traced back to the long-term historical processes of the institutionalisation of particular memorialisation agendas, through which both organisational and ideological power supposedly enabled and produced effective human rights values on the ground.

The Organisational Power of Moral Remembrance: The Emergence of the Structure

The institutionalisation proper of the human rights memorialisation agenda started with the United Nations' adoption of the Universal Declaration of Human Rights (UDHR) on 10 December 1948. The UDHR has no legal force and was not tailored to address memory issues per se. Nevertheless, as the single most important statement of ethics, its authority is unparalleled when it comes to memorialisation processes. Many legal experts suggest that it has acquired the status of international customary law, partially because of its almost unprecedented translation into approximately 360 languages. The UDHR, together with two binding treaties, the International Covenant on Civil and Political Rights (ICCPR) and the International Covenant on Economic, Social and Cultural Rights (ICESCR), adopted in 1966, forms the International Bill of Human Rights, which encapsulates a tradition of three centuries of human rights thinking and more than two millennia of natural law (De Baets 2009a: 20). However, at the beginning, the human rights understanding of memorialisation processes was developed on the side-lines of the core human rights agenda.

World War II, and in particular the Holocaust, led to a whole range of normative and institutional changes that primarily focused on preventing human suffering as a result of war and political persecution and took memory for granted. The importance of memory surfaced only gradually in the years afterwards. Immediately after the war, in 1945 and 1946, some of those persons responsible for crimes committed during the Holocaust were brought to trial in Nuremberg, Germany. The Nuremberg trials resulted in the sentencing of twelve prominent Nazis to death.

In contrast, others who played key roles in the Holocaust, including high-level government officials and business executives who used concentration camp inmates as forced laborers, received short prison sentences or no penalty at all. In the Far East, the International Military Tribunal for the Far East (IMTFE), also known as the Tokyo Trials, a military trial convened in 1946, was established to try the leaders of the Empire of Japan for 'Class A' crimes. Twenty-eight Japanese military and political leaders were charged with waging aggressive war and with responsibility for conventional war crimes. Trials of Nazis continued to take place both in Germany and many other countries. More than 5,700 lower-ranking personnel were charged with conventional war crimes in separate trials convened by Australia, China, France, the Netherlands, the Philippines, the United Kingdom and the United States. China held 13 tribunals, resulting in 504 convictions and 149 executions. Poland (with its most famous post-war national trial being held in 1947, in Krakow), the former Czechoslovakia, the Soviet Union, Hungary, Romania and France, among others, have tried thousands of defendants – both Germans and indigenous collaborators – in the decades since 1945. The Soviet Union held its first trial, the Krasnodar Trial, against local collaborators in 1943, well before World War II had ended. In Israel, after the introduction of testimony from hundreds of witnesses, Adolf Eichmann was found guilty and executed in 1962. The charges covered a wide range of crimes, including prisoner abuse, rape, sexual slavery, torture, ill treatment of laborers, execution without trial and inhumane medical experiments.

Those trials resulted in the establishment of permanent infrastructures such as the International Court of Justice (in 1945), the principal judicial organ of the United Nations. It was followed by creation of three major regional human rights instruments: the European Convention on Human Rights (1953), the American Convention on Human Rights (1969) and the African Charter on Human and Peoples' Rights (1979), all of which provided wider infrastructures for framing past human rights abuses in legal terms. Additionally, as the immediate effects of the post–World War II experience were felt around the world, the United Nations issued, in 1948, the Convention on the Prevention and Punishment of the Crime of Genocide, which for the first time recognised genocide as a crime under international law. Regardless of whether states have ratified the Genocide Convention, they all become bound as a matter of law by the principle that genocide is a crime prohibited under international law.

However, those legal foundations had a limited impact on the wider population. It was actually the foundations and institutionalisation of human rights activism that put forward a much wider agenda that gradually enabled the spread of the memorialisation agenda. Through networks of human rights activism, a widely diffused human rights infrastructure became increasingly embedded in a set of regional, international and global linkages. During the period from 1947 to the mid-1980s, the UDHR served as the foundation for the creation of an entire framework of international and transnational human rights discourses, within which the most important human rights instruments, non-governmental organisations (NGOs) and international publications were established, developed and grew in power and influence (Goodale 2006). Since the mid-1970s, the 'third wave of democratisation' has brought an explosion of previously suppressed collective memories and adjoining dilemmas of how to address past wrongdoings (Huntington 1991). Since the 1980s, the human rights vision of memorialisation as a process of remembering the wrongs of the past and honouring the victims has grown, together with the widely held idea that public and official recognition of crimes is 'essential for preventing further violence' (Hazan 2010: 5). One defining feature of the international human rights movement is the new concern for the suffering of specific others in distant lands – an agenda that, to some extent, displaces those earlier, very nation-specific struggles, even in the same places (Moyn 2012). To this end, certain necessary historical and social conditions had to take hold to bring about the rise of the moral state of compassion, defined by Sznaider (1998) as an active moral demand to address the suffering of others. The moral demand to act so as to lessen the suffering of others, across spatial and temporal dimensions, became possible only in the intersection between 'humanitarianism' and the emergence of liberal society, with its distinctive features of capitalism (the market) and democracy (civic equality and citizenship) (Sznaider 1998: 118). On the one hand, through democratisation and the lessening of profoundly categorical and corporate social distinctions, compassion becomes more extensive. On the other hand, the emergence of the market society, by widening the scope of exchange, unintentionally extended the public scope of compassion (Sznaider 1998: 119). Further, through memories of human rights abuses and their institutionalisation in international conventions, cruelty became understood as the infliction of unwarranted suffering, with compassion evolving as a public response to this evil and ultimately being transformed into an organised campaign to lessen the suffering of strangers (Sznaider 2015).

The rapid growth of memorialisation across the globe and the obsession with it during the 1980s and 1990s, which shifted from commemorating victories to commemorating massive past human rights abuses, might be explained by the fact that memorialisation became a crucial representation of the identity politics struggle (Winter 2007). In particular, since the 1980s and more so since the 1990s, when identity politics was a feature of the recovery of witnesses after the Soviet empire's collapse in 1989 (Winter 2007), it became clear to all parties involved in the process of memory construction that memory is not a guaranteed right but a privilege. The 1990s were filled with illusions generated by the collapse of Communist regimes, the retreat of social democracy in Europe and the abandonment of socialist ideals in post-colonial Asia and Africa. The ethical vacuum was filled by human rights, which were entrusted, as Moyn (2012: 9) wrote, with 'the grand political mission of providing a global framework for the achievement of freedom, identity and prosperity'. The increasing importance of memory also has to do both with developments in information technology and the inclusion of post-traumatic stress disorder (PTSD) in 1980 as a recognised medical diagnostic classification. Once accepted as a syndrome, PTSD validated not only rights to pensions, to medical care and to public sympathy, but also to the commemoration of traumatic memory (Young 1995).

These processes coincided with dilemmas for 1980s human rights activists, lawyers and legal scholars, policymakers, journalists, donors and comparative politics experts – dilemmas that were raised in regard to places such as Korea, Chile, South Africa, Brazil, the Philippines, Uruguay, Guatemala, Haiti, Poland and Czechoslovakia, and that relate to human rights and the dynamics of the 'transition to democracy' (Arthur 2009). A new sort of human rights activity was generated, labelled 'transitional justice', which was 'the full range of processes and mechanisms associated with a society's attempt to come to terms with a legacy of large-scale past abuses, in order to ensure accountability, serve justice and achieve reconciliation'.[4] It includes criminal prosecutions, truth commissions, reparations programs and various kinds of institutional reforms. The paradigm of transitional justice, which included not only juridical but also political and social mechanisms (with a strong focus on memorialisation), was intensively promoted from the late 1980s and has become the main ideological force behind the human rights agenda in conflict and post-conflict settings. Particularly for the 'third wave' democratic transitions in Eastern Europe and Latin America, which helped shape the core paradigms and normative assumptions of the field, the desired endpoint of the transition in question typically resembled a Western liberal market democracy (Sharp 2013). Transitional justice is reflective of, and contributes to, cosmopolitan imperatives, as it revolves around

---

[4] United Nations Regional Information Centre, Transitional Justice. (2014). Available at www.unric.org/html/english/library/backgrounders/transitionaljustice.pdf.

judicial procedures and memory practices addressing legacies of human rights abuses. Facilitating that transition from an authoritarian regime to stable democratic governance has come to involve some degree of recognition of the 'other': in the context of international legitimacy, cosmopolitan imperatives command a narrative that acknowledges past injustices (Levy and Sznaider 2010).

Transitional justice practices and related legal memories have emerged as a central political-institutional mechanism and cultural-normative arena in which the legal domain is not only about the institutionalisation of universal claims on which nation-state sovereignty and the self-understanding of a political community rest, but also figures as a strategic site of their transformation (Held 2002). With the establishment of international tribunals to prosecute those responsible for crimes in the former Yugoslavia (ICTY in 1993) and Rwanda (ICTR 1994), and the International Criminal Court (ICC in 1998), transitional justice became deeply institutionalised and a powerful ideological tool intended as a guiding model at the world polity stage.

Transitional justice, as a field and practice, has grown tremendously over the past decades. It now includes the institution of international criminal tribunals, hybrid courts and the International Criminal Court; the development of a 'right to truth' and a 'right to reparation' under international law; the transnational proliferation of truth and reconciliation commissions (TRCs); the expansion of transitional justice scholarship, peer-reviewed journals, research centres and academic programs; and the birth of international and regional transitional justice NGOs (Nagy 2008). With its institutionalisation and its status as an established fixture on the global terrain of human rights, it became potent with organisational power and able to put pressure on states to comply with norms set by transitional justice institutions, which included memorialisation processes framed in a particular way.

However, the appearance of transitional justice as a novel legal framework was followed by a broader spectrum of ideas, concepts and practices that, gradually, clearly defined the memorialisation agenda. It developed parallel to the notion of restorative justice developed by a criminologist, Howard Zahr (1990), who viewed any crime primarily as a violation of people and relationships that need and can be repaired. Based on the positive results of efforts in the late 1970s and 1980s at victim–offender mediation in the United States (Van Ness and Strong 2010: 27), by the 1990s restorative justice had become a global movement (Johnstone and Van Ness 2007) – one that moved well beyond a narrow criminal justice paradigm and became implemented into human rights advocacy to redress legacies of human rights abuses in post-conflict settings. The restorative justice framework proposed mediation between the victim and the offender, along with accountability, as necessary steps to bring justice and healing to victims. With the adoption of the Working Party on Restorative Justice (1998) and the United Nations' adoption of 'Basic Principles on the Use of Restorative Justice' into the ICC agenda, the ICC – a 100-member-state, permanent court that tries persons accused of genocide, crimes against humanity and war crimes –became a main vehicle by which NGOs have adopted, promoted and disseminated restorative justice practices globally from the 1990s onward. In doing so, the focus has shifted from a criminal justice discourse to a human rights discourse on reconciliation, peacebuilding and memory.

The notion of 'accountability', in particular, enabled new frameworks (other than legal) to supposedly inflict human rights values on states in 'transition' from conflict-ridden or totalitarian systems to democracy. Transitional justice adopted accountability principles to fight impunity as the main approach for dealing with difficult legacies. Having said that, accountability mechanisms and restorative justice were broadened to include not solely juridical but also political and social mechanisms (Bell 2009; Teitel 2003). The original focus of transitional justice, rooted in the discipline of law, was that human rights law requires accountability to fight impunity among transitional societies. In a ground-breaking article, M. Cherif Bassiouni (1996),[5] one of the leading promoters of the centrality of criminal prosecution for transitional justice, placed accountability at the very heart of transitional justice. Building the accountability approach as a pillar of justice for victims, he provided a long list of examples where there was 'a high level of victimization, including genocide, crimes against humanity, and war crimes for which there has been no accountability'. More importantly, he expanded the legal notion of accountability, framed as being the antithesis of impunity, arguing that accountability is not only a putative measure but also 'integrally linked to prevention and deterrence' (Bassiouni 1996: 26). In recent years, the notion of legal accountability has given rise to a new model of criminal accountability, in which individuals are held responsible for human rights violations (Sikkink 2011) along with the responsibility to protect (R2P). Used by states acting collectively through the ICC to hold individuals responsible for human rights violations (Sikkink 2011), R2P refers to the responsibility of the international community to intervene (Borzel and Risse 2012).

---

[5] Professor of Law and Former Chairman of the United Nations Commission of Experts Established Pursuant to Security Council Resolution 780 (1992) to Investigate Violations of International Humanitarian Law in the former Yugoslavia.

Once the human rights infrastructure was in place, to impact memorialisation processes on the ground, different organisations and institutions, through the work of knowledge-based expert groups, gradually developed policy recommendations and briefings. Together with the principles underlying the idea of reparations, as drafted by the Special Rapporteurs van Boven and Bassiouni and adopted by the UN General Assembly in 2005, they discussed at length the principles underlying the idea of memorialisation standards as pillars of the broader issue of reparations, arguing passionately that these principles may bring about reconciliation in divided societies, and should be considered as the best roadmap for memorialisation processes. Culminating in 2013 and 2014, memorialisation become the main stream within the field of cultural rights. Two important reports, one on history textbooks and the second on memorialisation in general, were presented at the UN General Assembly as part of dealing with the promotion and protection of human rights. Both policy papers were written by the Special Rapporteur in the field of cultural rights, Farida Shaheed, as mandated by the General Assembly in 2009. Her 2014 final report on memorialisation processes, written after a series of expert meetings, 'stresses the significance of actions in the cultural field for achieving the overall societal goals of transitional justice, while noting that entire cultural and symbolic landscapes are designed through memorials and museums, which both reflect and shape, negatively or positively, social interactions and people's cognition of identities – their own as well as that of others' (UN General Assembly 2014: 1).

By the time the United Nations had published those two distinct policy briefings with regard to memorialisation processes, several other initiatives promoting the importance of memorialisation policies had already taken place. The first was published in 2007 and based on the international conference on 'Memorialization and Democracy: State Policy and Civic Action' that was held on 20–22 June 2007 in Santiago, Chile. This effort was largely propelled by the notion that, for victims of violence, memorialisation initiatives were the second most important form of state reparation, after financial compensation (Kiza, Rathgeber and Rohne 2006). Around the same time, a US Institute of Peace working group published a report with detailed recommendations as part of its Stabilization and Reconstruction series: *The Urge to Remember: The Role of Memorials in Social Reconstruction and Transitional Justice*. This report 'focused on the role of memorialization in promoting, jeopardizing, or impairing social reconstruction and reconciliation in societies emerging from violent conflict' (Barsalou and Baxter 2007). The same ideas proliferated in other parts of the world, and in 2013, an additional memorialisation policy report was published by INGO Impunity Watch (IW)[6] following the International Memory Initiatives Exchange Forum 'Breaking the Silence', which was held in Phnom Penh, Cambodia. This report went even further than earlier documents by providing a set of 'Guiding Principles for Memorialization' (IW 2013), as did another report a year later in 2014 – 'Memory for Change Memorialization as a Tool for Transitional Justice'. Similarly, the US Institute of Peace Memorialization Report (Barsalou and Baxter 2007) ascribes to memorialisation a plethora of functions, such as truth-telling or documenting specific human rights violations; creating a specific place to mourn victims; symbolic reparations to honour the victims of violence; a symbol of a commitment to values of democracy and human rights; and the promotion of reconciliation by repairing damaged relations among groups. All of these memorialisation briefings are meant to provide practical guidance for places after periods of state repression or violent conflicts that were characterised by massive human rights abuses. The briefing reports claim that memorialisation is 'commonly understood in terms of commemoration, the non-recurrence of violence and symbolic forms of reparations[;] research now demonstrates that memorialization must be considered beyond these traditional understandings and as contributing in much more dynamic and diverse ways to attempts to deal with a violent past, including truth and justice' (IW 2013: 3).

Attempts to incorporate memorialisation processes as an integral part of transitional justice mechanisms, and to move from 'duty to remember' as a moral instance to the policy-oriented 'proper way to remember', are designed and envisioned through *standardisation of memory*. According to the authors of the UN Report on Memorialization Standards (UN General Assembly 2014), memorialisation has become a core principle and is developed as a set of policies for combating injustice and promoting reconciliation. Thus, the United Nations' adoption of 'memorialisation standards' that promoted Western memorial models as a template for the representation of past tragedies or mass crimes seems to be a logical step. The UN document explains: 'Western memorial models commemorating the victims of Nazism,[7] while not always the most adequate or

---

[6] Impunity Watch is a Netherlands-based, international non-profit organization that conducts periodic and sustained research into the root causes of impunity and obstacles to its reduction; this research includes the voices of affected communities in an effort to produce research-based policy advice on processes intended to encourage truth, justice, reparations and the nonrecurrence of violence.

[7] Alluding here to German Chancellor Willy Brandt's emotional gesture of falling down on his knees in front of the Jewish ghetto in Warsaw in 1970 as a sign of deep regret and apology.

appropriate, have become a template or at least a political and aesthetic inspiration for the representation of past tragedies or mass crimes' (UN General Assembly 2014: 8). Another report, dating from 2007, reflects this same attitude, noting that certain 'standards concerning the role of states in dealing with the past are starting to emerge' (Brett et al. 2007: 20).

Standardisation is a crucial feature of the process of the emergence of global moral remembrance. It is precisely this shift from context-based memorialisation to abstract models of memorialisation that is generated through the process of gradual standardisation that is allegedly applicable worldwide. Standardisation is always about aggregative knowledge that, due to budgetary concerns and impact measurements, is meant for collectives that are defined through a categorical key, and not for individuals, who rarely fit solely into one particular category. This emphasis, I suggest, exposes the cumulative and coercive bureaucratic nature of the human rights regime, which tries to homogenise and monopolise the way we are supposed to frame and remember our past.

Moving from the legal framework, human rights broadened its spectrum from solely legal mechanisms to include various explicit and implicit memorialisation agendas and practices, such as reparations, truth committees, commemorations, museums and memory sites, to name but a few, and finally to memorialisation policies that have narrowly defined the canon of proper remembrance. This several-decades-long historical process put in place the infrastructure for the appearance of moral remembrance. As previously stated, moral remembrance is based on three grounded principles: 'facing the past', 'duty to remember' and 'justice for victims'. These three principles have become deeply rooted in human rights memorialisation practices and norms.

The Ideological Power of Moral Remembrance: The Promotion of Content

Once the organisational power was set in motion, what was the content that was pushed forward? And what is the memory-frame in which this content is being promoted? 'Memory-frame' describes a specific positioning of, and relationship between, an object of study and its 'surroundings' (Burke 2002: 152). It pertains to 'the setting within which specific content is presented to us' when we recall images of the past, 'providing a unique ambiance for this content in each case' (Casey 2000: 68). Indeed, this memory-frame serves as the setting in which the specific content of a memory is situated and, when situated in a certain way, is imposed through the normative schemes of moral remembrance.

What is the memory-frame that moral remembrance imposes? As the human rights memorialisation agenda is crafted through the prism of universalism, standardisation of memory requires a shift from concrete memories to abstract remembrance. This, however, always occurs at the expense of complexities and moral ambiguities. Three main principles have crystallised over the years and become pillars of the human rights memorialisation agenda: the 'facing the past' principle, the 'duty to remember' principle and the 'justice for victims' principle. Those principles have become so deeply rooted into human rights memorialisation practices and norms that their historical–political context has been whitewashed and misinterpreted as being apolitical and 'natural' and the only proper way to remember the past. It is precisely this seemingly 'natural' and 'logical' way to treat past human rights abuses that hides the particular context and politics under which those principles have been produced. Hence, one should be well aware that the naturalisation of those principles, promoted through the organisational and ideological power of moral remembrance, does not make them ultimately right, but instead helps to hinder and de-historicise their wider meanings and applications. In other words, what we might perceive as 'natural' are, in fact, social forces and context in disguise.

To unveil those blind spots, it is crucial to understand the ways in which certain events and discourses have been adopted by human rights activists and promoters and further translated into principles, practices and norms. In particular, to understand the adoption of the 'duty to remember' and 'facing the past' principles as major forces in the human rights memorialisation agenda, it is necessary to reflect upon several historical events, different in their intent and impact but very significant for the expansion of the human rights memorialisation agenda at both the ideological and practical levels.

Facing the Past

The rationale for placing the notion of 'facing the past' at the heart of post-conflict processes and massive human rights abuses has been established and rationalised based on three primary assumptions. The first, borrowed from individual psychology, is that working through the past is necessary for healing, forgiveness and reconciliation. The second, a political position, argues that accountability fosters democracy and promotes peace and human rights. The third posits processes of dealing with the past as a moral duty, to remember the victims and acknowledge their trauma (Dragović-Soso 2010). Those assumptions developed gradually as an important counter-effort to World War II, with the ultimate goal to 'heal the nation' and to reconcile so as to move beyond the troubled past. The moral grounds for the idealistic assumption of 'healing' and 'reconciliation', rooted in religious Christian thinking, were that 'reconciliation', as a genuine alternative to war, is a long-term process and a movement forward towards making peace. In that sense, reconciliation refers to a process by which countries can establish structures and procedures for establishing durable peace with their adversaries (Ackermann 1994: 229). Reconciliation was to be achieved, similar to the later-developed transitional justice mechanism, through a variety of forms and practices such as education, memorials, and written and verbal dialogues about the past (Gardner Feldman 1999: 335).

The most influential reconciliation project that has been impacted by memorialisation processes and practices, beyond recognition, is to be found in the post–World War II Franco–German partnership. In the Franco–German instance, a clear moral imperative emerged for societal and political leaders to confront the past. In this partnership, religious leaders played a primary role in unfreezing relations, not only via the well-known Roman Catholic efforts, but also through equally influential, though less heralded, Protestant voices and actions (Gardner Feldman 1999). The Franco–German case is rightly depicted as an inspiring model and even sometimes as 'the biggest product of reconciliation in history' (Kurbjuweit 2010). In 1964 alone, the Franco–German Youth Office contributed to the coming together of 180,000 youths from both countries at 6,500 gatherings, seminars and study trips – a process that gradually affected all levels of society. In just a couple of decades, from being bitter adversaries, the Franco–German relationship had been upgraded on multiple levels. The countries became each other's most important trade partner. In addition, more than 2,500 towns are involved in twinning programs and partnerships, with almost 75 per cent of the French and German populations living in twinned cities or towns. More than 7 million young people have been involved in student exchange programs (Rosoux 2016). The impact of what is today known as the German model of human rights understanding and promotion of memorialisation processes is gargantuan.

Human rights activists and politicians from South Africa and elsewhere closely studied what the Germans had done by way of trials, public commemorations, schoolbooks and their partnership with France. Indeed, the Chinese would at one point admonish Japan that, in dealing with World War II, it should adopt the 'German model' (Werner Müller 2015). Further, the human rights memorialisation agenda was greatly shaped by historian debates in the 1980s in Germany and was further developed and adapted to fit the policy-oriented frameworks of transitional justice. The *Historikerstreit*[8] ('historians' quarrel') was an intellectual and political controversy in the late 1980s in West Germany about the crimes of Nazi Germany, including their comparability with the crimes of the Soviet Union. In the famous German *Historikerstreit*, German historians debated at length the notions of *Vergangenheitsbewältigung*: 'dealing with the past,' 'treating the past,' 'working over the past' or 'overcoming the past.' In particular, the historians' debate questioned how and when the memory of violent events might be 'overcome' or 'mastered', and how accountability supposedly facilitates democratisation processes and liberal peace. The debate, which focused on the process of turning remembrance into public awareness, took place in media outlets in West Germany at the same time as discussions in Latin America explored how to deal with former right-wing regimes. The centrality of the 'facing the past' approach was much promoted by Adorno's 1959 influential article 'What Does Coming to Terms with the Past Mean?,' in which he argued that a culture of forgetting threatens democracy because real democracy requires a self-critical working through of the past. Similarly, Habermas (1997) argued that one must accept the presence of the past as a 'burden' on moral accountability. The *Historikerstreit* in Germany and human rights activism in South America – both of which, in many ways, shaped and promoted such notions – were inspired by the rise of Western individual psychology in general and specifically by Freud's psychoanalytical approach to retrieving repressed painful memories as part of a healing process (Misztal 2003: 140–143). The highly influential book *The Inability to Mourn: Principles of Collective Behavior*, written by Margarete and Alexander Mitscherlich (1967), applied Freudian theory to explain post-war Germany's failure to come to terms with its wartime guilt; it became a key text during the student unrest in 1968, leading to demands that the wartime generation face up to the past. The Mitscherlichs, both psychoanalysts and co-founders of the Sigmund Freud Institute for psychoanalytic research in Frankfurt, contended that, unless Germans confronted their past and worked through the memories and implications of what had happened, they could not begin to move on.

---

[8] The *Historikerstreit* spanned the years 1986–1989, and pitted right-wing intellectuals against left-wing intellectuals. The positions taken by the right-wing intellectuals were largely based on the totalitarianism approach, which takes a comparative approach to totalitarian states, while the left-wing intellectuals argued that fascism was uniquely evil, arguing it could not be equated with the crimes of Soviet communism. The debate attracted much media attention in West Germany, with its participants frequently giving television interviews and writing op-ed pieces in newspapers.

This approach echoed and was further established though a series of conferences that took place in the late 1980s and early 1990s: the 1988 Aspen Institute conference on 'State Crimes: Punishment or Pardon'; the 1992 conference in Salzburg, Austria, on 'Justice in Times of Transition'; and the 1994 Institute for Democracy in South Africa conference on 'Dealing with the Past'. In these conferences, 'political actors, human rights activists, and observers from around the world were convened in order to compare experiences' and discuss transitions to democracy (Arthur 2009: 325). During the 1990s and continuing today, coming to terms with the past has emerged as the ultimate imperative, providing a scheme that can help transitional societies move forward into democracy. The previously mentioned conferences gave full legitimacy to the 'facing the past' approach, as remembering became intimately tied to a preventive vision of 'never again!' in which suffering and sacrifices have not happened in vain (Olesen 2012: 337).

The German model was not the only one proposed, though it became the most dominant approach after the late 1990s. For several geo-political regions, the Spanish model of *consenso* (consensus) proved to be a blueprint for addressing mass human rights atrocities. The Spanish model produced another concept of 'dealing with the past' that has been most often characterised as a deliberate, but largely tacit agreement to 'forget' the past – a pact of oblivion or *Pacto del Olvido* (Davis 2005). The idea of reconciliation was promoted through the notion of a peaceful handover of power in return for silence about the past. For two decades, from the late 1970s until the mid-1990s, the Spanish model proved appealing to both Latin American and East European countries, as it offered a roadmap for concrete political action. The Spanish model of *consenso* was also part of the debate across Eastern Europe – from Poland and Hungary to the Soviet Union – over the nature of the transformation away from communism (James, Baby and Kassel 2019). Notably, it advocated 'pardoning without forgetting' the criminalities of the antecedent regime.

All over Latin America, Spanish politicians, publicists and academics promoted their vision of collective amnesty and official oblivion with the putative assumption that it would be the only appropriate approach to peaceful democratisation. However, while the Spanish model of dealing with the past informed the Chilean transition of 1988, neighbouring Argentina instead appropriated the model of the truth commission (established in 1983), proposing a new vision of dealing with the past based on 'truth without justice' (Kressel 2019). Yet, between 1996 and 1998, an abundance of evidence on human rights abuses was gathered with the assistance of numerous human rights NGOs, both in Spain and abroad. Part of a much broader investigation into the human rights crimes of Latin America's southern cone dictatorships, a formal inquiry was initiated in July 1996, when charges of genocide and terrorism were filed in a Valencia court against former Chilean dictator Augusto Pinochet and a number of his associates (Davis 2000: 6–7). The Chilean government's diplomatic engagement to secure Pinochet's repatriation became a topic of worldwide debate. The transnational mobilisations of Latin American activists and their cooperation with European and American partners not only led to the reopening of trials against former military leaders in Latin America, but also prompted the revival of pro-accountability discourses as a necessity for healing nations: the revisiting of General Francisco Franco's crimes in Spain, in return, influenced memory processes in Eastern Europe (Baer and Sznaider 2017).

By the mid-1990s, the fascination with the Spanish transition was in decline. However, for almost twenty years, the Spanish model of *consenso* had been a powerful transmittable experience which had been incorporated into political debates in many countries undergoing transition (James, Baby and Kassel 2019).

The decline of the Spanish model was also due to the extensive transnational activist networks and victim groups that pushed for accountability and the German model, rather than impunity. However, from the 1990s, two models of 'dealing with the past', both deeply rooted in the assumption that proper 'dealing with the past' is necessary for a transition to democracy and for better appreciation of human rights, prevailed: the reconciliation model, which stemmed from the Franco–German model and was later utilised in the South African experience, and the truth model, which originated from Latin American experiences. Those approaches to past human rights abuses also created a global movement for historical justice – acknowledging and redressing historic wrongs – which represents one of the most significant moral and social developments of our times and which has been actively promoted in both scholar and activist circles. The 'growing importance of pursuing retroactive justice is also a result of the increased valorisation of memory as the essential element of collective identity' (Misztal 2001:63). Global injustice memories are thus intimately connected to an implicit or explicit global 'we', with moral responsibilities that extend beyond national boundaries and identities (Olesen 2012: 377). Based on the historical experience of the oppressed and oppressors, those new global movements for historical justice often form new solidarities based on those dichotomies.[9]

---

[9] However, the global solidarities of the oppressed are often grounded in narrow nationalist agendas.

The 'Duty to Remember' Principle

It is hard to distinguish which developed first: the 'duty to remember' or the 'facing the past' principle. The histories of these two concepts intertwine in multiple ways. The universalised notion of 'duty to remember' appeared in the aftermath of World War II, with mediatised criminal proceedings, most famously during the international military tribunal in Nuremberg (1945–1946), the Israeli trials of Adolf Eichmann (1961) and Ivan Demjanjuk (1986–1988), and the French trial of Klaus Barbie (1987) (Belavusau and Gliszczyńska-Grabias 2017: 8). However, the expression 'a duty to remember mass crimes' first appeared in German Chancellor Helmut Schmidt's speech delivered in a Cologne synagogue at the Kristallnacht commemoration, on 9 November 1978. This notion also echoed during the *Historikerstreit* in Germany in a way that can be read as a criticism of this culture of 'remembering to forget and forgetting to remember' (Zehfuss 2006).

All of this set a tone and developed a belief in redemption through memory. Since the 1980s, historians, politicians, political scientists, human rights lawyers and activists have all advanced this idea either directly or indirectly. The question was not whether to forget, but rather how to engrave memory into the flesh of a nation. For example, the Truth and Reconciliation Commission, a court-like restorative justice body assembled in South Africa after the abolition of apartheid in 1996, was 'established with the hope that it would bring social catharsis – that the truth about the past, by being revealed, will bring reconciliation' (Margalit 2002: 5). The seemingly simplistic phrase 'duty to remember' became both a political slogan for redemption and a panacea for digesting atrocities committed in the past. This assumption, developed mostly by human rights lawyers, activists and political scientists, was based on an idealised view: that by compelling the honouring of the memory of those who died, the 'duty to remember' would act as an insurance policy against the repetition of such crimes. In fact, virtually no evidence supports this presumption, yet it remains one of the most deeply embedded ideas that impact not only day-to-day politics and policy-making but, more profoundly, the meaning-making processes of selfhood and nationhood.

The shift from awareness-oriented 'duty to remember' to policy-oriented 'proper way of remembrance' (David 2017a), along with the institutionalisation of human rights ideology, altered the ways in which we understand the memorialisation process and contributed to the rise of moral remembrance – a demand that, for the sake of morality and preventing the recurrence of violence, collectives must comply with certain memorialisation forms, norms and values. The impact of this shift is far reaching. For example, recent developments in EU law indicate a substantial evolution of the activist citizenship discourse on historic memory from 'invitation to remember' towards 'duty to remember' (Fronza 2006). In a similar trend, Jenna Thompson (2009) claims that citizens are obliged to remember the deeds of their predecessors and to apologise and make recompense for historical injustices. Those claims are important as they reflect the overreaching practical implication of this deeply embedded notion of 'duty to remember' and its shift towards ethics of moral remembrance.

The 'Justice for Victims' Principle

The main authors of the human rights discourses, including Western UN states, international NGOs and senior Western academics, constructed a three-dimensional prism consisting of victims, perpetrators and bystanders (Matua 2001). An important milestone in enrooting this division came in 1985, when the UN General Assembly adopted the following definition of victims:

> 'Victims' means persons who, individually or collectively, have suffered harm, including physical or mental injury, emotional suffering, economic loss or substantial impairment of their fundamental rights, through acts or omissions that are in violation of criminal laws operating within member States, including those laws proscribing criminal abuse of power.

Throughout the 1990s, victim-oriented memorialisation started appearing in UN reports, at first as a side remark to the various forms of reparation for the victims of past human rights abuses. The former Special Rapporteur of a 1993 Sub-Commission, Theo van Boven (1993: 57), in his sixty-five-page report, under 'general principles concerning the right to restitution, compensation and rehabilitation for victims of gross violations of human rights and fundamental freedoms', included certain forms of memorialisation. He noted that 'satisfaction and guarantees of non-repetition shall be provided' (to victims), among other means by 'Apology, including public acknowledgment of the facts and acceptance of responsibility', and 'Commemorations and paying tribute to the victims.'

Louis Joinet (1996: 253), the former Special Rapporteur of the Sub-Commission on Prevention of Discrimination and Protection of Minorities, listed a 'set of principles for the protection and promotion of human rights through actions to combat impunity', focusing on four pillars of transitional justice: the rights to know, to justice and to reparation, and guarantees of non-recurrence. Joinet's work brought to the fore the notion of 'the duty to remember', placing it under 'the victim's right to know'. He explained: 'its corollary is a "duty to remember" on the part of the State: to be forearmed against the perversions of history that go under the names of revisionism or negationism. ... These, then, are the main objectives of the right to know as a collective right'. Under principle 2 of 'The Duty to Remember', he further elaborated: '[a] people's knowledge of the history of their oppression is part of their heritage and, as such, shall be preserved by appropriate measures in fulfillment of the State's duty to remember. Such measures shall be aimed at preserving the collective memory from extinction and, in particular, at guarding against the development of revisionist and negationist arguments' (256). Joinet based this understanding on the notion that 'collectively, symbolic measures – annual homages to the victims or public recognition by the State of its responsibility, for example – besides helping to restore victims' dignity, also help to discharge the duty of remembrance' (258).

Joinet's effort was pioneering work because, up to that point, victims were rarely the focus of attention – in legal terms. Instead, victims were perceived as random casualties. Only during the 1990s did that status begin to change. NGOs such as REDRESS that, from the beginning, placed survivors at the top of their agenda, moved gradually from defining victims of torture in the narrow sense[10] to emphasising 'women, men and children who have been tortured during relative peace and in times of conflict, including human rights defenders; members from marginalised ethnic, religious or other minorities; survivors of sexual and other gender-based violence; LGBTI people targeted for their sexual orientation and suspects of ordinary crimes'.[11] Only during the 1990s, and after learning from victim experiences in Bosnia in particular, including not only their mistreatment by the state but also their re-traumatisation by the ICTY, did human rights NGOs succeed in lobbying to redirect the focus from crimes to victims. Introducing terms with legal ramifications such as 'remedy' and 'reparations' gave victims a platform for acknowledgement of their sufferings.

By the 1990s, a triad matrix of simplified categories of victim, perpetrator and bystander were already well embedded into discourses on guilt, accountability and remembrance. Raul Hilberg (1993: ix), one of the greatest historians of World War II, framed the entire Holocaust through

---

[10] Redress was founded in 1992 by Keith Carmichael, a British torture survivor who sought justice for how he had been treated while a prisoner in Saudi Arabia from November 1981 until March 1984.
[11] https://redress.org/about/impact/

categories of victim–perpetrator–bystander. In his words, 'these three groups are distinct from each other and they did not dissolve in their lifetime'. Hilberg described perpetrators as participants who ascribed the act of doing something impersonal to their position and duties. Victims, he argued, as a whole remained an amorphous mass and are remembered mainly for what happened to them (as opposed to who they were). Bystanders were not willing to hurt victims, nor did they wish to be hurt by perpetrators. However, one way or another, they were involved (Hilberg 1993). The schematic conceptualisation of past human rights abuses, based on simplified and purified categories of victims–perpetrators–bystanders, became an ideological infrastructure conceptualised as a universal pattern and as the only framework through which memorialisation should take place when considering past human rights abuses.

Moral Remembrance and Its Impact on the Ground

The ethics of remembrance as conceptualised and promoted by human rights advocates is 'victim oriented' and seemingly brings back justice and equality. However, for a number of reasons, the triad categorisation of victims, perpetrators and bystanders, rooted in moral remembrance, often brings more inequalities and new forms of violence. This is because, to apply certain memorialisation standards, one has to erase complexities from the categories of victims–perpetrators–bystanders and keep them purified and normative. Moral remembrance requires a shift from concrete memories to abstract remembrance. This shift cements numerous erroneous assumptions and ideas that, once incorporated into moral remembrance, in many ways produce opposite results than those desired by the human rights activists in the first place.

First, the main principle of 'facing the past', borrowed from individual psychoanalysis, is embedded and encoded as a therapeutic remedy that allegedly has beneficial psychological consequences for the 'healing' of post-totalitarian or post-conflict societies. This means that moral remembrance has adopted the logic of translating and applying notions of illness and healing to entire societies, making no real distinction between the ways in which individuals reckon with their traumatic memories and the ways in which collectives engage with their painful past. Moral remembrance promoters have adopted the false assumption that Freudian-derived individual psychology is based on universal human needs, which effectively obscures ideological roots deeply embedded in Western(ised) cultures, persistently ignoring cultural, religious and societal differences. Applied medical diagnostic categories of mental illness are shaped by psychological explanatory models and therapeutic discourses of treatment and recovery (Herman 1992). This deficient approach based on clinical psychoanalysis, whose main potency lies in its catchy metaphor of an 'ill nation' contaminated with its contested past, became the bedrock of the 'facing the past' agenda. Further, culturally embedded differences regarding the perception and expression of suffering, pain, illness, memory and forgetting may often result in silence that is, in the transitional justice discourse, explicitly understood as detrimental to post-conflict collective and individual healing. Silence is perceived as a negatively marked absence, and thus is problematic because it deviates from the Eurocentric psychosocial norm of voice (Kidron 2009: 6). However, evidence from Bosnia shows that silence can be a form of communication, as multifaceted as speech and conveying a broad range of contextually situated social meanings such as respect, recognition and coexistence (Eastmond and Mannergren-Selimović 2012).

Second, moral remembrance freezes only one set of events of the past as being critical – nothing else can be mentioned and must, ironically, be repressed. Thus, the past becomes captured in motionless pictures lacking any dynamics or fuzziness. The same sanitised logic of victims–perpetrators–bystanders is being applied in moral remembrance when the vast differences and idiosyncrasies present in any victim community are forgotten, and it is generally assumed that all those affected by the same kind of violations form a homogenous group that has identical needs, motives and aspirations (Malkki 1996). This universalist, purified and ahistorical logic thus ignores the specific histories, political and economic conditions and contexts of individual victims. Such a definition reflects the humanistic universalism of the victim as an embodiment of pure humanity. At the same time, this tendency to universalise victims as a special kind of people serves the human rights agenda of depoliticising victims and defining them as ahistorical, universal humanitarian subjects (Mutua 2001). Moreover, in human rights discourse, victims and perpetrators are usually referred to as two completely separate and homogenous sets of people, while in reality not all victims are the same, not all perpetrators are the same, and some victims are also perpetrators (Borer 2003).

Though all moral remembrance practices allegedly encourage victims to speak, this categorical framework forces them to adapt their stories to fit the matrix, to filter and de-contextualise certain memory contents (David 2015a, 2015c; Močnik 2019) to maintain the purity of the classification system. For example, members of the third generation of Hutu in Belgium are still marked as perpetrators, even though many of them have never been to Rwanda. Similarly, not just the descendants of Holocaust survivors are still regarded as victims: practically all Jews, regardless of their geography or age, are regarded and treated as victims. Paradoxically, under the pretence of moving beyond ethnic divisions, such logic advances the generational transmission of those fixed categories, making them almost impossible to escape. It actually binds a categorical system of victims, perpetrators and bystanders to their ethnic and religious identities, rather than to human beings as a whole. Thus, moral remembrance produces, on the ground, endless struggles and politics over victimhood, actively promoting hierarchies of suffering, and ending up in promoting some victim groups while many others are completely marginalised. Consequently, we often witness the re-eruption of ethnic hostilities because, as Mann (2004b) powerfully explained, ethnicity often trumps class and becomes the main form of social stratification, bringing to the fore class-like sentiments towards ethno-nationalism.

Finally, the false logic of the necessity of 'facing the past', which is gradually transformed into the policy-oriented standardisation of memory, is apparent in the absence of significant, unambiguous proof that once the past has been faced, the result will be 'the non-recurrence of violence' and the adoption of human rights values. At least two separate problems arise with this assumption. First, it would need to be tested, but what is an appropriate time frame for such a test: ten years? a generation? a century? Second, once conflict emerges, it is hardly possible to isolate processes of facing the past from wider geo-political, economic and societal contexts so as to test its relationship to the outbreak of conflict. It seems to me that the notion of facing the past for the sake of the non-recurrence of violence is just a wishful ideological construct based on false premises.

Conclusion

The ideological expansion of human rights produced similar fractal-like forms of memorialisation around the globe. Moral remembrance emerged gradually, acquiring its might during the last four decades, through the rise of the organisational and ideological power of human rights. Moral remembrance matters greatly because the entire human rights peace industry is built on those assumptions. Transitional justice, conflict resolution, transformation, management, peacebuilding and historical dialogues have all not only developed rich scholarship but also contributed to the formation of moral remembrance. However, regardless of their differences, all have developed (from) the same core human rights memorialisation agenda based on three core pillars: 'facing the past', 'duty to remember' and 'justice for victims'. Under those core

Conclusion

human rights ideas, they advance the notion of 'proper remembrance', claiming that it allegedly enables the adoption of human rights, thereby paving the road to democracy and preventing the recurrence of violence. To put it bluntly, this sounds more like 'wishful thinking' than well-established facts: both of those assumptions actually have little or no evidence on the ground. In particular geo-political contexts, the importance of the emergence of moral remembrance became invisible, with its principles being transformed, through processes of standardisation in global governance, into abstract, morally grounded values. This matters greatly: once those principles, dressed up in a variety of memorialisation practices, 'land' into small societal groups, they have almost entirely opposite effects – often, in fact, strengthening nationalist sentiments. This effectively means that moral remembrance is not capable of implementing human rights values as predicted, hoped and envisioned. My argument, developed further in the coming chapters, is that the core intention of the human rights memorialisation agenda, to prevent further violence by promoting human rights and democratic values in post-conflict societies, results precisely in the opposite outcome – the strengthening of divisions on the ground. This, I suggest, has to do with one major issue: moral remembrance is constructed on experiences based on historically grounded events that, once transformed into policy-oriented memorialisation efforts, become abstract, producing a long list of false premises along the way. It becomes further filtered and reduced through nation-states' interests and ends up enforcing the ethnic animosities that it was supposed to dissolve.

In the coming chapters, I will look closely at two different geo-political regions to examine first, how moral remembrance became institutionalised through peace agreements, and second, what happens once the principles and the logic of moral remembrance become promoted in local communities. Is the human rights memorialisation agenda truly capable of carrying people into a moral action based on human rights values and norms? Finally, I will address some wider and undesired implications that moral remembrance produces on the ground.

4 The Institutionalisation of Moral Remembrance
Case Study of Palestine and Israel

Introduction

Moral remembrance, as explained in detail in Chapter 3, refers to the process of memory standardisation at the world polity level, and includes dozens of practices that are grounded in the ideological agenda of human rights. All of those practices obtain their power and legitimacy from three interrelated and historically contextualised principles: (1) as a precondition for adoption of human rights and the healthy development of a democracy, society needs to face, and deal with, its troubled past; (2) there is a duty to remember past human rights abuses and (3) those processes of redress have to be victim-centred. However, the promotion of the moral remembrance framework is always conditioned on current power relations and local geopolitics. The main focus of the two upcoming chapters is to describe local settings on the ground and the ways in those realities have shaped, absorbed, filtered and promoted certain human rights memorialisation practices, while including some and excluding many others.

To start with, I show how different peace agreements legitimised moral remembrance in two very different geo-political contexts: in the countries of the Western Balkans – Croatia, Bosnia-Herzegovina (BIH) and Serbia – and in the Middle East – Israel and Palestine. Despite the significant differences between those two geo-political regions and the localised versions of moral remembrance adopted in each of the settings, both not only enabled (though often for very different reasons) the adoption of moral remembrance, but also contributed to its further development and promotion. This comparison is based on the assumption that, in both conflict and post-conflict settings, the framing of the national past is a crucial element of the conflict itself. Moreover, the comparison between Israel and the Palestinian National Authority (PNA) and Serbia, Croatia and BiH is not random. Palestine is certainly not a state in a narrow sense, since it has neither a well-defined territory nor internationally recognised sovereignty. However, since Palestine

Introduction 67

does have a recognised government, it is still useful to work with the assumption that Palestine is a state, especially since diplomatic practice seems to be the most important argument for viewing Palestine as a state. The sharp imbalance in power between Israel and Palestine is significant because it provides us with some important evidence on both differences and similarities in the ways in which memorialisation isomorphism affected the creation of micro-solidarity in Israel and in Palestine. For Israel and Palestine, the centrality of the Holocaust legacy serves as a diversion from Palestinians' suffering, a fundamental issue in their already seven-decades-long conflict. For Serbia, Croatia and BiH, the Srebrenica genocide resolutions are part of their two-decades-long, uneven and largely externally forced processes of dealing with the contested legacies of the wars in the 1990s.

However, those two settings paint a different picture with regard to moral remembrance. While the countries of the Western Balkans became major consumers of human rights–promoted memorialisation practices, Israel and Palestine, due to the infrastructures that promoted their own historical suffering, over time shaped and re-modelled the human rights memorialisation agenda at the polity level in several different ways.

On the one hand, the dismembering of Yugoslavia, which was followed by bloodshed, pushed human rights promoters to pressure the United Nations into establishing the International Criminal Tribunal for Yugoslavia (ICTY). Over time, it became a symbol (though often contested) of transitional justice efforts to *properly* deal with massive human rights abuses. Probably one of the biggest achievements during the period of the ICTY trials was the acknowledgement of the need to place victims at the centre; this became the backbone of the moral remembrance framework. However, this framework was pushed forward and 'dropped' from above on Bosnia and, to a lesser extent, on Serbia and Croatia. In turn, they mostly reacted to the situation they were trapped in, rather than having any real power to impact the previously setup agenda of 'proper memorialisation' as envisioned by human rights promoters. In reality, placing victim agendas at the very centre of the *proper way* to deal with the massive human rights abuses produced endless competition between different victim groups on the ground, unequivocally adding fuel to the already well-embedded nationalist narratives.

On the other hand, for contextual reasons, both Israel and Palestine, due to the protracted nature of their conflict and the effectiveness of framing and promoting their suffering globally in terms of 'innocent and good' and 'bad and evil', adopted the very core of the human rights memorialisation agenda, albeit from significantly different positioning. Israel continued to institutionalise the Holocaust globally, not only as a distinctive Jewish experience of ultimate victimhood and the very foundations of the State of Israel, but also as a moral measurement of all of humanity. Thus, understanding the Holocaust in terms of human rights served Israel well, linking its political agendas and legitimising its actions in the Israeli–Palestinian conflict as part of the security/existential narrative threat. This linkage between the legitimacy of Israel, the uniqueness of Jewish suffering and Israel's involvement in legitimising the moral values of other countries became a tool for further promoting a narrow nationalist agenda. From the completely opposite position, Palestinians – faced with the Holocaust 'wall' that effectively nullified their own ongoing historical suffering caused by the same people who perfected the promotion of the Holocaust message 'never again' on the international stage – succeeded in framing their struggle internationally as an appeal to the free world to end colonialism, urging historical justice. From the Palestinians' side, binding their suffering to colonialism (which undoubtedly it is) and efficiently promoting their struggle for independence as a symbol of the oppression proved to be the key: it earned them wide global support and a consensus among the oppressed worldwide. In many ways, while the Holocaust trope became perceived as constructed and enforced from above, the Palestinian trope became widely appealing for groups whose suffering had never been acknowledged as envisioned by the memorialisation isomorphism logic. The Palestinian trope generated feelings for all of those peoples who see themselves as oppressed, gathering many, often diametrically different groups under the one umbrella of solidarity. Whereas the Holocaust trope became a tool for institutionalising democracies, the Palestinian suffering trope became a political tool for fighting institutionalised democracies and sponsoring struggles of identity politics.

However, over the past twenty-five years or so, in the Western Balkans and in Israel and Palestine, one can trace the institutionalisation of the human rights memorialisation agenda and the ways in which it became mixed and merged into different political contexts. Regardless of the astonishing differences in the ways that moral remembrance was localised, adopted, adjusted or reframed, in all settings, at the macro solidarity level, the erroneous logic of moral remembrance was used to enforce narrow ethno-nationalist feelings. The attempts to mandate a *proper way* to remember past human rights abuses actually ended up perpetuating conflicts, rather than promoting human rights.

This chapter proceeds in three parts. I start with the Oslo Accords and the human rights memorialisation agenda that was 'sneaked in' through the back door of the agreement. To fully grasp the realities on the ground onto which moral remembrance landed, in the following two parts I take several steps back to present the genealogies of both Holocaust and Nakba memorialisation efforts. This is important because memory is never a fixed category: what people choose to remember is always a selective process in which parts are forgotten while others are amplified and mythologised. Consequently, memorialisation efforts and claims over memory always mirror the needs of the present. Thus memories (via memorialisation efforts), rather than providing an accurate picture of past events, serve as a link between past events as landmarks and the notions of the selfhood, nationhood and identity within the boundaries of a collective to which one belongs. In this chapter, I look at how collective memory, often perceived as natural and omnipresent, is embedded in social structures that are, in fact, shaped by complex social processes and political actions. I focus on how those sentiments of loss and despair are used to promote certain political agendas. To that end, it is worth mechanically distinguishing three interconnected genealogical paths through which collective memories of the Nakba and Holocaust became hijacked by political (and intellectual) elites and evolved into both a homogenising factor and a recruiting force, albeit in significantly different ways. First, it is important to acknowledge that the Nakba and the Holocaust have their own unique transformative paths, which were very much dictated by the domestic political scene and memory agents. Second, as much as being independent, the Nakba and Holocaust memory constructions, due to the protracted and ongoing Israeli–Palestinian conflict, developed – in very different ways – in relation to one another. Finally, both were impacted by global trends and social movements.

The main purpose here is to describe the state of the memory constructions of the Nakba and the Holocaust and to give some suggestions as to how those memorialisation efforts resonate globally. I argue that the memory of the Holocaust became a top-down meta-narrative of our times and a measure for human rights in institutionalised democracies, whereas the Palestinian Nakba became a worldwide symbol and a recruiting force for many people around the world for fighting historical injustice and institutionalised democracies from the bottom-up level.

The Oslo Accords and the Memorialisation Agenda in Israel and Palestine

As will be discussed, while Serbia, Croatia and BiH were heavily pressured to shape their national histories in accordance with the mandates of a specific human rights regime, Israel and Palestine offer different dynamics. From a systemic perspective, and considering the numerous wars and conflicts in which Israel and Palestine have been and continue to be entangled, the formation of the State of Israel (1948) helped define some general patterns of larger power relations. Though the Israeli–Palestinian conflict is changing constantly and both Israelis and Palestinians consider themselves to be victims of each other, the Israelis are in a position of vastly greater political, financial and military resources and power compared to the Palestinians. Further, while the European Balkan states have faced financial conditionalities throughout the steps of the EU accession process, Israel and Palestine are much less pressured by the international community to exhibit even nominal acceptance of a cosmopolitan history, through which global concerns and values become part of local experiences. Having said that, the Oslo Accords, signed in 1993 and in 1995, which projected an independent Palestinian state by 1999, were of great importance for bringing to the fore new memorialisation agendas – never discussed per se in any of the legal documents, but indirectly promoted in multiple ways. After the signing of the Oslo Accords, many Palestinians, including Palestinian Liberation Organization (PLO) leaders, were able to make visits to Israel (as part of the 'Open Bridges Policy'). Nevertheless, the Palestinian public and the 'street' leadership reflected in the *Fatah* organisation – which originally was an enthusiastic supporter of the peace process and of the need to reach reconciliation with Israel – came to the conclusion that Israel did not, in fact, want to end the occupation and grant the Palestinian people their legitimate rights (Pundak 2001: 31).

The ideological discursive framework adopted in the Oslo Accords was based on a report by the former UN Secretary-General Boutros Boutros-Ghali, submitted to the Council just after the Rio Summit in 1992, entitled 'An Agenda for Peace: Preventive Diplomacy, Peace-Making and Peacekeeping'. It brought, for the first time, the concept of peacebuilding as a core principle of the Oslo Accords. In September 1992, Secretary-General Boutros-Ghali invited more than 1,000 non-governmental organisations (NGOs) to the United Nations to discuss their roles in regional conflicts (Chufrin and Saunders 1993: 156). In 'An Agenda for Peace', he defined post-conflict peacebuilding as an 'action to identify and support structures which would tend to strengthen and solidify peace in order to avoid a relapse into conflict'; in other words, 'post-conflict peacebuilding was to prevent a recurrence' (of violence) and the establishment of human rights. Beyond the need for traditional crisis management, mediation and negotiation, post-conflict peacebuilding requires a new focus on changing and building relationships between people – a process that allegedly transforms conflictual relationships so that parties can both end violence and build the peaceful relationships necessary for tackling post-conflict problems. The term 'peacebuilding' was first introduced by Galtung in 1976 as one of three approaches to peace. Galtung (1976) distinguished between peacekeeping, peacemaking, and peacebuilding, and argued that peacebuilding activities could produce peace at all levels of society by addressing the causes of war and creating institutions that could provide alternatives to war.

One of the Oslo constructors, Ron Pundak, described what he called the 'Oslo spirit', arguing that this positive Oslo spirit had influenced the highest levels of both the Israeli and Palestinian leaderships, but had permeated neither to the level of the Israelis who formulated the complicated implementation agreements (the Gaza and Jericho Agreement and the Interim Agreement of September 1995), nor to the Israeli officials who were in charge of negotiating with the Palestinians on translating the agreements into concrete actions. There has to be some sense of equity, or at least moving toward equity, for such reconciliation to take place (Said 2001). The 'Oslo spirit', Pundak (2001: 32) claimed, was based on the understanding that the baleful history between Israelis and Palestinians represents an almost insurmountable obstacle for conventional negotiations, taking, as a point of departure, the existing imbalance of power between the occupier and the occupied that impeded conventional negotiations. Moreover, 'for those involved in the initial discussions in Norway, the goal was to work towards a conceptual change which would lead to a dialogue based, as much as possible, on fairness, equality and common objectives' (Pundak 2001: 32). It was a widespread belief, spilling out from the scholarly community, that these values should be reflected both in the character of the negotiations – including the personal relationships between the negotiators – and in the proffered solutions and implementation. This new type of relationship was supposed to influence the type and character of Palestinian–Israeli talks that would develop between other official and semi-governmental institutions in the future, as well as future dialogue between the two peoples. The degree of exclusion from the political process of refugees and the discussion of the right of return or responsibility for 1948 has, since 1993, been matched only by the scale of international donor funding allocated to 'dialogue' between groups of Palestinians and Israelis. This subset of the broader human rights–sponsored 'peace industry' has supported and promoted the idea that mutual understanding between sectors of Palestinian and Israeli societies – typically youths, or academics, or women – would, if generalised to their respective societies, help each understand the other's narrative. Such understanding is portrayed both as a good in itself and as addressing a central difficulty of the conflict, represented as essentially consisting of a lack of mutual understanding rather than objectively incompatible narratives (Hill 2008: 156).

The closest the peace process got to addressing the Israeli and Palestinian narratives and memorialisation processes was the Taba Summit in 2001, where the parties unprecedently negotiated over numbers relating to the return of some Palestinian refugees into Israel, and considered acknowledging the Palestinian tragedy and Israel's share of responsibility for the exodus of approximately 700,000 Palestinians during the 1948 war (Hirsch 2007). The approach was encapsulated by Taba negotiator Yasser Abed Rabbo:

[At Taba] we asked for the principle of the right of return, but the implementation of it, it should be discussed in a very practical and even pragmatic way, without affecting or without – yes, without affecting – the Jewish nature of the state of Israel. We said it. This was our position. (Eldar 2001)

UN Special Representative Miguel Moratinos reported that both the Israeli and the Palestinian sides put a lot of effort into making a joint narrative for the tragedy of the Palestinian refugees; even so, the Taba Summit ended up without any agreement (Khoury 2016: 479). In essence, the peace process, with its endless parades of talks – Madrid, Oslo, Wye River, the Clinton Parameters, Camp David, Taba, the Geneva Initiative, the Road Map, Annapolis, Israel – was used and abused by Israel to actually seize land in the West Bank while appearing to discuss its fate (Spangled 2015: 153). All of those who later acknowledged the problems of 'historical propaganda' failed to suggest any solution to it and do not represent a significant attempt to tackle the matter of conflicting narratives.

The context of the Oslo Accords and the peacebuilding agenda promoted these guidelines as a way 'to prevent a recurrence of violence' (Boutros 1992), and created the assumptions held by Western donors about how peace would be achieved (Turner 2012). After 1993, the amount of aid and donors ballooned: by 2010, forty-two donor countries and twenty UN and other multilateral agencies were involved in peacebuilding activities, and aid rose yearly from US$178.74 million in 1993 to US$2.52 billion by 2010. Among the large number of donors and peacebuilding agencies involved in the occupied territories, the most important were the United States, the European Union (EU), the World Bank and the United Nations (EU) (Turner 2012). The objective of western peacebuilding in the occupied Palestinian territories was to underpin the peace process by building a Palestinian economy and state institutions in preparation for final status negotiations, guided by the assumption that the occupation would end and there would be a 'two-state solution'. Wider peacebuilding activities in Israel and Palestine that were meant to promote human rights, reduce tensions between the two peoples and support the official peace process – such as people-to-people programs, dialogue, contact groups, sports and film projects, and environmental programs – were some of the most extensive peacebuilding efforts in the world.

The failure of the Oslo Accords is generally put down to its erroneous strategy of separating and delaying three issues for future negotiation: sovereignty over Jerusalem, the borders of the future state of Palestine and, above all, the right of return of Palestinian refugees from the war of 1948. The exclusion of issues of truth and reconciliation from the political process of Oslo peace documents resulted in a resurgence of the status of memory in Palestinian discourse, which was manifested in an increasing number of commemorations of the Palestinian Nakba and oral history projects, and an upsurge in the use of 'memory' and 'truth and reconciliation' as political idioms in the discourse of Palestinian intellectuals, historians and civil society organisations (Hill 2008). Broadly speaking, from an Israeli perspective, Palestinian public opinion was unable or unwilling to acknowledge the historical truth about Jewish persecution and the relevance and magnitude of the Holocaust to the conflict in general and to the events of 1948 that led the refugees to flee. From a Palestinian perspective, Israeli public opinion was unable or unwilling to acknowledge the truth, both particular and general – about largely the same issues, with the addition of the nature of the forty-year occupation of the West Bank and Gaza – and will remain unable to reconcile itself to the changes in mindset, discourse and political structures required for sustainable peace until it acknowledges such truths (Hill 2008: 153).

Following the Oslo Accords and the establishment of the Palestinian Authority (PA), the EU was willing to tolerate authoritarian rule and human rights violations by President Yasser Arafat for the sake of keeping the peace process alive. The Barcelona Process was set up in 1995 in the wake of the Oslo Accords and was designed to foster political and economic reform in the Mediterranean, as well as to strengthen multilateral and bilateral relations. The Euro-Mediterranean Partnership was established at a Conference for Ministers of Foreign Affairs, held in Barcelona on 27–28 November 1995, and included 27 countries.[1] It aimed to create peace, stability and development in a region which is of

---

[1] The fifteen EU member states are Austria, Belgium, Denmark, Finland, France, Germany, Greece, Ireland, Italy, Luxembourg, the Netherlands, Portugal, the United Kingdom, Spain and Sweden; the twelve Mediterranean partners are Algeria, Cyprus, Egypt, Israel, Jordan, Lebanon, Malta, Morocco, the Palestinian Authority, Syria, Tunisia and Turkey.

vital strategic importance for Europe. The Policy Agenda for the Strategic Partnership includes a vast array of subjects – notably political and security dialogue, human rights, counter-terrorism, migration, economic reforms, social development and cultural dialogue – and makes significant but indirect efforts to address and bridge the gaps in the historical narratives on both sides.

The political and cultural institutions of the PA benefited from substantial European funding and financial assistance, especially in the post-Oslo period beginning in 1993. The main justification for the donor strategy revolved around the elusive notion of 'supporting the peace process' (La More 2005: 992). Between 1993 and 1997, donor pledges to the PA continued to increase regularly (their value had risen to approximately US$3,420 million as of the end of October 1997) as a result of the faltering peace process, along with the needs and subsequent assistance necessary for Palestinians to survive (Al-Daqaq et al. 2004). This changed with the Second Intifada, as well as the 9/11, London and Madrid terrorist attacks. Both the George W. Bush administration and the EU changed course. Given the autocratic nature of the Palestinian political system and the lack of democratisation pursued by its political leadership, EU interest in domestic stability stands, more often than not, in direct contradiction with the goal of supporting the establishment of a viable democracy in Palestine. Additionally, since the 9/11 attacks, fears of increasing Islamic fundamentalism, which could profit from democratisation, have pushed the pendulum of EU policies towards greater emphasis on stability (Stetter 2003).

Whereas the policy had hitherto been built on the belief that a successful peace was a condition for democratisation, this presumption was now reversed, and the democracy agenda received a boost (Huber 2011). Yet interestingly, though all parties involved had agreed that the Oslo peace process had failed, and even after the failure of the Road Map (based on a speech by US President George W. Bush on 24 June 2002), the failure of initiatives to establish clear steps to a two-state solution, the attempts by the Geneva Initiative (2003) to go even further and deal with problematic issues such as the status of Jerusalem and the issue of refugee return, and even the Second Intifada (2000–2005), donors continued to support and sponsor dialogue projects in the hope of promoting human rights. Following the logic of the connective path, the European Neighbourhood Policy (ENP) – a strategic partnership with the Mediterranean and the Middle East, and the Middle East peace process – was established in 2004. The ENP policy involved 'a significant degree of economic integration and a deepening of political co-operation, with the aim of preventing the emergence of new dividing lines between the enlarged EU and its neighbours' (Newman and Yaakobi 2004: 14). Over the years, the EU has devoted significant funds to Israeli–Palestinian conflict resolution, focusing on three objectives: politics and security; economy; and cultural, social and human partnership so as to improve 'mutual understanding among the peoples of the region and the development of a free and flourishing civil society'.[2]

From 2000 to 2006, from EU aid sources alone, came the bulk of funds for democracy promotion (€20 million). The focus of the EU was on building strong state institutions. Bottom-up democratisation through civil society bodies received a maximum of €1.2 million per year through the European Instrument for Democracy and Human Rights (EIDHR) (Huber 2011). From June 2001 to 2002, the EU provided €10 million per month in direct budgetary assistance to the PA (Newman and Yaakobi 2004). In 2006, the PA received US$1.5 billion in net official development assistance (World Bank 2008) from Western states. Between 2007 and 2015, the EU allocated more than €2.5 billion to the occupied Palestinian territory (OPT), mainly as direct budget support, or 43 per cent of the OPT's total funding (Norwegian Directorate for Development Cooperation [NORAD] 2017). Since 1993, the European Commission and the EU member states combined have been, by far, the largest aid contributor to the Palestinians (Le More 2004). More than US$7 billion has been disbursed to the OPT since 1993, with considerable donations also coming from the Arab League states (La More 2005). Hence, it is important to point out that it is comparatively easier for the EU to pressure the PA to reform than other governments, as the EU enjoys a high shadow of hierarchy due to the fact that Palestinians are highly dependent on Western aid.

However, the ability of the EU to use its leverage as a means of influencing the process of conflict resolution was (and still is) limited. Given the United States' support for Israel, the fact that Israel is not a candidate for full membership in the EU, and the significant trade between the two, the EU has as much to lose from downgrading its current level of trading and cultural relations as Israel does. The nature of the trade and cultural relationships between the EU and Israel are different from those between the EU and the PA. While EU relations with Israel are based on trade cooperation between two highly developed first world and modern economies (Ahiram 1995), the organisation's relations with the PA are mainly based on the provision of significant financial assistance and aid packages. The potential influence of the EU is far greater with respect to the

---

[2] See more in External Relations: EUR–LEX: https://eur-lex.europa.eu/summary/chapter/external_relations.html?root_default=SUM_1_CODED%3D28

PA, as it depends on substantial EU economic assistance for the daily existence and management of its fledgling institutional structure. This takes place in a number of areas, such as assistance for Palestinian refugees, shaping the Palestinian educational curriculum and the issue of Palestinian governmental reforms (Newman and Yaakobi 2004).

The power relations between Israel and Palestine and their particular positioning with international actors have defined, to a large extent, the ways in which moral remembrance was adopted, filtered and promoted locally from the Oslo Accords onwards. However, to understand the complex paths through which moral remembrance became diffused into local realities, through peacebuilding and dialogue projects, first we need to understand the complex and unique genealogies of the Holocaust and the Nakba memorialisation efforts.

Genealogies of the Nakba and the Holocaust

The Nakba: A Collateral Damage of the Zionist Project

Zionism, as a national project that sought autonomous polity for Jews, took shape within the framework of a colonising enterprise. It sealed its national independence through what remains the Zionist movement's greatest diplomatic achievement, aside from the 1917 Balfour Declaration: the UN partition plan of 29 November 1947, which accorded it 56.47 per cent of British Mandatory Palestine for the creation of a Jewish state. In 1967, it extended this achievement by extracting retroactive legal recognition, courtesy of UN Security Council Resolution 242, for its military conquests in 1949 of a further 22 per cent of Mandate territory (Usher 2005). As Israeli historian Baruch Kimmerling (1983) wrote, the Zionist 'miracle' of the 1948 war was not so much the expansion of Israel's territories far beyond the borders traced by the 1947 UN partition plan, but rather that these territories were massively cleansed of their Palestinian inhabitants, and their society destroyed to prevent their return.

Beginning in March 1948, Israeli armed forces and Jewish militias razed some 400 Palestinian villages, expelling or forcing the flight of some 650,000 (Gelber 2006), 750,000 (Usher 2005: 27) or 750,000–900,000 Palestinians (according to BADIL).[3] The day 15 May 1948 recalls the dispossession and displacement of Palestinians who were violently usurped from their land to facilitate the creation of the modern-day State of Israel. Sanbar (2001) notes, 'the contemporary history of the

---

[3] The leading refugee rights group operating in the region.

Palestinians turns on a key date: 1948. That year, a country and its people disappeared from maps and dictionaries'. The Nakba (Al-Nakbah) is a Palestinian event and a site of Palestinian collective memory; it connects all Palestinians to a specific point in time that has become for them an 'eternal present' (Sa'adi 2002). The Palestinian encounter with the Zionist colonial project, with its varying historical forms and expressions, is a focal point in Arab discourse in general and in the national Palestinian discourse in particular. The year 1948 saw the establishment of a settler-colonial Zionist state on 78 per cent of Mandatory Palestine at the expense of the destruction of historic Palestine and 'ethnic cleansing' of the Palestinians. The Nakba is associated with a rapid de-Arabisation of the country. This process has included the destruction of Palestinian villages[4] as well as the confiscation of Palestinian-owned land by the Israeli State (Sa'adi 2002). The ongoing dismemberment of historic Palestine led to the unprecedented fragmentation of Palestinian society. The Nakba created a division between the minority of Palestinians who remained in Israel and the refugees forced outside its borders. The 1967 war fostered further splits: between East Jerusalem and the West Bank, and between the West Bank and Gaza. Even the Oslo Accords, which were promoted as a peace process meant to end the conflict, turned out to be a factor in creating new divisions – between the leadership of the PA, refugees and the diaspora communities. However, for all of the different factions of Palestinian society, the Nakba has remained the main site of Palestinian collective memory for various reasons. Sa'adi (2002: 196) rightly points out that:

First, the event itself changed Palestinian society beyond recognition; moreover, it has had a lasting impact on the lives of Palestinians since its occurrence. Second, Al-Nakbah represents a decisive breaking point between two qualitatively different realities, with different rules that govern before and after. Third, Al-Nakbah is the beginning point of the current history of the Palestinians. The roots of the other sites of memory are firmly anchored in it.

Today some 70 per cent of Palestinians are refugees. There are more than five million Palestinian refugees in the Middle East and many more worldwide (Masalha 2009).

With such deep fragmentation, where different segments of Palestinian society became subject to different and often even conflicting histories, the Nakba trope became an important identity marker and unifier. However, though the memories of the Nakba were present and vivid at the

---

[4] About 418 villages were erased. Out of twelve Palestinian or mixed towns, a Palestinian population continued to exist in only seven.

bottom-up level from the very beginning, unsurprisingly the making of a more utilised, homogenising and (most importantly) political-recruiting version of the Nakba was a slow and generative process that gradually become a major force in the process of forging contemporary Palestinian identity. In fact, Foster (2011) showed that, prior to the Nakba events, local loyalties to cities and towns were the most significant identity markers in the 1920s, followed by Arab and religious loyalties in the late 1920s and early 1930s. In the mid-late 1930s and 1940s, the territorial identification with Palestine emerged as a key source of loyalty, a process often understood as 'Palestinian particularism' – the tendency to prioritise Palestinian solidarity over pan-Arab or Islamic identification (Sorek 2013). The Nakba events, featuring catastrophe, loss and humiliation, created a rupture of volcanic proportions in Palestinian society.

The commemoration of the Nakba has been ongoing since the events took place in 1948, albeit as spontaneous acts of smaller communities at the grassroots level in villages and refugee camps. Villages, towns and cities remembered long before any 'official' events were established (Browne 2016). Although the Palestinian elite was well aware of the importance of these markers for identity formation, its ability – as an agent of memory – to nurture them was limited by an institutional weakness and a lack of political sovereignty. While Palestinian national identity took root long before 1948, Palestinian memory accounts of the post-Nakba period became a major factor in the reconstruction of Palestinian national identity and the emergence of the PLO in the 1960s (Masalha 2012: 206). Since the birth of the PLO in 1964, the Nakba memory and the right of return associated with the refugee issue have been seen as mainstays of Palestinian nationalism. The right of return of refugees is listed as one of the founding principles of the movement. The refugee camp, as an icon of the nation, became central to Palestinian thinking. Within the rhetoric of the PLO, the refugee camps have figured as key symbols of the struggle for return and restitution (Farah 2009). Indeed, for much of its existence, the PLO conducted operations from exile bases in Lebanon, Syria and Jordan. Therefore, the events to which Palestinians refer as their Nakba have significantly shaped the political and nationalistic aspirations of the Palestinian leadership. Interestingly, Browne (2013: 152) points out that the PLO, in those years, deemed 'official' or state-sponsored commemorations unnecessary because 'Our whole resistance and movement was based on the need to reverse what had occurred during the Nakba and so the commemorations continued at a local, community level'.[5]

---

[5] An interview with a Palestinian activist, cited in Browne (2013).

However, emerging in the early 1990s, a new process of identity construction seemed to deviate from the previous emphasis on 'victim identity' and raised questions about how to go about revitalising the Nakba discourse in the process of Palestinian identity formation (Koldas 2011: 950). The signing of the 1993 Oslo Peace Accords and the move towards preparation for Palestinian statehood (based on a list of principles agreed upon by the Israeli government and the PLO), as far as the fledgling Palestinian leadership was concerned, pushed the issue of Palestinian refugees and their right of return further down the list of priorities. For many Palestinians living within the OPT and in the wider diaspora, it is the crucial issue of redressing the effects of the 1948 Nakba – and bringing an end to the ongoing exile of the refugee community – that dominates their political thinking. Thus, the exclusion of the refugee issue from the Oslo agenda engendered great disappointment, anxiety and fear. In the absence of any feasible political solution to the refugee issue, the Nakba day commemoration has taken on new meaning (Browne 2013: 153).

The end of the 1990s witnessed a process of revitalisation of Palestinian collective identity and national consciousness among Palestinian citizens of Israel, in which the Nakba was transformed into an important reference point in the politics of memory within the Palestinian–Israeli public sphere (Koldas 2011). In the OPT, annual commemorations have become a powerful tool for highlighting the ongoing plight of Palestinian refugees. Since 1998, with an agenda of keeping the refugee issue alive, BADIL, the leading refugee rights group operating in the region, has been a key organiser in planning the annual Nakba events (Browne 2013: 152). In 2007, under the auspices of the PLO, a National Committee for the Commemoration of the Nakba and the Palestinian Right of Return Coalition was established to ensure a more coordinated and structured commemoration of the Nakba. The main goal of this enterprise was to bring a wide range of stakeholders together, including Palestinian NGOs, refugee camp leaders, memory activists and political representatives, to agree on the format and substance of the commemorative activity (Browne 2013). As a result, the commemoration of the Nakba is the most widely attended event in the crowded Palestinian commemorative calendar, with remembrance marches, parades and similar practices taking place on the same day across the OPT, among the Palestinian diaspora and globally – all as part of a solidarity movement with the Palestinians.

For the Palestinians in Israel, the dominant discourse regarding the Nakba at the civil and political societal levels has either greatly neglected or suppressed the Palestinian perspective. The development of the collective identities of the Israeli and Palestinian societies has been a dialectic process based on 'the negation of the other' (Sagy, Kaplan and Adwan 2002: 27) through the destruction and delegitimisation of the other's narrative memory. Any implication of a link between the collective memories of the Palestinian community in Israel and Palestinians in the diaspora in the West Bank and in Gaza has been interpreted as a serious challenge to the dominant discourse that the Zionist political leadership has taken to represent the unity and integrity of Israeli political and civil societies.

Until the late 1990s, Palestinians in Israel commemorated the Nakba as a 'nostalgic grief' and largely remained passive, but the Oslo Peace Accords pushed Palestinians in Israel to affirm their own identities as separate and distinctive from other Israelis. In fact, as a result of the Oslo Accords, the 'Palestinianisation' of the 1948 events inside Israel was intensified and achieved by linking them with a Nakba discourse (Koldas 2011: 949). Additionally, interpretations of the Nakba have been fuelled by an internal crisis in the dominant Zionist discourse that deepened as a result of the historical revisionism that took place in Israel at the beginning of the 1990s (Masalha 2003). The 'new Israeli historians' such as Benny Morris, Ilan Pappe, Tom Segev and Avi Shlaim have challenged the dominant discourse in Israel of the Zionist narrative regarding the alleged exodus of Palestinians. According to this narrative, some of the Palestinians left willingly (due, for instance, to partial calls by the Arab/Palestinian leadership to leave as well as to fear and societal collapse), while others were expelled by the Jews/Israelis (Nets-Zehngut 2015). This challenging of the firm Zionist narrative has enabled Palestinians in Israel to build a Nakba discourse. In particular, some Palestinian members of the Israeli Knesset (MKs) began mentioning the political significance of the Nakba in public and political debates.

By the turn of the century, the memory of the Nakba had become a major element in the political struggle of the Palestinians in Israel, moving from personal memories to a generative, politically useful and legitimate tool against oppression and inequality. For example, in 2001, the Palestinian MKs organised a 'public relations' event to meet Palestinians from the West Bank and Gaza, marching from the opposite direction during the commemoration ceremonies (Koldas 2013: 925). Rouhana and Sabbagh-Khoury (2014: 218) pointed out that the Return Marches have become a living reminder of the settler-colonial actuality that underlies Israel's 'Nakba Law', enacted in 2011, which calls on the government to deny funding to any organisation, institution or municipality that commemorates the founding of the Israeli state as a day of mourning. The shift to more calculated, instrumentalised uses of the memory of the Nakba is also evident in the Palestinian NGO sector in Israel. Although varying in their levels of intensity, most Palestinian NGOs have been involved in this discursive activism and since the late 1990s, it has become instrumental in mobilising the political and civil societies of the Palestinian community.[6]

For Palestinians in the refugee camps, where the dramatic rupture in the continuity of space and time in Palestinian history was probably most apparent, Nakba commemoration and memorialisation were, from the beginning, understood and promoted as a form of resistance (Khalili 2005). Nakba events in 1948 led to some 726,000[7] Palestinians fleeing or being expelled from Palestine, some of whom settled into refugee camps in Syria, Lebanon, Gaza, the West Bank and Jordan. According to Al-Awda, the Palestinian Right to Return Coalition:

More than half the refugee population lives in Jordan. Approximately 37.7 percent live in the West Bank and Gaza Strip, comprising about 50 percent of the population in those areas. About 15 percent live in almost equal numbers in Syria and Lebanon. About 355,000 internally-displaced Palestinians reside in present-day Israel. The remaining refugee population lives throughout the world, including the rest of the Arab world. Of the 4.3 million refugees registered with the United Nations Relief and Works Agency (UNRWA), 33 percent live in UNRWA's 59 refugee camps throughout the West Bank and Gaza Strip, Jordan, Syria and Lebanon.[8]

Nearly one-third of registered Palestine refugees – more than 1.5 million individuals – live in fifty-eight recognised Palestine refugee camps in Jordan, Lebanon, the Syrian Arab Republic, the Gaza Strip and the West Bank, including East Jerusalem.[9] According to Khalili (2005), since the descendants of these original migrants have inherited their refugee status, the number of Palestinian refugees registered with the United Nations Relief and Works Agency (UNRWA) in Lebanon in 2005 was just under 380,000, half of whom live in twelve refugee camps administered by the UNRWA.

From the onset of the Oslo negotiations in 1993 and the carve-out of the refugee question from the agreement, Palestinian refugees have found themselves increasingly excluded from the political processes that

---

[6] The Haifa Initiative, a movement in Israel composed of Israelis and Palestinians, has appeared as an example of inter-communal civil societal activism based on an alternative Nakba discourse.
[7] As suggested previously, this number varies, ranging from 650,000 to 950,000 Palestinians.
[8] See Al-Awda: The Palestinian Right to return Coalition. Available at http://al-awda.org/learn-more/faqs-about-palestinian-refugees/
[9] UNRWA. Available at www.unrwa.org/palestine-refugees

affect their fates. This stands in contrast to the situation during the PLO's heyday, when Palestinian camps emerged as national signifiers derived from a pronounced emphasis on armed struggle and complementing their reputation as repositories of Palestine's pre-1948 rural memory and ethos (Farah 2009: 86). After the Oslo agreements, the feelings of abandonment and betrayal were heightened. The Palestinian refugees believed that the PLO leadership had sacrificed their right of return to their original homes and land for a shredded statelet in the West Bank and Gaza. These political shifts, which threatened to damage the meaning of camps as national signifiers, injected a troubling note of disorientation into the stable narratives of identity that had nourished a sense of collective belonging among refugees and exiles (Farah 2009). The Oslo Accords unsettled the camps' symbolic, rhetorical and political location and marginalised refugees in the political process, effectively producing new political divisions between the refugee camp leadership and the PLO.

Every Palestinian community had its own distinct genealogical route in making the linkage between the memory of the Nakba and political action that was subject to local politics, the Israeli–Palestinian conflict and global trends such as post-colonial theory, de-colonialisation methodologies and oral histories. On the one hand, memory accounts and endless narratives on the landscape and everyday life, captured in oral history collections, poetry, autobiographies, novels and photograph collections, brought to the fore the symbolic as well as the emotional connection with the lost past: valleys, wadis, hills, tombs, shrines, springs and distinctive flora. For example, after signing the Oslo agreements, when Palestinians were finally allowed to enter Israel, *Al-Karmel* – the Palestinian cultural journal – devoted considerable space (in addition to autobiographies) to a section called 'The Memory of Place and the Place of Memory', where many Palestinians described their encounters with Al-Nakbah sites (Sa'adi 2002: 189). On the other hand, the intellectual endeavour of bringing the notion of Nakba into the intellectual, political and activist sphere was an accumulative process that, over time, gained legitimacy and power at the international level. It started with Constantine Zurayk's 1949 book *The Meaning of the Nakba*, six volumes (in Arabic, translated into English in 1956) on the Nakba and Jerusalem by Arif Al Arif. It subsequently included Walid Khalidi's articles in the late 1950s and early 1960s; the establishment of an academic peer-reviewed journal – *Journal of Palestine Studies* – in 1971; a research centre on Palestinian studies; Edward Said's (1979) *The Question of Palestine*; the proliferation of academic articles on different topics in relation to the Nakba during the 1970s and 1980s; the increasing production of, and interest in, Palestinian films; the rise of memorialisation projects on Palestine; the availability of archival databases; and the top-notch research from around 2000 onwards by scholars such as Lila Abu-Lughod, Ahnad Saadi, Nur Masalha, Lelah Khalili and Rashid Khalidi.

This brief genealogy of the institutionalisation of the Nakba memory amongst Palestinian communities in the West Bank and Gaza, in refugee camps and in Israel has been a product of three interconnected social processes. First, memories of the Nakba were vivid, from the beginning, in small communities – in families, villages and refugee camps. As they gradually became a distant past and began to be reshaped through the narratives of the second and third generations, this profound memory of the loss of the homeland transformed into a symbol of a golden era of the pre-Nakba Palestinian past. As such, it served the needs of the domestic political elite to settle political agendas and defeat rivals. The PLO embraced this memory framework, as it became a potent recruiting tool to achieve particular political goals (some of which served to maintain the narrow political elite).

Second, the Nakba memory was shaped in relation and in opposition to both the protracted Israeli–Palestinian conflict and the Holocaust memory. The conflict not only dictated the sentiments and the understanding of the Nakba, but also shaped educational curricula, including who gets to learn/teach what and where. For example, the term 'Nakba' has never been introduced into the Jewish school curriculum. Israeli Prime Minister Binyamin Netanyahu has even stated that the use of this term is tantamount to spreading propaganda against Israel (Masalha 2012: 241). Similarly, in Palestinian history textbooks, there is no mention of the Holocaust, though it is important to stress that we cannot talk here about symmetric omissions in any way: while there should be an expectation to talk about the Nakba and consequences of the 1948 Israeli independence war in Israel – because it is at the root of the ongoing conflict between Israel and Palestine – the Holocaust in Palestine should be understood as part of the global history of human suffering. However, the Nakba discourse is limited and restricted in Israel to identity politics. (In fact, since 2011, an Israeli 'Nakba Law' has banned the commemoration of Israeli Independence Day as a day of mourning, thereby actively continuing the policy of denying identity). Unsurprisingly, as the Holocaust is endlessly used and abused in Israel for narrow political gains and manipulated in various ways to justify Israeli political and military actions, perceptions of the Holocaust in Palestine vary from 'apparent indifference' about isolated cases of Holocaust endorsement and denial, to the more frequent charge that Israel exaggerates 'the scope of the genocide,' to the most common attitude, which accuses Israel of imitating or reproducing atrocities and, sometimes, of going one better than the Nazis (Achcar 2010). Furthermore, a phenomenon of Holocaust denial has emerged among Palestinians, as was evident in a recent speech by Palestinian President Mahmoud Abbas, in which he said that the Holocaust was not caused by anti-Semitism, but by the 'social behaviour' of the Jews. Conversely, Israeli Prime Minister Binyamin Netanyahu has accused Grand Mufti Haj Amin al-Husseini, a principal Palestinian leader in Mandatory Palestine, of being responsible for the Holocaust by having persuaded Hitler to carry out the genocide of the Jews – an example of delegitimising Palestinians (Bar-Tal 2018).

Third, the institutionalisation of the memory of the Nakba into discourses, practices and political structures happened partly because of, and in spite of, the prevailing success of the Holocaust memory both at the local and international levels. On the one hand, since the 1990s, newly adopted general scholarly and activist trends – such as the settler-colonial paradigm, feminist theories, citizen paradigm rights and the legitimacy of oral histories – have become major tools of widening the scope of Nakba visibility. On the other hand, some more specific practices that stemmed first and foremost from the development of the memory of the Holocaust at the global scale (but predominantly in Israel, Europe and the United States), such as witness testimonies (in particular. after the fall of the Berlin Wall), oral databases and different strategies in framing the Holocaust as a globally relevant issue, were adopted over the years within Nakba research and activism, helping to frame the memory of the Nakba not as an a local event, but rather as an event that has a potency to reflect global historical injustice elsewhere. By adopting Holocaust remembrance as a template for commemorating atrocities and historical injustices across the globe, human rights institutions have provided legitimacy for bringing to the fore the denied and oppressed Palestinian memory of the Nakba. Nur Masalha (2009: 79), a leading Palestinian historian, writer and activist, put it bluntly: 'There is a need for various grassroots projects such as educational workshops on the Nakba, a Nakba Museum and perhaps the institutionalisation of a Nakba Memorial Day as a *worldwide* event' (his italics). In other words, it was the gradual adoption of the memory of the Nakba by the Palestinian political elite as a unifying and homogenising force, the reaction to the denial of Palestinian history as a result of the Oslo peace process, and the gradual institutionalisation of the memory of the Holocaust on the global scale, as well as new scholarly trends on the importance of decolonialisation theories, oral histories and especially the rise of human rights agendas, that framed the Nakba as a symbol of a justified struggle to promote narrow nationalist goals in the name of human rights and peacebuilding.

The Holocaust and the Spill-Over Effect of the Phantom Limb

Israel's 1948 Declaration of Independence (State of Israel: Proclamation of Independence, 14 May 1948), refers to the Shoah (Holocaust) as 'proof' of the need to solve the problem of the homelessness and lack of independence of the Jewish people by means of the re-establishment of the Jewish state. However, the immediate aftermath of World War II was marked by a silence concerning the destruction of European Jewry which, at that time, did not even have a name yet. It was perceived as part of a larger practice of war crimes. Furthermore, the Holocaust did not permeate public discourse, nor was its commemoration institutionalised. On the contrary, the rejection of the exilic past was clearly reflected in the Sabras' attitude towards the Holocaust. This attitude of psychological distancing was tinged with an air of superiority towards the Holocaust victims who 'went like lambs to the slaughter', although the Yishuv and its leadership did express concern for, and identification with, the fate of the Jews under Nazi-controlled regimes (Zerubavel 2002). Israel's commemorative approach to the Holocaust was marked by ambivalence from its very beginning. Zionism, as a movement of national independence, was based on the assumption that Jewish assimilation in Europe had failed. This negative view of Jewish life in exile stands at the core of Israel's initial reluctance and the subsequent formula of commemorating the Holocaust (Levy and Szaider 2002). Ambivalence towards the Holocaust survivors continued after their immigration to Israel, and Israeli public culture was slow in incorporating the commemoration of the Holocaust (Zerubavel 2002). The nascent Israel, with almost half of its population consisting of Holocaust survivors, tried to minimise memories of Jewish victimhood (Segev 1993). In the eyes of the Sabras, the Holocaust survivors represented victims as typical examples of Jewish passivity; instead, they commemorated those Zionist martyrs who actively resisted the Nazis. Israel's sovereign politics was associated with active decisions, while the Holocaust was a reminder of helpless passivity, typical of Jewish existence outside the sovereign space of the territorial state (Levy and Sznaider 2002: 94–95).

During the 1950s, this perception gradually started to change. Since its inauguration in 1953, Yad Vashem museum has become part of Israel's official remembrance culture, which includes commemoration events and memorials first and foremost. In 1959, the Israeli parliament, the Knesset, made Holocaust Remembrance Day (Yom Ha'Shoah) a national public holiday. In 1961, another law was passed that closed all public entertainment on that day; at ten in the morning, a siren is sounded when everything stops and everyone stands in remembrance of the Holocaust victims. Further, the opening of negotiations with West Germany for compensation of the material losses to Jewish people in Europe and later the establishment of full diplomatic relationships between the two countries, along with the 1961 Eichmann trial, had a profound effect on the ways in which the Holocaust became understood and narrated. Hence, this phase of silence and shame was transformed during the 1960s, gradually building a direct link between the Holocaust-based existential threat and the Israeli–Palestinian conflict. Since the 1961 Eichmann trial, reminders of Hitler's annihilation 'prophecies' against the Jews of Europe have been brought up again and again by Arab and Palestinian leaders' threats against the existence of Israel. The trial brought the Holocaust to the centre of public attention.

On the back of the Eichmann trial and the Six-Day War in 1967, the Holocaust assumed a new and prominent role in Israel's political culture. It became a symbol for existential fears and the necessity to construct and maintain a strong military state. This 'existential' agenda remains pervasive in the education system, the army and the mass media to this day. The Holocaust came to be understood solely from the point of view of Jewish existence and as such, it became immediately imprinted onto the Arab–Israeli conflict and has remained there ever since.

Fear and uncertainty were, at the same time, real and instrumentally constructed. Terrorist attacks produced constant feelings of vulnerability, fear and anxiety, while the demographic disadvantage played on an old, yet deeply present Holocaust trauma of extinction. Fear, as a collective theme, plays an important role in the construction of walls between Israelis and Palestinians as a security-providing material body. The perception of boundaries as necessary for securing a national, ethnically Jewish identity is tightly linked to the memory of the Holocaust, which is a powerful psychological force that has framed the feeling of isolation and accentuated the perception of threat (Shlaim 2000).

In multiple ways, and through a dialectical process of appropriation and exclusion, remembering and forgetting, Israeli national identity has defined itself in relation to the Holocaust experience (Zertal 2005). Jewish powerlessness and vulnerability, epitomised by the Holocaust, became transformed into a fantasy of absolute power exercised against the Palestinians as a substitute for the European goy (Loshitzky 2006: 329). By evoking memories of the Holocaust as a justification for Israel's existence and actions, the Palestinians were placed behind a double barrier of emotion and memory – locally and globally (Huyssen 2003: 99). Thus, since the 1960s, the Holocaust has been misused in Israel's conflict with the Palestinians and the neighbouring Arab states to the extent that the Arabs have been 'Nazified' (Zertal 2005).

The gradual adoption of the Holocaust memory into state-sponsored memorialisation projects started in the mid-1950s. The custom of holding Holocaust Day and Memorial Day ceremonies in schools, which began in the early 1950s, did not appear by chance. Fixing Holocaust Day as the 20th of Nisan (five days from the end of Passover, one week before Independence Day) was designed to separate it from other days of Jewish mourning, as well as to use it to commemorate the Warsaw Ghetto uprising (Ben-Amos and Bat-El 1999: 268). A survey conducted in March 1960 by the Yad Vashem Holocaust Memorial Authority (to which only one third of the schools responded) found that Holocaust and Heroism Memorial Day was observed by less than 66 percent of Israeli schools (Porat 2004). Until 1954, Israeli students did not learn about the Holocaust at all. When the topic did enter the curriculum, the Holocaust was taught within the context of non-Jewish history. It was put forward that Holocaust victims lacked individuality; they acted as a passive mass. The Holocaust remained a marginal memory in Israel's educational system in the 1960s, as it had been in the 1950s; that memory came from rebellion, from the Jews' war against the Nazis.

At the national level, Holocaust Day was marked by solemn ceremonies, especially at Kibbutz Yad Mordechai and Kibbutz Lochamei HaGhettaot (many of whose members were Holocaust survivors), and at the Yad Vashem Holocaust Museum in Jerusalem. In 1953, Yad Vashem, officially named 'Yad Vashem to the Shoah and Heroism', was legislated as the official State Memorial Authority. Located on the western side of Har Ha'Zikaron, it is within sight of the Palestinian village where the Dayr Yasin massacre took place on 9 April 1948, in which more than 100 Palestinians lost their lives. Through these efforts, together with the adoption of the reverse thesis that promotes a comparison between the Holocaust-based experience of a constant existential threat and the Arab threat to the survival of the Jews (in the eyes of the Palestinians, seen as an excuse to conduct a massive ethnic cleansing of the local Palestinian population), the Holocaust became a major state-sponsored project.

Following the Six-Day War in 1967, and especially after the Yom Kippur War in 1973, Israeli youth became increasingly engaged with Holocaust history. In fact, in 1970s Israeli curricula, the Holocaust was divorced from World War II, remained part of non-Jewish history and was placed alone within a sequence of Jewish events, altering both the significance and the meaning of the term 'Holocaust'. Even so, Israeli students could graduate from high school having learned about the Holocaust in only a handful of history classes interspersed throughout their school years. In fact, only a few students chose to study the Holocaust

(Porat 2004). All of the history textbooks presented a picture of the Jewish people as victims of anti-Semitism. Jewish history was presented as an unbroken sequence of pogroms, special taxation, libel and forced conversion, with the Holocaust forming its climax (Bar-Tal 1998).

Beginning in the 1980s, Holocaust education further intensified: the Holocaust joined the history of the diaspora, Zionism and the Israeli–Arab conflict as the only three mandatory topics (out of a total of twenty-six) in the high school history curriculum. Israeli school students would study the Holocaust in no fewer than thirty history lessons in one school year alone (Porat 2004: 631). In Israeli history curricula from the 1980s onwards, the Holocaust was portrayed as a unique event with no precedent in world history, an event that symbolised uniqueness. In the early 1980s (following the approval of the 1980 Holocaust Law), a single Holocaust textbook, *The Holocaust and Its Significance*, was introduced for all high schools to homogenise and bring together different Jewish diasporas in Israel under one meta-narrative; the text dominated the market for fifteen years. Both the school curricula and the Holocaust Day school ceremonies served a dual function: they reflected the position of the initiators and organisers at both the national and local levels, and they also contributed to moulding the pupils' Zionist outlook (Ben-Amos and Bat-El 1999).

Additionally, to further imprint the memory of the Holocaust onto the Jewish national body, delegations of pupils travelled to Poland to visit concentration camps. The trips, which became almost a mass movement beginning in 1987, brought to the young 'pilgrims' experiences that awakened them to their Jewish link with the diaspora (Segev 1993). The trip to Poland has gradually become a central rite of passage for Israeli Jewish youth. More than 100,000 Israeli youngsters have visited the death camps in Poland since the mid-1980s, through trips organised either by schools under the auspices of the Ministry of Education or by youth movements or private tour agents. Jackie Feldman (2002) rightly argued that visits to Poland by Ministry of Education groups are designed to inscribe upon Israeli youth the sense of belonging to an egalitarian collective with well-defined but constantly threatened boundaries. The main purpose of those educational trips is not framed in terms of understanding the Holocaust in terms of human rights abuses, but rather is intended to strengthen the willingness of Israeli youths, just before their conscription into the Israeli army, to sacrifice themselves for the state and prove themselves worthy heirs to the legacy entrusted to them. The importance of the Israeli Defence Forces (IDF) in the eyes of Israeli youths is best seen in the readiness of the state to closely link their Jewish identities to the Holocaust experience, framing it in terms of

Jewish security and danger, where the most precious lesson from the Holocaust is 'never again to us' (as opposed to a universal 'never again').

An astonishing number – 40,000 – of Israeli Jewish students were expected to visit Poland's concentration camps in just 2019 (Datel 2018).[10] As just noted, such visits are used as emotional chargers to prepare youngsters for their military service, providing a link between real threats, the Holocaust and Palestinians (framed in terms of danger) in Israel. Even in school, Israeli Jewish youths are prepared to join the military forces. Members of the defence forces hold lectures to give information and impressions of life in the Israeli army. Some youths volunteer for special units or undergo pre-induction courses. This is particularly significant for the male recruits, as they are expected to become defenders of the nation (both literally and symbolically).

Whereas the Oslo Accords served, in many ways, to push the memory of the Nakba forward as a tool for intensifying the homogenisation of the Palestinians in the occupied territories and in Israel, Jews in Israel (with the emphasis on secular Jews) were much more receptive to peacebuilding efforts that addressed memorialisation issues. This was, first and foremost, due to structural and power differences, but also due to the hyper-inflation of the Holocaust and Zionist state-sponsored memory. From the 1980s onwards, cracks in the Zionist narrative started to appear, accompanied by the emergence of the New Historians – Benny Morris, Ilan Pappé, Avi Shlaim and Simha Flapan – who dared to challenge the official state-promoted Zionist narrative, in particular with regard to the events of the 1948 war and the forced expulsion and ethnic cleansing of the Palestinians. In the 1990s, many joined this effort, such as Tom Segev, Baruch Kimmerling, Idit Zertal and Shlomo Sand, trying to break down the one-sided historical narrative of the circumstances leading to the creation of the Palestinian refugee problem. Their challenges to the mainstream narrative echoed loudly and opened up political space for a fresh approach to memory and memorialisation practices.

At the end of 1980s, Israeli civil society started promoting various initiatives to deconstruct the ossified state-sponsored narrative. In combination with the Oslo Accords and its peacebuilding agenda, those efforts were pushed forward, adjusted and fine-tuned to fit the peacebuilding guidelines – as understood and promoted by the international community. Within this framework, previously taboo subjects such as the dialectical relationship between collective memories of the Holocaust and the Nakba have been discussed 'as part of a critical deconstruction

---

[10] ליאור דטל (2018) למרות סערת החוק הפולני: המסעות למחנות ההשמדה יזנקו – וההורים ישלמו ביוקר. דה מרקר Available at www.themarker.com/news/education/1.5827250

of the manipulation of collective memory in the service of nationalism' (Shlaim 1995: 288).

Having said that, those were only relatively minor cracks in the Israeli discourse: the Holocaust was (and still is) perceived as a lynchpin of Jewish identity, deeply linked with the Israeli–Palestinian conflict, and successfully providing a framing for Arabs in general and the Palestinians in particular, not only as an immense security threat but as an existential threat. Two separate, yet inter-related processes shaped identity perceptions on the ground. On the one hand, the official state-sponsored efforts that enforce Holocaust remembrance as the cornerstone of the Jewish DNA – through educational projects such as school curricula (not only in history and Jewish studies but also in literature, geography and social sciences textbooks), trips to the Polish concentration camps, Holocaust Day, commemorations and ceremonies, museums, annual sirens and popular culture (movies, songs and Holocaust survivor biographies) – were predominant and were an untouchable agenda, leaving little or no room for multiple narratives. The well-cemented meanings of the Holocaust became even more pronounced, bringing new meanings and importance to the Holocaust framework in the international arena. The historians' dispute in Germany during the 1980s, which generated a great deal of academic and public attention, addressed the ontological status of the Holocaust (Olick and Levy 1997). Further, the shift at the beginning of the 1990s from the publicly oriented 'duty to remember' to the policy-oriented 'proper way of remembrance' (David 2017b) at the world polity level gave birth to a standardisation of the memory of the Holocaust, bringing to the fore memorialisation policy briefs on how to 'properly' remember the Holocaust (David 2017a). Holocaust museums were already in place in numerous places, with the US Holocaust Memorial Museum (USHMM) opening in April 1993. The International Holocaust Remembrance Alliance (IHRA) – an intergovernmental organisation which unites governments and experts to strengthen, advance and promote Holocaust education, research and remembrance worldwide – was established in 1998. Through such efforts, the Holocaust became a unit of moral measurement in relation to human rights violations (Levy and Sznaider 2002). It served as a reference point for the 'moral community of shared memories' (Margalit 2002), which resulted in the opening of dozens of Holocaust memorial museums, not only in Europe, but in distant places such as Uruguay, Argentina, China, Hong Kong, South Africa and elsewhere.[11] The effort to establish the Holocaust

---

[11] A partial list of the museums can be seen here: www.nj.gov/education/holocaust/resources/world.pdf

remembrance as a meta-narrative of human rights efforts was also apparent in the UN General Assembly's 2005 adoption of International Holocaust Remembrance Day, an international memorial day on 27 January commemorating the victims of the Holocaust. In practice, this means that every UN member state is obligated to commemorate the Holocaust at the state level regardless of its own nationally contextualised histories. The rapid growth of global memory, framed through a normative lens of human rights and expressed through the framework of 'proper' Holocaust remembrance, is best seen in the fact that, by 2013, the Association of Holocaust Organizations included more than three hundred worldwide organisations located in thirty-three countries that are linked to Holocaust education (Goldberg and Hazan 2015). Currently, the prestigious EU-based IHRA[12] has thirty-one member states and an additional nine observer states in the process of becoming members. Furthermore, for EU countries, the memory of the Holocaust became an important glue in the attempt to forge a more homogenised European identity. The 'Europeanisation' of the memory of the Holocaust is promoted by transnational agents such as the European Parliament, the Council of Europe, the Organization for Security and Cooperation in Europe (OSCE) and its Office for Democratic Institutions and Human Rights (ODIHR), and the United Nations, but most significantly by the IHRA (Kucia 2016).

This trend did not occur solely as the 'natural process' of the institutionalisation of human rights, but rather represented an active and persistent effort on the side of the Israeli government. Make no mistake, the Israeli delegation pushed vigorously for the establishment of the International Holocaust Day at the United Nations. Painting it as an issue of 'human rights promotion', the international memorial day was understood, rightly, as an effective way to promote Jewish suffering for political gains – first and foremost, as leverage in the ongoing Israeli–Palestinian conflict. In fact, it was an initiative of Silvan Shalom, then head of the Israeli delegation to the United Nations, that led to Resolution 60/7 establishing January 27 as a day to honour the memory of Holocaust victims.

This linkage is even stronger now: in 2015, the IHRA accepted the Israeli delegation's initiative to broaden the scope of the definition of anti-Semitism to anti-Zionism, stating that the manifestation of anti-Semitism 'might include the targeting of the state of Israel, conceived as a Jewish collectivity' (IHRA 2016). This alteration was partially based on the *Antisemitism Worldwide* report (Moshe Kantor Database 2014: 65), written by a group of scholars from the Moshe Kantor Database for the Study

---

[12] Previously known as the Task Force for International Cooperation on Holocaust Education Remembrance and Research (ITF).

of Contemporary Antisemitism and Racism at Tel Aviv University (Israel). They provided the guidelines for when to equate anti-Semitism with anti-Zionism:

- If the State of Israel is equated with Nazi Germany and its actions and policies are equated with a 'genocide' of the Palestinians
- If the Israeli policy towards Palestinians and Arab Israelis is equated with 'apartheid'
- If one acts to promote the boycott of Israeli goods and institutions (such as the Boycott, Divestment and Sanctions [BDS] movement)

One of the main conclusions of the *Antisemitism Worldwide* report is that anti-Semitism has intensified globally today as never before, often as a disguised form of anti-Zionism, which in many places has become infiltrated into mainstream discourses, particularly among left-wing activists and the far left. This is, of course, not to say that anti-Semitism and anti-Zionism cannot be linked and interconnected, but submerging anti-Zionism under the umbrella of anti-Semitism has an immediate boomerang impact on the Israeli–Palestinian conflict. It both further shrinks the legitimate space for Palestinian actions (delegitimising, for example, the BDS movement) and legitimises Jewish militants' narrative of the existential security threat.

Levy and Sznaider (2002) recognised that different people at different places frame the Holocaust in different ways; whereas those differences might be subtle, they are also crucial. In Europe and in the United States, the Holocaust is understood either as a history of racism that can happen to anyone who is different or as a crime against humanity that is considered a crime against the human condition. In contrast, in Israel, the Holocaust is framed exclusively as the culmination of a history of anti-Semitism that happened only to Jews. Thus, whereas globally the Holocaust serves as a warning subsumed under the slogan 'never again', in Israel it serves to promote the diametrically opposite, ethnically narrow message of 'never again to us'. In Israel, in terms of the promotion of the remembrance of the Holocaust, research and education were part of Israeli state efforts of 'Hasbara' (propaganda, explanation) intended, first and foremost, to position Israel in the international arena as a victim nation that is entitled to defend itself. Over the years, well-grounded arguments have been raised arguing that Jews both inside and outside Israel have abused the Holocaust for political reasons, using it to justify the state's territorial expansion, the suppression of the Palestinian people and the state's use of aggression and torture as legitimate acts of self-defence (Stannard 1996).

Conclusion

The recent shift in the ways in which the memory of the Holocaust, as opposed to the memory of the Nakba, resonates globally matters greatly. It results from not only local politics, but also the interplay between memory entrepreneurs as well as global trends. Israel continues to institutionalise the Holocaust globally, not only as a distinctive Jewish experience of an ultimate victimhood and as the very foundations of the State of Israel, but as a moral measurement of humanity in its entirety. In the past, understanding the Holocaust in terms of human rights served Israel's interests, linking its own political agendas and legitimising its actions in the Israeli–Palestinian conflict as part of the security–existential narrative threat. This linkage between the legitimacy of Israel, the uniqueness of Jewish suffering and Israel's involvement in legitimising other countries' moral values became a tool for further promoting a narrow nationalist agenda. From the completely opposite position, Palestinians were faced with the Holocaust wall that effectively nullified their own ongoing historical suffering, caused by the same people who perfected the promotion of the Holocaust message 'never again' on the international stage; the Palestinians succeeded in framing their struggle internationally as a global appeal to end oppression and colonialism. From the Palestinian side, binding their suffering to colonialism (which it undoubtedly is) and efficiently promoting their struggle for independence as a symbol of oppression worldwide proved to be the key to achieving a consensus among the oppressed.

On a grand scale, in many ways, the Oslo Accords and the gradual implementation of the moral remembrance framework enabled new instruments to continue the conflict through the means of memory. While the Holocaust trope became perceived as constructed and enforced from above, the Palestinian trope became widely appealing for groups whose suffering was never acknowledged, as envisioned by the logic of memorialisation isomorphism. The Palestinian trope spoke to the feelings of all those people who see themselves as oppressed, gathering many, often diametrically different groups under the umbrella of solidarity. Whereas the Holocaust trope became a tool for institutionalising democracies, the Palestinian suffering trope became a political tool for fighting institutionalised democracies and sponsoring the struggles of identity politics.

Those two very different, yet interconnected, genealogical trajectories shaped the local settings and the perspective through which people responded on both sides, on the one hand, to their own national histories and, on the other hand, to the demand (promoted via moral remembrance) to reframe the ways in which they perceive their own sufferings. In Chapter 6, we will see the true power of those layers of memory, intersected by both of the narratives on suffering and state-promoted memorialisation efforts, once people from different sides of the conflict start to negotiate their contested past. Challenged by, and structured according to, the logic of the human rights memorialisation agenda, once they meet in 'facing the past' dialogue encounters, pushed by the facilitators to reconsider their own roles and positioning in the conflict, do participants internalise moral remembrance as a foundation for a moral action? What is the nature of the transformation achieved by adopting the principles of 'facing the past', 'duty to remember' and 'justice for victims' as imposed through the framework of moral remembrance? And how do interpretations of symbols and their historical narratives shape the ways in which they understand, internalise and shape human rights values in the long run?

5 The Institutionalisation of Moral Remembrance
Case Study of the Western Balkans

The Dayton Agreement and the Memorialisation Agenda in Serbia, Croatia and Bosnia-Herzegovina

Three peace agreements ended the conflict in Croatia and Bosnia-Herzegovina (BiH): the Washington Agreement, which created the Muslim–Croat Federation; the Erdut Agreement, which intended to peacefully reintegrate the last Serb-held territory into Croatia; and the Dayton Peace Agreement, which established a detailed framework for peace in BiH (Galbraith 1997). The most significant amongst them, the Dayton Agreement, came as a result of the intensive North Atlantic Treaty Organization (NATO) bombing campaign between 30 August and 20 September 1995. Finally, in December 1995, the Dayton Agreement, which provided for the immediate cessation of hostilities as well as an institutional framework for a Bosnia and Herzegovina nation-state, was signed. It was meant not only to bring back peace and stability to the region, but also to heal the wounds of ethnic division by introducing extensive programs of peacebuilding, transitional justice and reconciliation.

The Dayton Agreement represents one of the most ambitious experiments ever undertaken in the constitutional engineering of ethnic conflict. It took the form of a territorial bargain: the division of Bosnia through the trading of territorial shares, borders and areas of strategic or economic importance. The condition of retaining a single state of Bosnia and Herzegovina within the old republican borders saw the creation of a loose federation with a weak central government, leaving each ethnic group substantially autonomous within its own territory (Cox 1999). The absence of a decisive military victory – by any of the warring parties – constrained the architects when it came to formulating treaty terms which all parties would accept (Caplan 2000). The agreement created an independent Bosnian state divided between two separate entities – the Muslim (Bosniak)–Croat Federation, occupying 51 per cent of the territory, and the Serb-held area, Republika Srpska (RS), occupying 49 percent – and Brčko District, a self-governing administrative unit in north-eastern

Bosnia and Herzegovina. The framework created at Dayton was an extremely flexible one, which has enabled international actors, unaccountable to the people of BiH, to shape and reshape the agenda of post-war transition. The Dayton Agreement's flexibility has been the key factor in enabling external powers to permanently postpone any transition to 'local ownership' (Chandler 2005). Though proclaimed as a sovereign state, BiH was a de facto protectorate of the international community and EU bodies, with the Office of the High Representative being directly in charge and having the responsibility of overseeing the implementation of the agreement. None of the warring parties was satisfied with the outcome of the negotiations, much of which had been conducted over their heads and behind their backs (Caplan 2000).

However, those agreements effectively facilitated the ending of the wars. The consequences of those wars were enormous. Mass violations of international humanitarian law were reported, including mass killings; the massive, organised and systematic detention and rape of women; and continued 'ethnic cleansing'. Following those peace agreements, all parties formally committed to the Europeanisation process, which was conditioned upon, among other things, all sides involved facing their 'criminal past' of human rights abuses.

In Bosnia, where the agreement played a key role in homogenising ethnic groups, it was agreed that a UN International Police Task Force (IPTF) would be established, but only to monitor, advise and train local law-enforcement personnel. The IPTF would help ensure that the parties provided a 'safe and secure environment' for all persons in their respective jurisdictions and that law enforcement agents conducted themselves in accordance with 'internationally recognized standards and with respect for internationally recognized human rights' (Caplan 2000). The nearly 20,000 UN forces in Bosnia, which would be replaced by 60,000 NATO troops, including 20,000 US soldiers, were assumed to be well equipped and empowered to respond effectively to any attacks and to ensure against any resumption of hostilities between the parties.

The Dayton Agreement meant the end of the physical violence, but ordinary people woke up into a reality that was twice hijacked: once by the international community, which had made Bosnia a de facto protectorate, and a second time by the local nationalist governments on all sides, which had closed off any possibility that people would be differentiated in any way other than under very clear ethnic lines. Although the agreement ostensibly supports a unitary Bosnian state underpinned by democratic values, it effectively favours partition and ethnic apartheid (Caplan 2000). In many ways, it reflected the failure of the idea of a single Bosnian state gaining acceptance by most members of two of its three largest constituent peoples (Hayden 2017). With approximately 70 per cent of the region's industrial capacities and infrastructures ruined during the war, extreme poverty, and harsh war legacies of wartime rape, killings, mass graves and traumas to deal with, the official end of the war was, for all sides involved, just the beginning of settling their disputed historical accounts.

The fact that ethnic division in Bosnia was institutionalised and closely monitored internationally (with different degrees of success) produced two effects on the ground. First, the international community played a significant role in pressuring not only BiH's entities but also (to a lesser extent) Serbia and Croatia to shape their national histories in accordance with its own agenda which, though changing and evolving over time, was always dressed in human rights garb. Second, through enforcement by state institutions developed along ethnic lines, the Dayton Agreement cemented the importance of ethnic categories, disabling any formal ambiguity with regard to ethnic identities, a fact that had spill-over effects on the realpolitik in both Serbia and Croatia. It meant that, effectively, Serbs and Croats in Bosnia were directly connected to – and both influencing and influenced by – the nation-states of Croatia and Serbia. Consequently, the structural embedding of ethnic divisions reduced the complexity of Western Balkan society from the previous socialist class system to its ethnonational dimensions.

This outcome is important because, whereas the Oslo Accords tried to bring Israeli Jews and Palestinians closer together (though with clear geographic and ethnic boundaries), the Dayton Agreement effectively erased the parties' previous multi-ethnic past, which had been based not so much on ethnic distinctions (though in some parts of Yugoslavia those differences were more pronounced than in others) but on class distinctions. This matters greatly. As we will see, the memorialisation agenda that followed those agreements further promoted solidarities based along ethnic lines and not what would have been a more inclusive policy – based upon their previous class experience.

Similar to the Oslo Accords in Israel and Palestine, the peacebuilding agenda took centre stage as an irreplaceable feature of consolidating democracy and human rights through civil society and the commitment to the Europeanisation process. The notion of civil society became inextricably linked to democracy, along with the argument that civil society has 'the capacity to generate political alternatives and to monitor government and state, can help start transitions, help resist reversals, help push transitions to their completion, and help consolidate and deepen democracy' (Linz and Stepan 1996: 18). Thus, in the aftermath of the wars, donors started inflating money to encourage post-war reconstruction, peacebuilding and reconciliation. The EU made a substantial financial commitment to civil society projects in the Balkans under its Instrument for Pre-accession Assistance (IPA). It also developed the Civil Society Facility (CSF), which implemented different strands of interventions to strengthen the development and dialogue of civil society in the region, with a clear focus on the People 2 People Programme (P2P). With the exception of Croatia, where the state provides significant support to the civil society sector (that, to a large degree, lined up with the official narrative), other countries in the region were (and still are) largely dependent on assistance from Western European and US development programs, such as USAID, the Swedish International Development Agency (SIDA) and especially the EU (Balfour and Stratulat 2011). The BiH-pseudo international 'protectorate' is operated through the executive management of external actors: the Office of the High Representative (OHR) of the Peace Implementation Council; the United Nations; the missions of both the Organization for Security and Cooperation in Europe (OSCE) and the EU; the International Management Group (an EU-funded body that undertakes reconstruction evaluations); aid agencies; and international financial institutions (IFIs). They provide executive governance that reflects the values and norms of the powers that dominate the global economy.

An estimated 46 per cent of the population in the Federation of Bosnia and Herzegovina and 75 per cent in Republika Srpska were living in poverty in 2000, and most people were getting poorer. In 2000, donors had to allocate funds to meet a revenue deficit of more than US$360 million, with Republika Srpska having a 73 per cent shortfall on expected revenue and the Federation 31.5 per cent (Pugh 2002). Roughly 95 per cent of Bosnia's non-governmental organisations (NGOs) received foreign funding in 1999 (Hyatt 2000: 54). A similar trend is observed in Serbia. Foreign donors represent the largest single source of support for local NGOs, accounting for 47 per cent of their funds. However, in 1999–2000 a large number of donors either left altogether, moving to other conflict areas, or significantly reduced their presence. In Croatia, most donors pulled their peacebuilding funding between 1998 and 2008 – three to thirteen years after the conflict ended (Heideman 2016). Having said that, the civil sector has continued to grow. For example, in 1996, only ninety-eight local NGOs were registered in BiH, but by 2004 that number had jumped to more than 8,000 (Micinski 2016).

This should not be surprising. In many ways, forming an NGO in the post-war reality was the only way not just to apply for funding, but to be employed. For example, in 1997, an astonishing 400 various voluntary groups and civil society organisations were already registered in Bosnia.

The number of projects conducted in the past twenty-five years is voluminous, to say the least. However, not all geographic areas and segments of the population were included in the same way: some areas and segments of people were well exposed to human rights projects, while others were deeply marginalised. According to the USAID NGO Sustainability Index for Central and Eastern Europe and Eurasia, in 2008, there were an estimated 12,198 NGOs in BiH, and 37,000 NGOs in Croatia. According to the European Commission's 2011 progress report on Serbia, there were a total of 8,500 registered organisations.[1] Within the scope of peacebuilding, it is important to stress that international donors largely prioritised NGOs that promoted a reconciliation agenda (Micinski 2016), based on the 'facing the past' and 'victim-centred' agenda.

In Israel and Palestine, there was not, and could not have been, any acceptance of the transitional justice or reconciliation paradigm for all kinds of political and structural reasons where the international community was not able (or willing) to force sides into it. For Serbia, Croatia and BiH, the pressure posed by the international community in general, and by the EU in particular, was a given from the very beginning: following the wars of the 1990s, they all formally committed to the Europeanisation process and transitional justice mechanisms. Each state's entrance into the EU was supposedly conditioned upon, among other things, facing its criminal past of human rights abuses. The main request posed to Croatia and Serbia by the EU was cooperation with the International Criminal Tribunal for Yugoslavia (ICTY). The Croatian government mostly cooperated selectively and reluctantly. Nevertheless, in 2005, it successfully transferred the last ICTY indictee to the Hague Tribunal, effectively fulfilling its obligations to the tribunal (Subotić 2009). This resulted in opening Croatia's path for EU candidacy. Croatia ultimately joined the EU in 2013, ending its transitional phase on the conditionality path. For Serbia, cooperation with the ICTY was even more contested, and still is: it was only in 2008 that the Serbian government arrested and extradited Radovan Karadžić, the president of Republika Srpska during the war in Bosnia, and, in 2011, Ratko Mladić, a former Bosnian Serb military leader. However, three radical party officials are still wanted on charges of contempt of the tribunal, rather than for any crimes committed during the wars, and have not been extradited to the ICTY.

In Bosnia, the 1995 Dayton Agreement served primarily as a freeze-frame that acknowledged territorial consolidations achieved by Serbs,

---

[1] Those figures should be taken with reservations: not only does each country have its own regulations on how to register NGOs, but there are many phantom NGOs that do not operate in reality.

Croats and Bosniaks and solidified them with a constitutional framework which made Bosnia a de facto international protectorate, ruled by the OHR with almost limitless executive power. What is more, during the first two decades of its mandate, the OHR had the power not only to decree resolutions but also to enforce them, including to praise and criminalise all sides involved.[2] Under this authority, the OHR has issued a large number of decisions on issues of monitoring, coordinating and promoting state capacity building in accordance with the Dayton Agreement. Several decisions, however, were directly related to identity and memory formation. First, as early as 1998 and 1999, the OHR issued three important decisions regarding national symbols: *Decision Imposing the Law on the Flag in BiH* (1998), *Decision on the Flying of the Flag in BiH* (1998) and *Decision Imposing the Law on the National Anthem of BiH* (1999). Second, Wolfgang Petritsch, the third High Representative for BiH, in October 2000 issued a *Decision Designating in Perpetuity a Plot of Land at Potočari to Be Set Aside As a Cemetery and As a Solemn Place for the Erection of a Memorial to the Victims of the Srebrenica Massacre*. In May 2000, he issued a *Decision Establishing and Registering the Foundation of the Srebrenica-Potočari Memorial and Cemetery*, which received and disbursed funds to build and maintain the memorial and cemetery. Third, Annex 8 of the Dayton Peace Agreement provided for the formation of a commission to preserve national monuments, whose mandate was to receive petitions to designate property of 'cultural, historical, religious or ethnic importance' as national monuments. In 2002, the OHR issued its *Decision Amending the Federation Law on Preservation of Assets Declared National Monuments of BiH under Decisions of the Commission for Protection of National Monuments* and *Decision Imposing the RS Law on Implementation of Decisions of the Commission to Preserve National Monuments Established under Annex 8 of the Dayton Peace Agreement*. All of those decisions, promulgated from the top down, promote the human rights memorialisation agenda in which the 'facing the past' and 'victim-centred' principles were meant to establish a new regime of memory by promoting a 'proper' way to remember the past.

A good example of the ways in which different forms of pressure are used to enforce particular visions of the past can be seen in the ways in which the European Parliament (EP) drafted the Srebrenica genocide resolutions.[3] The EP adopted three resolutions on the Srebrenica genocide: on 7 July 2005, 15 January 2009 and 7 July 2015, respectively.

---

[2] The OHR's power is in constant decline and is currently not effective in many ways.
[3] The Srebrenica genocide refers to the July 1995 killing of 7,000 to 8,000 Bosnian Muslim males in the town of Srebrenica during the last months of the Bosnian War (1992–1995).

All three resolutions outline *the proper way* to remember Srebrenica. Moreover, each resolution 'Calls on the Council and the Commission to commemorate *appropriately*[4] the anniversary of the Srebrenica-Potočari act of genocide by supporting Parliament's recognition of 11 July as the day of commemoration for the Srebrenica genocide all over the EU, and to call on all of the countries of the Western Balkans to do the same'. The policy framework of proper memorialisation standards was tailored through a precise wording that was meant to establish orders of power for the moral community of righteous. Thus, the EP 'stresses', 'recalls', 'regrets', 'expresses', 'praises', 'urges', 'condemns', 'reaffirms' and 'instructs' – for the sake of drawing moral lines between four distinct communities: ethnically bounded victims; their opponents; ethnically bounded perpetrators; and bystanders, personified and embedded in the international community in general, and in the EU in particular.

These and many other formal and informal measures (first and foremost, their commitment to the Europeanisation process) were used over time to push Serbia, Croatia and BiH to take responsibility and officially reframe their positions on what actually transpired in the wars of the 1990s. Memorialisation agendas are enforced though different forms of international pressure that are never constant in their intensity, sustainability and reliability. What defines the strength and tenacity of the external influence on local memorialisation processes is the mechanism through which international pressure is applied and enforced. Coercive pressure directly ties compliance with international demands to material rewards such as financial aid and/or membership in international organisations. Symbolic pressure induces compliance through appeals to the state's desire to be perceived as a legitimate international actor. Bureaucratic pressure works when states choose to comply with international requests because they believe international actors can solve their domestic problems (Subotić 2009: 7–8). Demands for dealing with the past, together with other political, social and economic requests and conditions, place enormous pressure on nation-states and currently play a central role in the process of memory construction. However, all states (to varying degrees) comply with those demands not only because it enables them to access funds and memberships, but also because, in terms of international relations, it proves to be beneficial to belong to the community of countries that position themselves as morally righteous. It is precisely this desire to be part of the global polity that facilitated the process in which all parties in the Western Balkans

---

[4] My italics.

tried to project their alleged commitment to the norms promoted through moral remembrance.

Europeanising the (Savage) Balkan Past

Europeanisation includes complex and strongly disputed processes wherein the amalgamation of knowledge, attitudes and values is emphasised (Karlsson 2010: 38). The most parsimonious definition of Europeanisation is that of a process by which 'states adopt EU rules' (Schimmelfenning and Sedlemeier 2005: 7). Radaelli (2003) describes Europeanisation as follows:

a process involving, a) construction, b) diffusion and c) institutionalization of formal and informal rules, procedures, policy paradigms, styles, 'ways of doing things' and shared beliefs and norms which are first defined and consolidated in the EU policy process and then incorporated in the logic of domestic (national and sub-national) discourse, political structures and public choices.

In the Western Balkans, Europeanisation is connected to applying for EU membership, a process supervised and monitored by the EU (Orlović 2007: 92). The European Union has been the most powerful political and economic agent in the post-socialist Balkans, Europe's most varied political landscape. But Europeanisation also has its price. According to its 1993 Copenhagen policy, the EU is supposed to educate, discipline and punish while offering EU membership as the prize. In other words, EU superiority is built into this process and, being at the top of the hierarchical pyramid, the EU dictates the conditions, tempo and changing logic of the 'game'.

In the countries of the Western Balkans, the conditional joining with the EU comes with imperatives for implementing certain forms of the memorialisation agenda – first and foremost, transitional justice. Transitional justice refers to a set of judicial and non-judicial measures implemented to redress the legacies of massive human rights abuses; both directly and indirectly, it dictates the frameworks of memory. The proscribed measures include criminal prosecutions, truth commissions, reparations programs and various kinds of institutional reforms, such as compensation for victims, lustration, establishment of museums and other commemorative activities. The politics of regret and formal and informal community initiatives are other examples of this phenomenon (Subotić 2009: 18). Transitional justice, as a praxis of the human rights memorialisation ideology, frames memorialisation as a tool for achieving a particular vision of the past – assuming that once crimes are faced and victims are officially recognised, this step will prevent violence from recurring and will lead to an appreciation of human rights values. Transitional justice is understood to serve the honour of those who died during conflict or other atrocities, to examine the past, to address contemporary issues and show respect to victims, and to prevent denial and help societies move forward. Thus, adjusting and manipulating values and ideologies by changing the image of the past was (and still is) an important part of the Europeanisation process.

Layers of Memory in the Western Balkans: The Threefold Nature of a Contested Past

Unlike in Israel and in Palestine, where the past has always been understood as a continuous narrative of nationalist ideologies, Serbia, Croatia and BiH, with the wars of the 1990s and the fall of socialism, were all forced to tailor the past to fit their new/old visions of their self and nationhood.

The violent ethnic nationalisms which replaced Yugoslavia's communalist ethos of 'brotherhood and unity' (*bratstvo i jedinstvo*) in 1991, when the Socialist Federal Republic of Yugoslavia (SFRJ) fragmented into its constitutive republics, annulled Yugoslavia's distinct socialist path. Up to that point, in the capitalist West and across much of the Third World, Yugoslavia, as a leading member of the Non-Aligned Movement, was often perceived as demonstrating a more 'human' socialism. The 1948 split, and the subsequent threats against Yugoslavia from the Moscow-aligned bloc, put Yugoslav socialism onto an independent and promising path. Massive industrialisation, modernisation and education took place, accompanied by workers' self-management agenda, which positioned Yugoslavia highly in international arenas, with major infrastructures being built from the post–World War II period until the late 1980s.

Prior to World War I, Slovenia and Croatia had belonged to the Austro-Hungarian Empire and had benefited from the wider economic modernisation the empire had experienced over the nineteenth century. These republics entered the socialist period with the tools needed to rapidly develop light industry. In contrast, Bosnia and Herzegovina, Montenegro, Macedonia and the southern parts of Serbia had either been part of, or dependent on, the Ottoman Empire and had remained largely agrarian and undeveloped. Hence, the Yugoslav socialist project promised to annul those differences and bring significant development to all.

Though some of the infrastructure was inherited from the pre–World War II period, the Yugoslav period was marked by the extension and electrification of the rail network, with the main two projects being the electrification of the Zagreb–Belgrade railway and the building of the highly challenging Belgrade–Bar railway. The core of the road network in Yugoslavia was the Brotherhood and Unity Highway, which stretched over 1,182 km. In addition, urban bus networks were put in place in all cities. In addition to Yugoslav Airlines Transportation (JAT), which was established in 1927, by the 1970s more airlines had been created – namely, Aviogenex, Adria Airways and Pan Adria Airways, focused on the growing tourist industry. Education and literacy were placed high on the national agenda. Hence, between 1945 and 1992 numerous schools and universities were established throughout the country, such as the Universities of Pristina, Skopje, Novi Sad, Osijek, Split, Rijeka and Titograd, along with dozens of others.

In many ways, the Yugoslav project provided extraordinary opportunities for personal as well as cultural, artistic, scientific and ideological development. The children and youth of Yugoslavia were exposed to classic cultures, through literature, theatre, museums and movies, and the newest events in culture from all over the world, including new popular youth music, avant-garde theatre, international film festivals and the newest literary works. Yugoslavs enjoyed a relatively greater freedom of speech, gathering and activism than most of their counterparts in other socialist countries, and they had opportunities to travel abroad and interact with people from all around the world who visited Yugoslavia.

To achieve all of these advances, the institutionalisation of the organisational and doctrinal power of socialism was heavily supported through the projects that enabled the internalisation of ideological, cultural, generational and ethnical mixing and merging. Many of the modernisation projects were achieved through voluntary 'work actions' (*omladinske radne akcije*) which aimed to strengthen the might of the socialist party and the 'Titoist' ideology of 'brotherhood and unity', and which were perceived by many as both a duty and a privilege. For example, the first section of the railway between Zagreb and Belgrade was built through the efforts of the Yugoslav People's Army (JNA) and the volunteer Youth Work Actions and was opened in 1950. The section between Ljubljana and Zagreb was built by 54,000 volunteers in less than eight months in 1958 (Lubej 2008). The JNA was the epitome of this mixing and merging politics: it was purposely structured in such a way so as to bring together geographically, culturally and ethnically distant peoples into one organisational and ideological framework.

In every single aspect of their lives, the memory of the Communist Yugoslav Partisans' victory against fascists and nationalists, and the rebirth of the Yugoslav people with Tito (Josip Broz) as the leading figure, were the central themes celebrated through commemorative events, memorial architecture, various art forms, the national calendar, official speeches, youth and workers' rallies and military parades. The celebration of anti-fascist struggle and the victory of the partisans of Yugoslavia during World War II was an omnipresent theme. This conflict was portrayed as a struggle not only between Yugoslavia and the Axis Powers, but also between good and evil within Yugoslavia, with the multi-ethnic Yugoslav Partisans being depicted as the 'good' Yugoslav partisans fighting against the manipulated 'evil' Yugoslavs – the Croatian Ustaše and Serbian Chetniks (Flere 2007).

Though the creation of the Yugoslav identity was politically motivated, many people did attach themselves to this identity during the 1960s, 1970s and 1980s (Petrović 2000: 166). 'Yugoslav' was an admissible category for self-declared censuses. It was used by three categories of people: those who were committed Yugoslavists, those who were members of the Communist Party and wished to eschew ethnicity, and those who were Muslims or who belonged to other ethnic minorities and wished to avoid ethnic identification (Hammel 2000: 26). However, Markowitz (2007) showed that state census categories do not necessarily reflect longstanding cultural practices, forge common-sense social categories or present an objective picture of the ethnic distribution of the population. Urban residents, Communist Party members, the younger generation, and people from minority nationalities or from nationally mixed parentage were most likely to identify themselves as Yugoslavs (Sekulić, Hodson and Massey 1994).

The deconstruction of the Yugoslav identity, ideology and legacy was omnipresent in all former Yugoslav states but was most extensive in Serbia, BiH, Croatia, Macedonia and Kosovo. For Croatia, Serbia and BiH, the wars of the 1990s led to a rupture not only because of the extensive use of violence and the collapse of socialism, but also because of the breakdown of the unique ideology of the Yugoslav project. Yugoslavia was framed within the partisan narrative that was supposed to depict a civil war between the different ideological groups on the ground – first and foremost between the partisans, Serbian Chetniks[5] and Croatian Ustaše.[6] Thus, after World War II, the message stressing 'brotherhood and unity' together with 'the immediate solution of class identity' (Bjelić 2002: 53) was intended to replace previous national

---

[5] A Serb nationalist and monarchist paramilitary organization, widely supported by the clerics of the Serbian Orthodox Church, that acted as an anti-Axis movement carrying out a tactical or selective collaboration with the occupation throughout World War II.
[6] A Croatian fascist, racist, ultranationalist and terrorist organization, active, in its original form, between 1929 and 1945.

identities, providing the political elite with a means of simplifying and explaining cultural and ethnic differences. It has been argued that Yugoslavia survived so long mostly because of the regime's firm grip over the national question (Prošić-Dvornić 2000). Thus, to unite these diverse ethnic groups, who had massacred one another during World War II, the Communist Party, as the governing entity, glorified World War II and the partisan narrative as the myth of the Yugoslavian nation's inception through an organisation called the Association of Fighters of the National Liberation War (SUBNOR).[7] The purpose of this war veterans' organisation, which had nearly a million members, was to propagate myths of homogenisation regarding partisan bravery and further a new collective memory as a means of building national Yugoslavian identity. This aim was illustrated by the scope of the organisation's activities: by 1961, it had erected 2,940 monuments, memorial sites and cemeteries for the purpose of infiltrating educational messages concerning the desired norms and values of the Yugoslavian nation (Bergholz 2007: 63). In addition, throughout his long rule, Tito stressed that the Yugoslav federation was a good space endangered by an antagonistic outside: from the initial opposition to fascism, to oscillating between the Soviet threat and the threat posed by the West (Bowman 2003: 45).

Thus, all ethnic identities were pushed aside in socialist Yugoslavia by the government project which sought to form a multi-ethnic nation – the Yugoslavian nation – while simultaneously and constantly instigating nationalism from above. However, by promoting a non-ethnic base for Yugoslav unity, the elite made nationalism the main rhetoric antipode to the dominant ideology of the regime. At the same time, by declaring everyone who opposed the regime a nationalist, the regime in fact promoted such nationalism as the main alternative (Jović 2017). There was an inherent ambiguity in the manner in which the Communist leadership in Yugoslavia treated nationality. Indeed, 'while communist states preached proletarian internationalism on the normative level, ethnonationalism was the cornerstone of their operative ideology and an important source of internal legitimacy' (Malešević 2006a: 399). In Yugoslavia, under Communist rule, sentiments were manipulated in the inauguration of a pan-Yugoslav national identity. The Titoist slogan 'brotherhood and unity' was intended to mend the rifts and fratricidal relations between Yugoslavia's ethnically defined 'nations' during World War II. Ethno-nationalism, which had generated the recent Yugoslav conflicts, was a dominant concept throughout the period of Communist

---

[7] Savez Udruženja Boraca Narodnooslobodilačkog rata Jugoslavije.

rule between 1941 and 1991 (Petrović 2000: 165). Brubaker and Cooper (2000) ascribed this to the fact that the strongly institutionalised ethno-national classificatory system made certain categories readily and legitimately available for the representation of social reality, the framing of political claims and the organisation of political action. Brubaker (1994: 48) claimed that institutional definitions of nationhood 'did not so much constrain action as constitute basic categories of political understanding, central parameters of political rhetoric, specific types of political interest and fundamental forms of political identity'. The government did not recognise the existence of Yugoslav nationality (as opposed to identity). Petrović (2000: 166) showed the depth of this paradox:

Even though the word 'Nation' was formally out of ideological favor as an inclusive category, the political leadership was too concerned with the so-called process of ethno-genesis so that in the second Yugoslavia (1945-1991) three new nations were created (Macedonian, Montenegrin and Muslim). This was possibly an attempt to balance the powers of the three 'old' nations (Serbs, Croats and Slovenes).

The paradox of institutionalised ethno-nationalism was manifested in the striking duality through which ordinary people perceived it. At the community level, even in places which were ethnically mixed, interethnic relations were judged to have been very good. However, at the inter-republic level, people saw relations between nationalities as being very bad (Gagnon 2010: 35). This was due to the fact that, by the early 1980s, the legitimacy of the Yugoslav Communist Party had been eroded and parties in the various republics began to portray themselves as defenders of the national interest. Each party blamed other republics for the economic problems their country was facing.

In fact, several other factors did play a role in the breakup of Yugoslavia and the violent wars that followed, such as unemployment (Woodward 1995), failures by the law and legal system (Lukić 1993; Ramet 2004) and the role played by the intellectual elite (Dimitrijević 2001; Dragović-Soso 2002). Thus, ethnic nationalism is as much a consequence of unsuccessful state-building as it is its cause.

The dissolution of Yugoslavia left in its wake ruptured memories and fomented mnemonic tensions over the legacy of the federation that had existed in various forms from 1918 to 1992. The nature of transition in the various successor states of the Socialist Federal Republic of Yugoslavia was marked, in Croatia and BiH above all, by mass violence, in wars that lasted for the greater part of the early 1990s. In the aftermath of the wars of the 1990s, all successor Yugoslav states suffered a delay in their transition to democracy and continued embracing and further institutionalising the ethno-nationalist category as the most important pattern for their national consolidation. However, the idea that the collapse of communism enabled the 'liberation' of private, national memories long suppressed under Tito must be regarded as highly dubious, not least because this was the way in which the new nationalist regimes themselves represented the situation (Jansen 2002).

In the aftermath of the wars of the 1990s, virtually all Yugoslav successor states chose the same pattern of memory politics – namely, embracing revisionist and anti-Yugoslav agendas. It was a triple-track process whereby all newly consolidated nation-states (1) revived elements from their ancient histories to legitimise their distinctiveness and uniqueness from neighbouring nation-states, (2) revitalised their right-wing movements and (3) reframed the Communist legacy and partisan struggle as oppressive.

Undergoing Transitions: Shifting Memory Politics

Transitions – whether we are talking about post-war, post-socialist, post-dictatorship or other transitory stages – are described as times of instability, ambiguity and crisis when animosities become particularly strained and marked by increasing degrees of intolerance (Prošić-Dvornić 2000). While undergoing their periods of transition, Serbia, Croatia and BiH had to re-narrate the moral and symbolic boundaries of their nationhood, as certain elements of their narrowly perceived ethnic past immediately became contested and were deemed unfit to serve their present nationalist agendas. In Serbia, Croatia and BiH, unlike in other parts of Eastern Europe, the contestation of the past took three forms: from a post-war state to a peacebuilding state, from a post-socialist state to a liberal democracy, and from a post-Yugoslav federation to an ethnically based state. However, the ways in which they all chose to address various layers of their national past has to be accounted for against the background of the rise of *moral remembrance*, as an influencing force to which all parties were pressured to align with.

The War Legacy

Wars necessarily entail ruptures in the fabric of identity on multiple levels, as they engender death and the personal experience of unimaginable horrors on the part of combatants and others. They also encompass the distortion of everyday life and the disruption of social and economic relations, as well as profound political change. Furthermore, wars leave obvious physical evidence of destruction in public spaces – destruction that is hard to mask.

The wars of the 1990s produced heavy losses and massive destruction. In Slovenia, 77 people lost their lives; in Croatia, the number of fatalities ranged from 17,000 to 22,000 (approximately 15,000 Croats and 7,000 Serbs). According to the head of the Croatian Commission for Missing Persons, Colonel Ivan Grujić, Croatia suffered 12,000 killed or missing, including 6,788 soldiers and 4,508 civilians (IWPR 2006). The Belgrade-based NGO Veritas listed 6,827 killed and missing from the Republic of Serbian Krajina, including 4,177 combatants and 2,650 civilians, and 307 Yugoslav Popular Army members who were from Croatia. Most of them were killed or went missing in 1991 (2,729) and in 1995 (2,348) (VERITAS 2014). In addition, according to Serbian sources, some 120,000 Serbs were displaced from 1991 to 1993, and 250,000 were displaced after Operation Storm (Štrbac 1999).

According to the Research and Documentation Center in Sarajevo, the number of dead or disappeared people during the wars in Bosnia total 101,040, of whom 62,013 were Bosniaks (61.4 per cent), 24,953 were Serbs (24.7 per cent) and 8,403 were Croats (8.3 per cent). Later those numbers were corrected by Tokača (2013), who has been taken as the most reliable source: this author suggests that the total number of people killed during the Bosnian War (1992–1995) was approximately 96,000. Out of that number, 38,239 were civilians and 57,701 soldiers. At least 30 per cent of the 2,007 confirmed Bosniak civilian victims were women and children. ICTY research in 2010, conducted for the Office of the Prosecutors at the Hague Tribunal, produced similar figures: a total of 104,732 killed, of whom 36,700 were civilians and 68,031 soldiers (Zwierzchowski and Tabeau 2010). An estimated 12,000 to 20,000 women were raped, most of them Bosniak (Crowe 2013: 343). Regarding the number of missing persons, it is estimated that, in Croatia alone, there approximately 2,400 missing persons (ICRC 2010). In Bosnia, there are more than 27,000 missing, according to Amnesty International. However, according to the BiH State Commission on the Search for Missing Persons and the International Red Cross of BiH (Radović 2004), in 2004 the number of missing persons was deemed to be 16,862 Bosniaks, 2,522 Serbs, 711 Croats, 35 Albanians, 11 Montenegrins, 19 Roma, 6 Ukrainians, 4 Slovenians and 2 Hungarians. In addition, in July 1995, more than 8,000[8] Bosniaks, mainly men and boys, were massacred in and around the

---

[8] Potočari Memorial Center Preliminary List of Missing Persons from Srebrenica.

town of Srebrenica during the Bosnian War, an event known as the Srebrenica genocide.

The wars in the former Yugoslavia all share three specific features: ethnic cleansing, prison camps and paramilitary formations (Radović 2004). While all parties involved in the conflict committed severe violations of international humanitarian law, such as the killing of civilians, rape, torture, and the deliberate destruction of civilian property, including cultural and religious properties such as churches and mosques, there were significant qualitative differences. Most of the violations were committed by Serbs against Bosnian Muslims.

Moreover, a large number of prison camps and places of detention were established (approximately 200): some were under the control of the regular armies, while others were of an unofficial, almost private character, under the control of local military and paramilitary heavyweights. While some functioned as ordinary places of detention, others had special purposes, such as the detention of women and their sexual assault and rape. Classical prisons and correctional institutions were used, as well as military barracks, police stations, primary and secondary schools, sports halls and various industrial, traffic and trade facilities, abandoned mines, warehouses, agricultural states, silos, catering establishments (hotels, motels, inns, disco clubs) and private houses.

Additionally, various paramilitary units operated during the Bosnian War. The number of paramilitary groups, and the size of each group, varied throughout the course of the conflict. However, reports provide only a rough approximation of paramilitary troop strength. They suggest that the number of persons in paramilitary groups fighting in support of BiH ranged from 4,000 to 6,000; between 12,000 to 20,000 supported the Republic of Croatia; and between 20,000 and 40,000 paramilitaries fought on behalf of the self-declared Serb Republics.

Hence, in Bosnia and Croatia, the destruction, with regard to both human life and infrastructures, was massive. In turn, it shaped the process of remembering in multiple ways. Wars are, in essence, extraordinary experiences that are traumatic and permeated with extreme emotions and actions. They possess a decisive function in building the nation as a 'sacred community of sacrifice'. The literature points out that warfare strengthens the connection between a nation and its homeland, and the creation of 'war myths serves multiple functions including the creation of meaning out of suffering' (Hutchinson 2009: 409). What is more, questions regarding the moral boundaries of a nation are often posed through wars. Thus, wars serve to reclassify people and ensure continuity, while signifying a group's inception, 'birth' or 'origins' (Nora 1996). War-related practices are intended to further valorise and promote the nationally suitable narrative in such a way as to justify it historically (Young 1993). The legacy of war is shaped by the nation-state, which exercises its power to recognise, commemorate and incorporate within its national narrative only certain war memories, whilst others are officially marginalised or forgotten. This is particularly true for nation-states that face serious obstacles in the process of 'making meaning out of suffering' (Hutchinson 2009) as a result of the problematic and contested elements of their past, which may include accusations of atrocities committed, the violation of international war laws and human rights violations.

After the wars of the 1990s, this assumingly 'natural' role of the state to selectively tailor its national past to fit its own political and ideological needs was, in many ways, reduced and outsourced to external, international bodies. The peace agreements that were put in place tried to push states to become accountable for massive human rights abuses during the wars of the 1990s. In multiple ways, those agreements were meant to restrict the freedom of political elites to engage solely in promoting one-sided narratives of the wars by conditioning governments to actively endorse the process of 'facing the past'. Through international bodies and the Europeanisation process, two interrelated strategies – that of transitional justice and that of peacebuilding and reconciliation – pushed forward the human rights memorialisation agenda. Through the discourses and paradigms of truth and justice and their importance for the transformation from war to peace, transitional justice mechanisms, followed by peacebuilding efforts and reconciliation, provided guidance for 'proper' memorialisation (as envisioned in moral remembrance). Though transitional justice mechanisms were not established or carried out with the clear purpose of defining memorialisation processes in Serbia, Croatia or Bosnia, memorialisation efforts were heavily influenced by the framework through which people perceived and understood the wars.

Generally speaking, both transitional justice and reconciliation projects produced two distinct mechanisms through which Serbia, Croatia and both entities in Bosnia responded to the international demands to reframe and adjust their historical narratives to fit a moral remembrance scheme. They all found themselves caught in the gap between domestic demands and those imposed by the international community. In an attempt to bridge the gaps between the opposing domestic and international demands, they all had to mediate and manoeuvre between the international demand to confront their criminal national past and the domestic demands to be validated as a righteous party in the conflict (David 2014b; Milošević 2017; Subotić 2009). Consequently, state-sponsored memorialisation projects, such as museums, commemorations, history books, monuments, national calendars and others, became platforms that were purposefully constructed to enable multiple functions and readings: on the one hand, to present these entities as democratic and progressive states, and on the other hand, to legitimise a wide range of emotions at the local level – first and foremost, gradiences and local patriotism. In other words, in all post-conflict countries across the Western Balkans, memorialisation projects were made and instrumentalised in such a way so as to meet European expectations and further the interest of states in joining the EU, but also to allow wider local audiences to express feelings of animosity, injustice and frustration as a means of settling historical accounts (David 2014a).

The most significant of all transitional justice mechanisms, the establishment and work of the ICTY, over the past two decades has impacted the ways in which the public perceives the externally promoted memorialisation efforts. According to the official site of the ICTY,[9] a total of 161 persons were indicted. There are 62 convicted Serbs, 18 convicted Croats, 5 convicted Bosniaks, 2 convicted Montenegrins, 1 convicted Macedonian and 1 convicted Albanian on this list. For Serbs, this disproportionality in convictions, fuelled by rhetoric manipulations from the political elite (in both Serbia and Republika Srpska), caused the general public to largely discredit the rulings of the ICTY as being biased. For the Croatians, any conviction of Croats was regarded as wrongful, as it collided directly with the official narrative of the 'righteous war for homeland independence' (Jović 2017). On the Bosniak side, the ICTY's work was too little, too slow and too late. Hence, the ICTY rulings were locally disputed and contested, and this shaped highly distorted perceptions on what moral remembrance is all about. Consequently, the fact that the ICTY provided an enormous database of fact-finding and a framework of reference for human rights NGOs and institutions was viewed and often treated locally with hostility and antagonism.

Furthermore, transitional justice and reconciliation efforts landed on local realities in which different ethnic groups understood the outcomes of the wars differently. For Croatia, the narrative presented from the very start – based on the conflict being a necessary war for achieving the long-standing dream of the independence of the Croatian people – instantly recruited Croats to justify its cause, even though in 1991, on the eve of the war, only 11 per cent were in favour of Croatia's secession (Jović 2017). Achieving an independent state and expelling Serbs was a

---

[9] International Criminal Tribunal for Yugoslavia (ICTY) Key Figures, www.icty.org/en/cases/key-figures-cases.

win–win situation for those who dreamed of Croatian independence. The Croatian defenders were immediately greeted and perceived as heroes and became a significant factor in the political life of Croatia. Instantly, the 'Independence War' replaced the anti-fascist narrative of the partisan struggle, and became the undisputed meta-narrative of Croatia's nationhood.

For Republika Srpska, the Serb entity of Bosnia, though it officially lost some of the territories gained during the war, the Dayton Agreement provided legitimisation for the development of an ethnically clean nation-state within the larger state. For the Federation of Croats and Bosniaks, the agreement proved to be more challenging. They had to balance two ethnically and religiously different groups, with the state of Croatia in the background, often intervening on behalf of the Croat minority. The inequality became even more transparent once Croatia joined the EU, consequently enabling dual citizenship for the Croats in Bosnia.

In Serbia, the situation was much more contested and ambiguous. Despite the extremely large number of dead and missing, for the Serbs living in Serbia, these wars were perceived as occurring somewhere else, away from home. On the one hand, until the overthrow of Milosevic in 2000, the authorities behaved as if Serbia and Montenegro had nothing to do with the wars. Despite the wars raging in the region and numerous informal indications as well as allegations of various international bodies that some citizens of Serbia and Montenegro[10] took part in the war in Croatia and BiH, the official state policy was that Serbia was not at war. On the other hand, for people living in Serbia, the 1990s was a decade of hardship and harsh economic sanctions, and they were deeply concerned with their own day-to-day survival rather than with the wars in the former Yugoslav countries. In addition to having lost three military conflicts,[11] the country was suffering from the highest level of hyperinflation witnessed in modern times as well as from international sanctions and isolation. Unemployment levels reached 50 per cent during the 1990s, and per capita income dropped by more than two-thirds after 1989. Furthermore, the flow of (unwelcome) Serbian refugees from Bosnia, but particularly from Croatia, made the hardship even harder. Thus, unlike in Croatia and Bosnia, where actual war was raging, for many people in Serbia, the end of the wars in Bosnia and Croatia seemingly did not change much of their ongoing reality.

However, the gradual proliferation of the human rights memorialisation agenda, with which the post-war states were expected to comply after the

---

[10] Until 2006, Montenegro and Serbia were parts of the same state.
[11] In Croatia, in Bosnia and later in Kosovo.

wars, directly collided with the narrow, nationalist narratives. This agenda prescribed and implemented the framework of 'proper' remembrance, based on the three embedded principles of 'facing the past', 'duty to remember' and 'victim-centred justice'. After the implementation of the international agreements and the beginning of the EU candidacy track for the new nation-states, numerous memorialisation efforts took place. On the part of nationalist governments, every success of the international community to pressure the differing sides into moral remembrance was immediately followed by counter-effects and a strengthening of historical revisionism. Taking the form of verbal pressure, resolutions, policy recommendations, prizes and awards, the international community negotiated the adoption of, and transition to, moral remembrance, assuming this would enable the much wider adoption of human rights values in the Western Balkans. This effort was headed by major human rights institutions such as the OSCE, the UN General Assembly, the European Parliament, the US Institute for Peace, the International Alliance for Holocaust Remembrance and Impunity Watch.

In some aspects, governments tried to satisfy the international community. With three Srebrenica Resolutions in place[12] and Serbia's formal submission for EU membership in 2009, in 2010 Serbian president Boris Tadić called on the Serbian Parliament to adopt a declaration that would unequivocally condemn the massacre in Srebrenica. However, because of a fear of losing domestic electoral voices, the Serbian Declaration did not use the word 'genocide' to describe the crimes committed in Srebrenica, thus going only halfway. At the official level, and under pressure from the international community, official apologies have been issued, with the most famous and questionable coming from Serbian President Alexander Vučić at the twentieth anniversary of the Srebrenica genocide commemoration – one that enraged the grieving participants who were present. Though Vučić was hit with stones and then used that response to his political advantage, Federica Mogherini, the High Representative for Foreign Affairs, tweeted: 'My solidarity to @avucic who made the historical choice of being present in Srebrenica. Peace can be built only on reconciliation'.[13]

The governments, however, never devoted serious effort to establishing the truth about the wars of the 1990s. There are still no official numbers of victims, refugees or soldiers that are verified from all sides. Hence, the pressured imposition of the moral remembrance framework, as part of the long-term peace agreement package, produced in reality a

---

[12] 2005, 2009 and 2015.
[13] https://twitter.com/federicamog/status/619864524611522560

turbulent situation where the same government that allegedly supports and is in favour of moral remembrance actively sponsors and promotes exclusivist nationalist (and often extreme-right) agendas. This means that, in the same breath, a government will allocate resources to 'facing the past' dialogue groups to discuss the contested past of the wars of the 1990s as part of the reforms demanded regarding civil society, while simultaneously paying for the legal expenses of a crime lord, promoting him domestically as a national hero.[14] In Croatia, the government invested money to bring the Jasenovac Concentration Camp Museum up to EU standards, yet also paid state funds to send official representatives to Bleiburg commemorations to commemorate Ustaše members killed by partisans. In Serbia, in the same open call, money was allocated for the commemoration of both Chetniks and partisans. The effect of such a dichotomous attitude towards memory is best seen in spatial and temporal markers. It resulted in the erection of literally hundreds of monuments and vast numbers of commemorative events – some sponsored by the state and some by local authorities, some built as local initiatives and some constructed illegally.

The Yugoslav Legacy

Reformulating the memory of past regimes and ideologies differs significantly from altering the memory of traumatic events and wars. Wars necessarily entail ruptures in the fabric of identity on multiple levels, as they engender death and the personal experience of unimaginable horrors on the part of combatants and others. They also entail the distortion of everyday life and the disruption of social and economic relations, as well as profound political change. Yet the collapse of regimes leaves far fewer physical traces and, over time, their legacies are always contested.

There are four predominant ways in which past regimes are remembered: anti-nostalgia, amnesia, cultural revisionism and nostalgia. The first strategy in dealing with the past is renunciation – anti-nostalgia. Where this strategy has been employed, the socialist times are almost completely blacked out and condemned. The second strategy is an amnesia that imposes silence about everything preceding 1989–1991, almost as though the past never happened. The third strategy of historical revisionism amounts to a complete reinterpretation of the socialist past. The fourth strategy is nostalgia, an uncritical glorification of past times, regardless of what they were really like (Velikonja 2009). These four

---

[14] This happened equally on all three sides.

strategies are found in varying combinations across south-east European post-socialist countries.[15] A similar situation is also found in the former Yugoslav Republics. On the one hand, large sections of the society embrace a specific form of nostalgia – Yugo-nostalgia and 'Titostalgy', as omnipresent mental representations of Tito (Velikonja 2008). On the other hand, other segments of society are hugely invested in revisionism (Kuljić 2002), in which Chetnik and Ustaše traditions are glorified and celebrated.

In the aftermath of the wars of the 1990s, one of the first legacies to be destroyed was the Yugoslav project, as the new states sought to relinquish and annul connections, symbolic and real, to this part of their past. It was institutionalised as an ad hoc project in Serbia and Croatia, and in both of the BiH entities.[16] Indeed, as a symbolic break from the previous regime, an intense project of erasing connections with the Yugoslav past began in the early 1990s.

Croatia, which declared independence in 1991 and officially became internationally recognised in 1992, was the first and most eager to annul and demonise its Yugoslav past. Zlatko Hasanbegović, President of the Committee for the Naming of Neighborhoods, Streets and Squares in Zagreb's City Council and a former Croatian Minister of Culture, explained the urge to disconnect from the previous socialist regime.

It's about fundamental facts – the Socialist Federal Republic of Yugoslavia and the Croatian state are mutually exclusive, and political, social, or any other form of continuity is unnecessary, because the modern Croatian state was created in opposition to the state that existed before, in a war that was initiated by the JNA [Yugoslav Popular Army]. (The Srpska Times 2017)

Starting from the early 1990s, street names, names of squares, city names[17] and names of schools and public institutions rapidly started to change, with the sole purpose of erasing traces of the Yugoslav past for the sake of claiming national continuity. Famous partisan heroes, dates, names resembling the socialist ideology of 'brotherhood and unity' as well as topographic references to cities in other former Yugoslav republics were targeted and renamed to fit the newly tailored nationalist pantheon. Approximately 500 streets in Zagreb, the capital of Croatia,

---

[15] There is often a huge gap in the strategic choices employed by the state as opposed to the approaches embraced at the grassroots level.
[16] The same trend appeared in all former Yugoslav spaces, including Macedonia, Montenegro, Kosovo and, to much lesser extent, Slovenia.
[17] For example, Titograd, the capital of Montenegro, was renamed Podgorica, and Titovo Užice, a city in mid-Serbia, was renamed Užice. In fact, all the republics and provinces in the former Yugoslavia had a city that was dedicated to Tito – and none of those names survived.

were renamed. In Split, a coastal city in Croatia, in the first three years after independence, 150 streets were renamed. Street names such as 'Belgrade Street', 'Brotherhood and Unity Square' and 'Tito's Boulevard' disappeared overnight. In Zagreb, the famous Square of Tito was finally changed in 2017 to 'Republic of Croatia Square'. In the Federation of Bosnia and Herzegovina (FBiH), with Bosniak and Croat majorities, streets dedicated to Tito and the socialist past, as well as streets with names that had any connection to Serbia, were renamed. In Sarajevo alone, out of 1,044 streets, 403 got new names. In the Serbian entity of Republika Srpska, both 'socialist' names and those referencing the legacy of the Bosniaks' presence were changed. In Banja Luka, the capital of Republika Srpska, out of 400 street names, 240 were altered (Kerbler and Stančić 2016).

In Serbia, the same trend appeared. In 1994, the main boulevard 'Marshal Tito Street' was renamed 'Street of the Serbian Rulers'. However, the Yugoslav past stayed pronounced for longer in Serbia than in the other former Yugoslav spaces, as the official Serbian position during the wars was that Serbia is defending the unity of Yugoslavia. Hence, the renaming in Serbia has been a much slower and more selective process. For example, in Belgrade alone, approximately 700 streets still have names suggestive of some connection to Yugoslavia. The museum of Yugoslavia and the House of Flowers (Tito's mausoleum) were never officially shut down but instead were selectively used to embrace nationalist politics. For example, in 2006, the body of the deceased Serbian President Slobodan Milošević, who died in the Hague during his trial, was presented there so that people could pay their respects. Today Tito's mausoleum is a prime tourist attraction.

Apart from re-marking public spaces to fit narrow nationalist agendas, temporal markers were altered. Commemorative calendars were tailored and adjusted to the new visions of nationhood (David 2014a), excluding all previously celebrated socialist holidays and commemorative dates and effectively erasing the legitimacy of anti-fascist legacy. This change, with regard to the World War II legacy, is blatantly apparent in the changing names of the streets, squares and public institutions (Mijatović 2008), as well as in the altered stances taken by history books (Stojanović 2009) and historical studies (Kuljić 2002).

It is not only Tito's name which was found to be problematic. Since the 1990s, any connections to people or events linked to the anti-fascist fight, workers' rights and generally the entire legacy of socialist Yugoslavia have been systematically erased, either by changing the names of streets, squares and public institutions, or by destroying or neglecting monuments and cultural heritage sites. During and after the wars of the

1990s, hundreds of World War II monuments and memorial sites were destroyed and defaced. For example, in Croatia alone, 2,964 World War II monuments and memorial sites were 'demolished or desecrated and removed' after the 1990s (Banjeglav 2012: 100). Similar examples can be found across Bosnia, where partisan monuments suffered the most damage (Karačić 2012: 29). The scale of destruction largely depended on the political and war-time environment in the 1990s, as well as on the makeup of the population in certain regions or cities (Horvatinčić 2017). Perhaps the best evidence of the attempts to erase the partisan anti-fascist struggle is the Makljen monument in Bosnia. In 2000, five years after the war in Bosnia was finished, the monument was mined and blown up. There has been no such systematic destruction in Serbia, but monuments there are in poor condition, neglected and left to be forgotten.

However, different polls show that the attitude of the people towards the Yugoslav legacy, as opposed to their political leadership, has stayed ambiguous. In a Gallup Poll conducted in 2017, 81 per cent of responding Serbs indicated that the breakup of Yugoslavia harmed their country, while 77 per cent of Bosniaks and 65 per cent of Macedonians agreed. Only 4 per cent of Serbs thought that the break-up of Yugoslavia was beneficial for their country, while just 6 per cent of Bosniaks and 15 per cent of Montenegrins felt positive about the split. Even in Croatia, which gained independence after the split, 23 per cent of respondents saw the break-up as harmful (Knežević 2016).

A study by IPSOS, a strategic marketing firm, showed that only 18.3 per cent of Croats regretted the dismemberment of Yugoslavia (IPSOS 2011: 63). In Bosnia and Herzegovina (22), 45 per cent of Croats, 70 per cent of Bosniaks and 75 per cent of Serbs regretted the break-up of Yugoslavia. In Serbia, this per centage rose to 70.9 per cent (81).

Another poll, conducted by the portal MojeVrijeme.hr (2015), asked, 'Was it better before the wars?' The results of this survey, which included 2,200 individuals in Bosnia and Croatia, further showed the troubled relationship people have with the Yugoslav legacy as well as the deep imprint it has on them. When asked about job security, 88 per cent of respondents in Croatia and 86 per cent in Bosnia replied that the situation was better during the Yugoslav period. Similar trends in favour of Yugoslavia were seen with regard to the Yugoslav health system – 78 per cent of those surveyed in Croatia and 83 per cent in Bosnia thought it was better before than it is now – and education – 61 per cent in Croatia and 75 per cent in Bosnia thought it was better before than it is now. On the issue of equality, 48 per cent of respondents in Croatia and 71 per cent in Bosnia preferred the previous system to the current one. Surprisingly, the poll showed that 39 per cent of those surveyed in Croatia and 75 per cent in Bosnia thought that human rights were better under Tito's regime.

Those trends are often regarded as Yugo-nostalgia, referring to a nostalgic emotional attachment to both subjective and objectively desirable aspects of Yugoslavia. These considerations include economic security, a sense of solidarity, socialist ideology, multiculturalism, internationalism and the policy of non-alignment, history, customs and traditions, and a more rewarding way of life (Luthar and Puznik 2010). This is not surprising, because the break-up of Yugoslavia led to the collapse of the social-care system, turning good medical treatment into a privilege for the wealthy delivered in private clinics. The state-run universities have introduced enrolment fees, which is why many remember the Tito era with fondness. Culture and art, once shared across all Yugoslav spaces, had to adjust to serve the nationalist environments after the wars in the 1990s, shrinking both their geographic and content impact. Hence, these grievances relating to Yugoslavia point to a generational gap: those who lived through Yugoslav times are still attached and deeply influenced by their own experience of growing up in Yugoslavia, while those who were born after its dismemberment, without any first-hand experience, see in it the reason for the wars and show no interest in embracing Yugoslav legacies.

The Socialist Legacy

When dealing with its socialist and Communist past, the officially framed tenor is anti-communism, mostly serving not as an order for remembering, but rather as one for forgetting, with the role of the Communist struggle in World War II being purposely downplayed (Kuljić 2005). Yet, other historical layers are being revitalised. After 2000, both the Serbian and Croatian governments officially revitalised the pro-fascist Ustaše and Chetnik legacies, which further echoed among the ethnically divided Bosnian entities. In Croatia, the erasure of the previous regime opened a space for a discussion that continues to this very day: which crimes are larger and more serious – those committed by Communists or those committed by fascists? In Serbia, in a similar way to Croatia, the major current public debates are focused on a reassessment of the role of Serbia in World War II, which serves to legitimate the Serbian monarchy and the Chetnik movement. There is a strong tendency to equate the partisans and the Chetnik movement, as has been in both professional historiography and history textbooks (Cvijić 2008).

The most striking examples of such revisionism, where ultranationalist movements were revived and officially supported, are found in Bleiburg, where partisans ended the political leadership of the Croatian Ustaše regime during World War II, and in Ravna Gora, where a Serbian general, Draža Mihailović, formed the Chetnik resistance movement. Since 2004, not only have Croatian official representatives participated in Bleiburg commemorations, but the state also funds both the commemorations and the memorial site. In Serbia, in 2015, Mihailović, a leader of the Chetnik movement, was officially rehabilitated. Hence, the replacement of the deconstructed Yugoslav identity with new nationalist identities was promoted by the restoration of the legacies of right-wing nationalist movements, first and foremost the Chetnik and Ustaše movements.

However, these revisionist tendencies have been followed by the adoption of the EU memorialisation agenda – primarily the largely artificial promotion of the Holocaust memory. The sudden burst of Holocaust memory enforcement in the Western Balkans should make us apprehensive since the Holocaust per se had almost been unrecognised in the former Yugoslavia. In socialist Yugoslavia, as in other Communist countries, the suffering of Jews was interpreted as a generic manifestation of the broader terror regime instituted by the Nazis against the civilian population. Nazi anti-Semitism was treated as an expression of racism directed not just at the Jews but also at the Roma and the Slavs. As a result, Jewish victims of the Holocaust were, for the most part, subsumed under the category of 'victims of fascism', which avoided the specificity of who killed whom; they were remembered only in the context of the broader memorialisation of the People's Liberation War and anti-fascist resistance (Bajford 2009).

However, as part of the Dayton Agreement that introduced the Europeanisation process, and consequently the human rights memorialisation agenda, Holocaust memorialisation practices were gradually adopted as yet another policy to be followed. According to a 2015 report on Holocaust memorialisation across the OSCE region, developed by the OSCE Office for Democratic Institutions and Human Rights (OSCE 2015a), Croatia is involved in Holocaust-related activities on multiple levels. The country observes 27 January as a Day of Remembrance of the Holocaust and the Prevention of Crimes against Humanity; this day marks the anniversary of the liberation of Auschwitz and commemorates the victims of the Holocaust and genocides of World War II.[18] Additionally, in Croatia, the Roma and Sinti genocide is officially commemorated on 2 August, the International Day of Remembrance of the Roma Victims of

---

[18] The date was established by a decision of the Ministry of Education, Science and Sports of the Republic of Croatia, adopted on 30 October 2003.

the Holocaust (OSCE 2015b). In April, commemorations are held at the Jasenovac Memorial site to mark the anniversary of the breakout by prisoners of the Jasenovac camp in 1945. Finally, 22 June is a national holiday in Croatia and marks Anti-Fascist Struggle Day, celebrating the beginning of the country's uprising against the fascist occupying forces during World War II. Those four commemorative dates are followed by numerous educational activities, regional and national seminars, and thematic museum exhibitions. In 2005, Croatia became a permanent member of the International Holocaust Remembrance Alliance (IHRA),[19] which further obliged it to enforce Holocaust memorialisation and education at all levels.

In Serbia, the revival of the memory of the Holocaust has followed a similar pattern. Serbia has observed Holocaust Memorial Day on 27 January since 2007. Additionally, on 17 August, Serbia commemorates the residents of Belgrade who were killed on that day in 1941. On 5 October, an official event takes place to commemorate the suffering of the Serbs, Jews and anti-fascists at the Jajinci execution site. Moreover, Serbia marks World War II Victims Remembrance Day on 21 October and the International Day against Fascism and Anti-Semitism on 9 November; the latter commemorates the anti-Semitic pogrom that took place in Nazi Germany on that day in 1938. However, the most important day is 22 April, the Day of Remembrance for all of the victims of the Holocaust, genocide and other victims of fascism in World War II; it, has been annually commemorated at the Jasenovac memorial site in Croatia since 2014. Since Serbia's acceptance into the IHRA in 2011, just as in the case of Croatia, various Holocaust-related activities, such as educational seminars and museum exhibitions, have been actively promoted through numerous school textbook lessons across multiple disciplines (David 2013).

Even in BiH, which is far behind in Holocaust memorialisation and education, there have recently been significant efforts to promote Holocaust remembrance.[20] In 2013, a large-scale project was launched to promote Holocaust education within 'the educational system of Bosnia and Herzegovina', as well as 'the maintenance of active public remembrance of the Jewish Holocaust victims from Bosnia and Herzegovina'.[21]

---

[19] Previously known as the Task Force for International Cooperation on Holocaust Education, Remembrance and Research (ITF).
[20] For example, in October 2006, the Goethe Institute and the Jewish Community of Bosnia and Herzegovina organized an international conference entitled 'The State of Holocaust Studies in South Eastern Europe: Problems, Obstacles and Perspectives'.
[21] Project: 'After the Traces of our Neighbors: Jews in Bosnia and Herzegovina and the Holocaust': www.jewsinbosnia.eu/.

Also, the Council of Ministers of Bosnia and Herzegovina marks 27 January as the International Day of Commemoration in Memory of the Victims of the Holocaust 'by addressing the public through a press release as part of its program of marking important human rights dates' (OSCE 2015a). However, according to the OSCE report, due to the absence of state-level legislation on official holidays, Bosnia and Herzegovina has not been able to establish an official Holocaust Memorial Day. Moreover, even though BiH had committed itself to incorporating Holocaust education into its school curriculum by 2005 at the 2000 Stockholm Conference, and is a participant state in the IHRA,[22] 'the country is still in the process of building a viable education system and Holocaust education is not its current priority' (OSCE 2014).

There are two reasons why Holocaust remembrance matters here. First, for the countries still waiting to enter the EU, such as Serbia and BiH, the promotion of Holocaust remembrance is a valuable public signifier of their moral boundaries. Embracing Holocaust remembrance is yet another policy that must be followed at least officially and, therefore, also a requirement for joining the European free market (Russou 2007). It is understood as a necessary step that improves the chances of the candidate states being accepted into the EU (David 2013). Second, the Holocaust has become, as Assmann (2007) suggested, the paradigm or template through which other genocides and historical traumas are often perceived or presented and the very foundation of globally promoted moral remembrance. The Western Balkans states all understand that complying with the imagined moral community of human rights is a necessary step to getting accepted into the EU (David 2013). Thus, the Holocaust has not replaced other traumatic memories around the globe, but has provided instead a language for their articulation, or a wider context that enables the reframing of selective fragments of the past (Byford 2007). In other words, it has suited all groups to use Holocaust-enabled language, through which their own victimisation can be framed and promoted, while sketching national boundaries of inclusion and exclusion. Just as with the revisionist agendas, the intensified memorialisation of the Holocaust has proved to be just another version of a nationalist outlook. All the current politics of memory in the former Yugoslav states are placed in the service of national interests.

It is not new for ethno-political groups to be deeply committed to embracing their victimhood. The role of victim turns out to be a comfortable one: if I am a victim, then I cannot be responsible for anything,

---

[22] 'Participant state' is a first step, before being an observer state, on the way to becoming a member state.

and no one can argue with me because that would be showing a lack of respect for a victim. It is actually a powerful position when one can play the role of an under-privileged and victimised nation that cannot be held responsible for the wars waged in the 1990s (Schauble 2011). However, what further legitimised the battles over victimhood is precisely the adoption of the human rights memorialisation agenda that glorified and enthroned the 'justice for victims' approach. In practice, this meant that the struggle, in both political and legal terms, changed from proving innocence to proving victimhood.

Conclusion

We have seen so far how moral remembrance has been heavily filtered through the state apparatus. In both Israel and Palestine, and in the Western Balkans, the human rights memorialisation agenda was introduced as part of the grab by promoters of human rights for control of the democratisation and peacebuilding processes. However, as we will see in the chapters to come, moral remembrance brought very little (if any) appreciation of human rights values – quite the opposite, in fact. The human rights memorialisation agenda was almost always hijacked by nationalist projects. This occurred for three different reasons. First, the human rights memorialisation agenda was developed on false assumptions, and this erroneous logic was replicated every time it was translated into a different geo-political context. Second, a narrow ethnically based key for forging solidarities was built into the peace agreements that were supposed to widen human rights and narrow nationalism. Third, moral remembrance, though institutionalised and capable of the coercive implementation of its organisational and ideological agenda, is not capable of competing on the ground with the infrastructures of nationalism. In the next chapter, I discuss what happens once moral remembrance, as a reconciliatory agenda, finally gets to the 'ordinary' people, explaining why, in any of those contexts, it never actually succeeds in producing human rights values.

6 Human Rights, Memory and Micro-Solidarity

Introduction

Up to now, I have focused on the macro level of world polity, and the mezzo levels of nation-states, to show the gradual penetration of moral remembrance. Moral remembrance refers to the accumulative process through which human rights memorialisation norms and practices have developed to form a toolkit for the 'proper' remembrance of past human rights abuses. Through its growing institutionalisation and organisational power, moral remembrance became potent with ideological might to enforce a global, human rights–sponsored memory regime. The question I address here is, what happens once moral remembrance hits the ground? How do people in conflict and post-conflict settings understand and perceive this widening of the scope of attachment – from one narrowly based on ethnicity to a not even pan-religious, but universal, global one, based simply on humanity? Of course, generalisations here are extremely dangerous: some people react one way and others in another. My sociological–historical inquiry is meant to show that certain patterns exist, and that the ways in which people understand and internalise the human rights memorialisation agenda are far from just being related solely to their education, age, gender, or religious or ethnic background. Phrases such as 'Jews are/should be more sympathetic to the suffering of others because of their own history' are simply baseless; they do not hold water. So, the main question remains: what happens when people – often those who were subject to great suffering and loss – are exposed to the human rights memorialisation agenda? Furthermore, once they are put in semi-staged or semi-structured environments, such as face-to-face groups of 'facing the past' projects, where they go through an intensive and, to some degree, controlled meaning-making process of their past sufferings, will they internalise human rights values in the long run? Here I will zoom in further to explore the connection between human rights, memory and solidarity in small groups.

It seems quite astonishing how little we know about human rights and the creation of solidarity – in particular, micro-solidarity, understood here as feelings of attachment in small group of face-to-face encounters. This stands in complete contrast to the taken-for-granted and, discursively, deeply embedded linkage between human rights and solidarity. The first thing that comes to mind when talking about human rights *is* solidarity. The United Nations even has an appointed expert on human rights and international solidarity whose mandate is just that – to promote human rights and international solidarity.[1] According to the UN calendar, 20 December is celebrated as the International Day of Human Solidarity. Several non-governmental organisations (NGOs) are called Human Rights Solidarity or a version thereof. The European Students Union has its own 'Human Rights and Solidarity Strategy' charter. The call for 'solidarity' is one of the most hackneyed, yet most central aspects of human rights. This appeal for solidarity was, and still is, the main recruiting machine for public support of any kind. Even within the human rights discourse, where some have criticised the overwhelming focus on individual rights within the first and second generations of human rights, from the 1980s onwards the focus shifted to 'solidarity rights' as a way to overcome the 'solitary autonomy of competing individuals and to achieve social solidarity' (Vasak, cited in Wellman 2000: 642). Karel Vasak, first Secretary-General of the International Institute of Human Rights in Strasbourg, France, argued that solidarity is a necessity and that it is required to achieve a coordinated response on a worldwide scale to the threats to human rights that arise from the global interdependence of all peoples and nations (Wellman 2000). The Polish leader Lech Walesa was awarded the Nobel Peace Prize in 1983 for his appeal for solidarity within the trade union movement in 1980 in opposition to the Polish government. His actions were instrumental in the collapse of totalitarian regimes in Central and Eastern Europe.

Whereas the literature on the dissemination of human rights is well established and evidence has been collected on various international solidarity human rights movements, research on human rights and micro-solidarity is truly scarce. Cases in which solidarity surpassed ethnic, religious, racial, gender or any other categorical divisions have been seen throughout history, whether we talk of male solidarity in the United States, which trumped racial solidarity when black men were given the right to vote (1870); the famous Polish Solidarity movement from the 1980s; the 'Save Darfur' campaign after the year 2000; or today's International Solidarity Movement for Palestine, to mention just

---

[1] For more information, see: The Independent Expert on Human Rights and International Solidarity, United Nations, Human Rights Office of the High Commissioner, www.ohchr.org/EN/Issues/Solidarity/Pages/IESolidarityIndex.aspx.

a few. Even the ghetto riots all over the United States in the 1960s or in Los Angeles in 1992, though not considered to be true movements, arose from a widespread sense of injustice and solidarity. It is the recognition of common interests by participants that translates the potential for a movement into action (Tarrow 1994: 11). Those examples, however, point to an anomaly – a short-term solidarity – rather than the rule. They cover an enormous number of movements that stay 'undiscovered' or 'not managed properly', as described in Clifford Bob's (2005) wonderful book on the need for proper framing and marketing of social movements to deliver on their success. Transnational–national–local linkages are mediated by power and resource disparities between movements and international NGOs (INGOs), and by the geo-political and national political contexts in which social movements operate (Flesher 2014). Many ideological movements, whether we speak of nationalist, pan-religious movements or large-scale ideological movements such as socialist, Communist or even fascist or Nazi movements, can also be partly understood as 'solidarity' movements.

Solidarity has made its way into the EU Constitution, and has been promoted by such rival movements as Marxism, social democracy, French solidarism, liberalism, Roman Catholicism and neo-fascism (Laitinen and Pessi 2014). This is because every ideology, apart from its organisational power, produces an ideological glue that binds together distant peoples with a particular worldview, under a pretence of solidarity. To understand the development of horizontal sentiments of attachment across the globe, we need to delve into the relationship between the micro and macro levels of social solidarity. It would be a mistake to think that the difference between them is just the scale of the phenomenon. In fact, the ways in which solidarity in small groups can be transformed into macro-solidarity is very much ambiguous and needs, first and foremost, a deeper understanding of how, if and when an ideology (in this case, that of human rights) is capable of producing sentiments of solidarity in face-to-face encounters.

We have relatively well-developed literature on micro-solidarity and violence, and their often-ambiguous relationship with nationalism, fascism and Nazism. Starting with Marshall's (1947) pioneering empirical studies on the behaviour of American soldiers in World War II, research by Shils and Janowitz (1948) on the significance of small-group cohesion in the Wehrmacht's early military successes, and decades of research on group cohesion (Collins 2008; White 2000) that show strong emotional ties and feelings of attachment are generated through friendship or immediate face-to-face encounters, micro-solidarity has been a key notion in explaining the recruitment of people into a social action.

Micro-solidarity in relation to violence (in events such as wars, ethnic conflicts, revolutions, protests, street violence and terrorist attacks) has been scrutinised to show how intimacy and feelings can push people into violent actions (Bartov 1991; Collins 2008; Laitin 2007; Malešević 2010, 2017; Malešević and Dochartaigh 2018; Mann 2004a, 2004b; Neitzel and Welzer 2012; Roy 2003; Weenink 2014). The similar blending of organisational requirements and microsocial attachments is just as present in other organisations specialised in the use of violence: from terrorist cells to genocidal units, revolutionary cliques and insurgency outfits. In all of these cases, the cumulative bureaucratisation of coercion and centrifugal ideologisation foster strong linkages with pockets of genuine micro-solidarity (Malešević 2017: 300).

The relationship between micro-solidarity and ideology, however, remains ambiguous. Researchers such as Bartov (1991) and Mann (2012, 2013) found ideology to be the most important recruiting factor in soldiers' decisions to keep fighting. Others, such as Malešević (2013a, 2013b), Brubaker and Laitin (1998), and Neitzel and Welzer (2012), showed the limited power of ideology in serving as an engine for violence, focusing on how organisational discipline, self-control, regulations and coercively imposed rules mould social action within military units (Malešević and Dochartaigh 2018). The explanations include both the strong emotions developed through face-to-face situations, where the sacrifice of the group members enables group bonding and emotional protection, and the bureaucratic and structural infrastructures in place. This ambiguity in relation to ideology is not only due to the fact that ideologies mix and merge partially conflicting and incoherent messages (Billig et al. 1988), but also reflects the reality that the ideological reception at the bottom-up level is always subject to particular symbols and perceptions of the generated past. Although internal legitimacy and a sense of solidarity are necessary for all social organisations and informal groupings, these qualities are often achieved differently by polities and groups (Malešević 2017: 17). Nation-states have a variety of mechanisms through which micro-solidarity is harvested: state-sponsored memorialisation projects such as annual commemorations and military parades, history museums, national calendars, educational curricula, monuments, military and honouree cemeteries, decorations, prizes, rewards and a wide variety of national symbols. All of those are used as a vehicle for ideologisation to bring distant peoples together, under a particular national meta-narrative, into one relatively homogeneous union. Nevertheless, to achieve an ideological unity, most forms of genuine, durable solidarity require a substantial degree of micro-level contact and face-to-face interaction (Malešević 2013a, 2013b).

If the state provides (relatively) successful infrastructures for the transformation of micro-level solidarities into macro-level nationalist narratives, then the question becomes: to develop and sustain horizontal transnational solidarity, which requires permanent affirmation and reinforcement among millions across the globe, are human rights capable of harvesting and sustaining micro-solidarity in the long run? Do human rights have the ability to harvest strong emotions and senses of loyalty in micro-solidarity pockets so as to promote and enforce their normative set of values? I ask here whether the human rights memorialisation agenda can reproduce and sustain human rights values by fostering genuine solidarity within small face-to-face encounters. In other words, to understand the ability of human rights to recruit distant peoples into a collective action, we need to treat it as an ideology to evaluate the creation of feelings of solidarity in small societal pockets.

Micro-Solidarity

To comprehend the relationship between human rights ideology and micro-solidarity, we need to take a step back. What, in fact, is solidarity? The word 'solidarity' derives from the Roman Law, where *obligatio in solidum* involved the group liability of joint debtors. The French word *'solidarité'* appears in a 1765 encyclopaedia, as well as in Napoleon's Civil Code of 1804. The word 'solidarity', which entered the English language in the middle of the nineteenth century, is derived from the French *solidarité*. It means a 'relation among persons who recognise a community of interests, and which leads to the moral obligation not to harm one another and to come to one another's assistance'. Cognate terms are 'association', 'mutual aid', 'reciprocity', and even 'companionship' and 'fellowship' (Laitinen and Pessi 2014). Solidarity has been often conceived either as a macro-level phenomenon of group cohesion or order, or as a micro-level set of behaviours, emotions and attitudes explaining such cohesion. As a micro-level phenomenon, solidarity has been conceptualised as prosocial behaviour across different situations – for example, helping and supporting in situations of need, doing one's share in situations of cooperation, ensuring fairness where the distribution of goods is concerned, avoiding a breach in situations of trust, and providing for moral repair when violations have taken place.

In sociology and social psychology, the term was introduced by August Comte, and further explored in Émile Durkheim's classic treatment of the distinction between the 'mechanic' solidarity of traditional communities and the 'organic' solidarity of modern societies. Durkheim (1997 [1893]) made a clear distinction between 'mechanical' solidarity, which was genuine for traditional, identity-bound societies that shared the same set of values and morality, and 'organic' senses of solidarity, which came about in industrialised, modern societies, highlighting the interdependence of individuals in the economic process as the source of this solidarity. In keeping with the age-old Durkheimian (1997 [1893]) query 'how do societies cohere?', we can ask 'how do compatriots bond with one another?' Durkheim points out two contrary forces – one centripetal, the other centrifugal – which cannot flourish at the same time. He argues that, if our ideal is to present a singular and personal appearance, we do not want to resemble everybody else. This is because at the moment when this solidarity exercises its force, our personality vanishes, as our definition permits us to say; that is, we are no longer ourselves, but the collective. For Durkheim, when solidarity comes from a similarity with other community members, it is always at the expense of a lively desire to think and act for ourselves.

Max Weber (Weber, Henderson and Parsons 1947) developed a different approach to solidarity. In his 'Theory of Social and Economic Organization',[2] he described 'Types of Solidary Social Relationships', which he divided into 'communal' and 'associative'. Contrary to Durkheim, who was certain that every solidarity is produced by forces outside the individual, for Weber, solidarity existed only when the individual believed in it.

Erving Goffman, who contributed greatly to our understanding of solidarity at micro-levels through his dramaturgic approach to the presentation of the self, expounded the Durkheimian approach. He stressed the importance of social structure, arguing that subjective consciousness is secondary and derivative. His central focus is grounded in his treatment of the interaction order as a distinct unit of analysis, where interaction occurs in contexts in which two or more individuals 'are physically in one another's response presence' (Goffman 1983: 2). In a way, his contribution partly represented his attempt to confront radical empiricists – first and foremost, Harold Garfinkel, who believed that ethnomethodology, based on principles of phenomenology, should replace symbolic interactionist theories (such as Goffman's). Garfinkel argued that symbolic interactionists were 'fooling themselves in thinking they are getting to the bedrock in social life in their situation and their role-making' (Collins 1994: 274).

Other theoretical approaches were developed as well. The positions of rational choice theorists, such as Hechter and Laitin, were grounded in

---

[2] Originally published in German in 1920 and in English in 1947.

rational-actor methodology and microeconomics. They utilised models developed by economists and game theorists, arguing that solidarity is a feature of the instrumental rationality of individuals who manage self-interest to maximise benefits for the entire group.

In contrast to explanations centred on rational choice and evolutionary biology, neo-Durkheimian theorists downplay individual rationality and emphasise collective affectivity as being decisive in explaining the relationships amongst war, nationalism and social cohesion (Malešević 2011a). Evolutionary psychologists, for their part, stress the capacity for solidarity as a fixed genetic inheritance produced by processes of natural selection by which hominoids who learned to cooperate were more likely to pass their genes then those who didn't (Hamilton 1964). Alen Fiske (1991), a social anthropologist who studied the nature of human relationships and cross-cultural variations between them, in his book *Structures of Social Life: The Four Elementary Forms of Social Relations* argues that humans define their social relationships based on four distinctive models: communal sharing, authority ranking, equality matching and market pricing. The essence of 'communal sharing', closely connected to solidarity, is understood as a relationship based on duties and sentiments generating kindness and generosity among people conceived to be the same kind (Fiske 1991).

Social psychologists, such as Ross and Nisbett (1991) and Van Lange (2000), have shown that it is not merely behaviour that varies situationally for the same person; rather, the core motivations to act vary situationally within the same individual. In many ways, these cognitive processes are linked to motivation by the fact that they are largely governed by overriding goals. Following the theory of goal framing and mental models of relationships, Lindenberg (1997, 2001) claimed that, in addition to the general formation of character or behavioural dispositions, situational cues are the key to understanding the difference between a behaviour affected by the salience of the solidarity frame as opposed to a behaviour motivated by either immediate gratification or long-term gain. Solidarity is thus precarious and needs to be supported by factors that increase the salience of the solidarity frame.

This last point is the focus of my inquiry. Whereas the vast majority of scholars ask, 'What is solidarity?', 'What is the scope of solidarity?' and 'Where does solidarity come from?' (Smith and Sorrell 2014: 227), I widen the scope of this investigation to consider the question 'When can solidarity enforce certain values (in this case, that of human rights) in the long run?' This is important in particular because solidarity is often understood as the bright side of human nature, referring to common sharing, friendship and care for others. However, research (as previously mentioned) tells us that those positive feelings are often translated into destructive and violent actions. In other words, the feeling of solidarity is used to promote certain group agendas, often at the expense of other groups. Morality and solidarity are symbiotically connected (Alexander 2014), but this does not necessarily apply to the morality of human rights. For human rights ideology, to accept the equal moral standing of all individuals is thus fundamental, albeit implicit, when discussing solidarity.

My understanding of micro-solidarity draws on extensions of Durkheim's work and the theories proposed by scholars such as Mauss, Goffman and, in particular, Randall Collins. Collins builds on Durkheim's explanation of what creates social membership, on Goffman's interaction ritual analysis, as well as on the social exchange theory put forward by Mauss, in an attempt to determine the situations in which people display solidarity with others. In his *interaction ritual chain* theory, Collins parts from Goffman's interaction ritual analysis, which assumes that sacred objects are already structured, arguing that 'intense ritual experience creates new symbolic objects and generates energies that fuel major social change' (Collins 2004: 42–43). Collins points out that emotional attachments play an indispensable role in human actions. He developed a theory of situations, arguing that interconnections among local situations and their embeddedness within larger structures across time and space, along with the extent of their spill-over, constitutes a micro-pattern (Collins 2004: 5). Individuals are much more motivated when their concerns are personal and involve people whom they know and care about. Interaction rituals generate a variable level of emotional energy in each individual over time. Emotional energy operates as the common denominator in terms of which choices are made amongst alternative courses of action. Individuals apportion how they invest in work and in ritual participation with a view towards maximising their overall flow of emotional energy (Collins 2004).

Collins argued that emotional energy is the main motivating force in social life, saying that the emotional, symbolic and value-oriented behaviour of any group participants is determined by chains of previous encounters, which he called *interaction rituals*. Human interaction shows a tendency for persons who establish a common focus of attention to become mutually entrained in a common rhythm of speech and bodily movements, and to intensify a shared emotional mood – that is, an interaction ritual. According to Collins, because interaction rituals vary in the amount of solidarity they provide, and in the cost of participating, there is a market for ritual participation that shapes the distribution of individual behaviour. The economy of participating in interaction rituals shapes individual motivation for participating in the economy of material goods and services (Collins 1993). Collins rightly pointed out that local encounters – micro-situations – have both agency and structure. Agency is understood as the energy appearing in human bodies and emotions, and as the intensity and focus of human consciousness that arises in interactions in local, face-to-face situations or that precipitates a chain of situations (Collins 2004: 6). Structure points to the existing infrastructures – in other words, what is in place to sustain this micro-solidarity.

To summarise, central to Collins's interaction ritual theory is the notion that a high degree of emotional entrainment results in feelings of membership that are attached to cognitive symbols, which further results in a desire for action that is considered a morally proper path (Collins 2004: 42). Simply put, a more shared emotional and cognitive action is likely to forge stronger and more durable bonds of micro-solidarity (Malešević 2017: 289).

Face-to-Face Encounters in Israel and Palestine and in the Western Balkans

At the centre of my explanation is not the individual but the situation – the context, both performative and situational, which predefines the outcome of the social solidarity being produced. To evaluate the impact moral remembrance has in face-to-face encounters in Israel and Palestine and in Serbia, Croatia and Bosnia-Herzegovina (BiH), I need to define (1) where to look and (2) what to look for.

First, human rights–sponsored memorialisation practices are voluminous and span a wide range of areas – they often include legal, political, societal, cultural and other means. Moreover, in both Israel and Palestine and in Serbia, Croatia and BiH, human rights memorialisation practices have been promoted and implemented for more than twenty-five years. Thus, the scope of my research is limited to selected projects that are (1) structured as face-to-face encounters and last a prolonged period of time and (2) grounded in the 'facing the past' and/or 'victim-centred' agenda. This means that other practices included in the moral remembrance repertoire, such as documentation projects, witness archives, oral histories, criminal prosecutions, reparations, virtual remembrance and many other human rights memorialisation projects, are not included here simply because they lack prolonged small-group encounters, the key to understanding the creation of feelings of solidarity in small-scale groups.

Second, within those small societal pockets, and relying on Collins's interaction ritual chain theory, to understand the development of micro-solidarity and its potential to grow into value-driven action, I elaborate on (1) the emotional energy produced in those face-to-face encounters,

(2) the rituals created in the group that enable emotional energy of high intensity and (3) the feelings of morality that serve to recruit group members into action. Let me start with what is included here and why.

In both the Israeli–Palestinian context and the Western Balkans context, I include two types of face-to-face human rights memorialisation projects that, loosely understood, promote an agenda centred on either 'facing the past' or 'justice for victims'. In Israel–Palestine, this 'facing the past' agenda is best (but not exclusively) echoed in the institutionalisation of dialogue groups. Building on co-existing projects that in the 1980s became a significant element in the Israeli education system,[3] under the agenda of peacebuilding, the Oslo Accords brought to the fore a plethora of new face-to-face projects. Those face-to-face projects infiltrated into already well-developed infrastructures of the 'co-existence sector' which diversified over the years and, during the mid-1990s, expanded dramatically. The Abraham Fund has been the largest funding organisation since the early 1990s (Abu-Nimer 2004). Though Binyamin Netanyahu's right-wing government sharply cut the budget allocated to co-existence projects in 1996, the 1993 Oslo Accords spawned a proliferation of face-to-face projects, primarily financed by EU and US agencies, that mainly focused on relations between Israelis and Palestinian subjects of the newly formed Palestinian Authority (Rabinowitz 2001: 67). Thus, one of the hallmarks of the Oslo process was the scores of peacebuilding projects initiated by local and international organisations to improve the relationship between the sides, not only at the official level of policy-makers, but also within grassroots communities (Maoz 2004: 566).

One of the most prominent institutions that adopted and developed a variety of face-to-face projects in the 1980s and early 1990s was the Van Leer Jerusalem Institute (VLJI), which operated in the co-existence field roughly between 1982 and 1992, and whose early work later became the conceptual backbone for the Ministry of Education's Unit for Democracy and Co-existence. Another was the Neveh Shalom/Wahat el Salam School for Peace (NSSP), which conducted dialogue workshops for Israeli Jews, Israeli Palestinians and Palestinians from the West Bank and the Gaza Strip – workshops in which issues and experiences relating to the conflict, power asymmetries, discrimination and oppression were discussed and studied. In the 1990s, those efforts were further multiplied by the work of a variety of human rights and peace-promoting

---

[3] The field was consolidated further with the establishment in 1986 of the 'Unit for Democracy and Co-existence' – a section of the Ministry of Education officially entrusted with funding and supervising research and the development and proliferation of educational packages concerned with co-existence.

institutions in both Israel and in Palestine, such as the Jewish Arab institute for Peace in Ramat Haviva, the Israel–Palestine Center for Research and Information (IPCRI), Middle East Children's Alliance (MECA), PRIME (composed of the Peace Research Institute in the Middle East and Neveh Shalom/Wahat El Salam), Bat-Shalom/ The Jerusalem Link and Palestinian women's organisations, situated in Jerusalem and in the West Bank. In addition, the Crossing Borders peacebuilding projects sought to convey a high degree of Jewish– Palestinian equality in several important dimensions (Maoz 2004).

Under the idea that any mutual understanding between sectors of Palestinian and Israeli societies – typically youths, academics or women – would be generalised to their respective societies to help each understand the other's narrative, those efforts were followed by multiple intergroup workshops initiated at various universities across Israel.[4] Dialogue encounter programs in Israel, among other activities, included simulation games explicitly designed to consider Israel's definition as a Jewish state, its character and laws, symbols and ceremonies, and the configuration of majority–minority relations. People-to-people peacebuilding activities took place in a variety of forms, especially dialogue projects between nonofficial yet influential individuals from both sides, such as academics, dominant non-governmental actors and individuals of close proximity to decision makers, but also meetings between school children, joint sports matches, and joint movie and theatre productions.[5]

The main purpose of what is called 'education for peace' was to show that the other side is just as human and that both sides seek peace and prosperity (Pundak, Ben-Nur and Finkel 2012). During such meetings, participants undergo a process in which they have to face their misconceptions to re-humanise the other side. Equipped with a variety of theoretical approaches,[6] all face-to-face encounters are meant to emphasise meeting the ultimate 'other'. Most dialogue encounters conducted were characterised by structural inequality and domination between two groups with asymmetric power relations, who are engaged in a competition over scarce resources: the Jewish majority (some 80 per cent of the

---

[4] In 1998, the Centre for Arab Jewish education established the first integrated school in Misgav. In 2004, another school was opened in a Palestinian Muslim village called Kfar Kara, and in 2007, in the city of Beer Sheva in the Negev desert. The next year, a school was opened in Jerusalem. By mixing Jewish and Palestinian students, those multicultural schools serve as an extension of the logic of dialogue groups: once different sides are in contact with each other, they will put a human face on the collective enemy.

[5] Many of these encounters are not based on the 'facing the past' agenda, such as dialogue groups and arts, sports or even IT. Those, however, are not covered by this research.

[6] The co-existence model, the joint projects model, the confrontational model and the narrative/story-telling model.

Israeli population) is in control of most material and political resources and determines the national character of the country.

With a turnover of tens of thousands of participants in workshops, meetings and other activities, these peace-promoting institutions became household names within the Israeli educational systems, attracting considerable public attention and scientific curiosity (Rabinowitz 2001: 68). A series of public opinion surveys of representative samples of the Jewish Israeli population in the years 2002, 2003 and 2005 indicate that about 16 per cent of the Jewish Israeli population (one in six) had participated in at least one program of planned encounters between Jewish and Palestinian citizens of Israel in their lifetime (Maoz 2011: 116). In fact, the smaller size of the Palestinian community compared to the Jewish Israeli community, and the fact that there are far fewer schools in the Palestinian sector, meant that at the height of the co-existence project, Palestinian schools were in high demand by their Israeli counterparts for joint encounters. Rouhana and Korper (1997) rightly pointed out that willingness to engage among the Palestinians was high – the typical situation when members of a minority group feel their perspective is under-told. Through the years, the Parents Circle–Families Forum (PCFF) alone has arranged almost 7,000 dialogue meetings, with more than 200,000 participating youth and adults.[7] The assumption was that, when personalised and personified in the interlocutor, the narrative would help listeners develop mutual empathy through which 'the otherwise silent underdog assumes a voice and becomes [a] raconteur ... expected to infuse the moment with emotional significance' (Rabinowitz 2001: 70).

Despite the volume and density of the encounters, the oxymoron of the Israeli–Palestinian 'dialogue industry' was that, on the one hand, if many Palestinians saw the Oslo Accords as having removed history from the conflict by reducing its resolution to a matter of negotiations within the status quo, many interpreted the face-to-face encounters as contributing, willingly and/or otherwise, to the removal of any politics from the conflict (Hill 2008). On the other hand, Jewish Israelis, at least in the first years after the Oslo agreement, tended to portray those dialogue groups as apolitical (Rabinowitz 2001), where the alleged main purpose was to help each understand the other's narrative.

Though dialogue groups continue to exist, and even to thrive, to this day, with the break-out of the Second Intifada and, in particular, the establishment of the Boycott, Divestment and Sanctions (BDS) movement in 2005, dialogue groups drew harshly criticism from

---

[7] The Parents Circle–Families Forum website: Dialogue Groups, http://theparentscircle .org/en/pcff-activities_eng/dialogue_meetings_eng/.

Palestinians, especially those living in the occupied territories. For many, the dialogue groups became synonymous with a 'normalisation' of the Israeli–Palestinian relationship that legitimised the asymmetric power relationship, instead of changing it. However, under the slogan 'more relevant than ever', NGOs in Israel and Palestine continued to pursue people-to-people programs, but had to face major challenges. During the Second Intifada, from September 2000 until early August 2002, at least 260 Israelis were killed, and more than 2,200 were wounded in suicide attacks (Moghadam 2003: 65). In the shadow of this uprising, Israel faced pressure for a quick fix solution to calm down the public. In March 2002, 135 Israeli civilians were killed in suicide attacks, with the most infamous being the 'Passover Massacre' at the Park Hotel in Netanya, in which 30 Israelis lost their lives. In his speech after the event, Prime Minister Ariel Sharon clearly stated that the Jewish state was at war with the Palestinians. After the Netanya attack and Prime Minister Sharon's speech, emotions were stirred up, with Israeli authorities exploiting the population's fears to suggest that Israel's very existence was at stake. Within 24 hours of the Passover massacre, Israel launched Operation Defensive Shield (Brym and Araj 2006: 1981).

Further, the perceived role of the barrier between Palestinian and Israeli settlements in reducing terrorist attacks inside Israel gained momentum, enjoying widespread approbation among Israelis (Jones 2009). In June 2002, Israel's then defence minister, Binyamin Ben-Eliezer, cut the ribbon on the first section of the West Bank separation wall near the Israeli village of Salem. This 'security fence/barrier' (as it was known on the Israeli side) and 'apartheid wall' (the term used on the Palestinian side), also known as the Separation Wall, became a physical barrier between the peoples. Thus, while people-to-people activities might stress physical interaction between people as a way to promote peace, the wall/fence and the permits regime became major obstacles for the local NGOs to overcome. Whereas groups of Israeli youth, for instance, could go to Tul Karm and meet with their Palestinian counterparts in the past, any joint activity was jeopardised under the permits regime.

There were attempts to organise meetings in neutral places, but these were quite scarce because of the wall/fence. Other attempts to get together included activities abroad, but these have their own problems, in addition to their heavy costs. For example, in January 2004, in the midst of the Second Intifada and under the slogan 'Breaking the Ice', an Israeli–Palestinian team (four Palestinians and four Israeli Jews) left the southern Chilean port city of Puerto Williams and begun a joint expedition to Antarctica. According to the Israeli daily newspaper *Haaretz* (2004), Shimon Peres as well as Yasser Arafat telephoned the expedition members to wish them a successful journey before they set off. Despite these symbolic and highly criticised actions, it has become a lot more difficult to conduct any type of joint work (Pundak, Ben-Nur and Finkel 2012).

Numerous international dialogue projects that were developed in the German–Franco post–World War II era partly replaced local dialogue efforts. European NGOs became critical actors in providing a platform for Israelis and Palestinians to meet face-to-face, often together with other participants from conflict-driven areas such as Serbs, Kosovars, Bosniaks, Croats, Turks and Kurds. Their participation has always been calculated based on the ethnic key and a meticulous quantitative balance between the participants. American NGOs also widely engaged in all sorts of face-to-face projects, although they often replaced and/or blurred ethnicity with religion, bringing Palestinian Americans together with Jewish Americans, as in the projects of the Abraham NGO.

In contrast to the Israeli–Palestinian context, where dialogue groups became well established and even institutionalised, in post-1990s war-torn Serbia, Bosnia and Croatia, the introduction of the face-to-face logic of mutual transformation by getting to know the significant 'other' reflected a reversed reality. Whereas in the Israeli–Palestinian context, co-existence is a barely tolerable fact, the experience of a benign co-living between Serbs, Croats and Bosniaks is still very alive. However, life in Yugoslavia, the mixed communities and the forced ideology of 'brotherhood and unity' were, in the post-war former Yugoslav countries, understood in various ways – largely depending on the outcomes and gains/losses of the wars of the 1990s. Until 1989, there was relatively free movement between Israel and the occupied territories and Gaza, as well as briefly after the Oslo agreement, and in Israel, in several cities, Jews and Palestinians lived side by side. But despite these interactions, they never truly mixed. In contrast, people in Serbia, Bosnia and Croatia had the experience of living together (to different extents), including sharing public spaces, health and education systems, workplaces, military service, and most importantly the same language and even intermarriages. The fact that national categories retained their salience for some people after the war should not lead us to conclude that such categories and war-time associations were dominant among a majority of people on an everyday basis (Bergholz 2013: 694). Hence, introducing dialogue groups in the Western Balkans was, in a way, oxymoronic: for the people born during or after the wars in the 1990s, the only reality they know is that of ethnic animosity; for those who lived throughout the Yugoslav period, though they shared some great memories, it ended up with bloodshed and wars. Thus, despite the common language (with different accents), the ethnic boundaries were sharp and well pronounced.

In post-Dayton Serbia, Croatia and BiH, face-to-face encounter projects became a frequent item in the repertoire of human rights peacebuilding and reconciliation NGOs. Peacebuilding and reconciliation, grounded in the principles drawn from the Franco–German reconciliation, assumed that regional cooperation and good neighbourly relations would lead to the overall success of regional reconciliation. As the Franco–German reconciliation lies at the very core of the founding myth of the EU (Guisan 2011), reconciliation is seen as a precondition for future development in the region and in different countries in the Balkans (Milošević 2017). The expectation is that efforts by ordinary citizens and those at grassroots level will follow changes at the top. Reconciliation processes are seen as something that will happen rather automatically in response to regional integration and economic cooperation, which is also reflected in the conditions that the EU has set, both formally and informally.

Consequently, the introduction of various face-to-face encounters aimed to follow the practice of human rights–oriented NGOs 'after similar initiatives in the Franco–German post-war context' (Youth Initiative for Human Rights [YIHR] 2015: 6). After the 1990s wars, the peacebuilding and reconciliation industry imported a dialogue groups model into the former Yugoslavian countries as part of this often blurred human rights/peace agenda. This particular model of face-to-face interaction was adopted as part of a moral remembrance framework, reflecting the agenda of 'a proper way of remembrance' (David 2017b). These practices were also strongly supported and sustained by EU mechanisms.[8]

Amongst the first organisations to start face-to-face initiatives were the Nansen Dialogue Network (NDN) and the Karuna Centre for Peacebuilding. The NDN started as an initiative of the former headmaster of the Nansen Academy, Inge Eidsvåg, who visited Sarajevo in 1994 during the siege. Once back in Norway, with the joint forces of the Norwegian Red Cross and Norwegian Church Aid, he initiated a project called Democracy, Human Rights and Peaceful Conflict Handling. Later, sponsored by the Ministry of Foreign Affairs of Norway, the Peace Research Institute Oslo joined in. In September 1995, the first group of students from around the former Yugoslav states participated in a seminar in Lillehammer, Norway. However, it was clear that dialogue groups structured in such a way can attract only the very privileged (those who had passports and visas and were fluent in English). Thus, in 1997, the group decided to set up a Nansen Dialogue Centre in Priština. Additional centres were opened in Podgorica, Skoplje and Belgrade, and later

---

[8] See, for example, Article 151 of the EU Treaty: https://cultureactioneurope.org/files/2015/02/CAE-ADVOCACY-GLOSSARY-13.pdf.

in Sarajevo, Mostar and Banja Luka. In 2001, offices in Osijek and Meštrović were opened and, in 2005, Bujanovac. Currently, ten Dialogue Centres are in operation, employing more than sixty people. Their main work is with politicians, journalists, teachers, parents and pupils from different ethnic groups on 'dialogue about their own conflict, exploring potential solutions and opening possibilities for institutional change, where the situation is no longer seen through ethnic or monocultural lenses, but with a view to a joint understanding that benefits all'.[9] According to their website,[10] between 1995 and 2010, the centres facilitated 150 dialogue seminars in the field; more than 1,000 dialogue workshops have been run in post-conflict areas; 25,000 people have participated in the workshops; and 1,500 people have been trained at the NDN headquarters in Lillehammer.

Karuna Centre for Peacebuilding, founded in 1994 by Dr Paula Green, is an INGO based in Amherst, Massachusetts. Working with Projekt Dijakom, it initially established the Project for Dialogue and Community-Building, offering education and training in conflict transformation, reconciliation and healing, and non-violent social change in cooperation with the Foundation for Community Encouragement, a Seattle-based NGO. Originally emphasising trauma healing for Muslim women, it slowly began to include women from Muslim Sanski Most and Serbian Prijedor. Thought modest in size, by the year 2000, the group had facilitated five inter-ethnic educators' seminars, with each dialogue seminar lasting three to five days and including about twenty participants – a mix of Serbs and Muslims from both cities, including teachers, school counsellors, principals and administrators, some new to dialogue and others returning participants (Green 2000).

One of the first local NGOs – the Centre for Nonviolent Action (CNA),[11] a regional peace organisation founded in 1997 by Nenad Vukosavljević, with offices in Sarajevo (BiH) and Belgrade (Serbia) – further developed this mission to promote 'a culture of non-violence and dialogue, trust-building between individuals and groups, as well as dealing constructively with the past, as one of the key elements of peacebuilding'.[12] By 2001, approximately 160 persons had been trained by the CNA (i.e., as participants in ten-day workshops). At least

---

[9] Nansen Dialogue Network website: http://nansen-dialogue.net/index.php/en/.
[10] Nansen Dialogue Network, 'Promoting & Facilitating Dialogue in Support of Peace Building Processes'.
[11] Centar za nenasilnu akciju: https://nenasilje.org/en/.
[12] Peace Insight. Center for Nonviolent Action: www.peaceinsight.org/conflicts/western-balkans/peacebuilding-organisations/cna/.

500 persons have attended other shorter training sessions: approximately forty of these introductory workshops have been conducted by CNA staff members (Fischer 2001: 18). Starting in 2002, the CNA increasingly began to focus on activities intended to initiate and support a self-critical process of 'dealing with the past' in Yugoslavia's successor states. For this purpose, the CNA organised public discussion forums in which war veterans from all sides spoke about their personal experiences and opinions. Fourteen such public forums were held between 2002 and 2004 in BiH and Serbia-Montenegro. Sixteen war veterans of Serbian, Bosnian and Croatian origin have gone through the process of preparing themselves for such public debates, together with the CNA (Fischer 2001). In subsequent years, the CNA brought together a number of war veterans from different ethnic backgrounds to participate in face-to-face encounters. While some went through intense training to themselves become 'peace ambassadors', the CNA's main activity remained bringing a mixed group of war veterans to the sites of suffering. It developed a model that included both face-to-face encounters of veterans from different ethnic backgrounds and intense emotional trips to various sites of remembrance. Participants visited numerous commemoration sites, including Bihać, Doboj, Busovača, Vitez, Srebrenica, Trušina, Aleksinac, Goražde, Varivode, Gospić, Hrastova Glavica, Trnopolje, Novi Grad, Lanište, Sijekovac, Velika Kladuša, Stog, Donji Vakuf, Pakrac, Lipik and Daruvar, to mention just a few.

Those first NGOs imported and further developed the face-to-face model to serve their peacebuilding agendas. It took a decade to get to the point where enough local facilitators were trained, and able to secure funds, to start multiplying those and similar methodologies of face-to-face encounters. In 2003, the Youth Initiative for Human Rights[13] was established in Belgrade, Zagreb, Sarajevo, Priština and Podgorica. The YIHR, with a mandate for dealing with the past, addressing its legacy in the present and learning its lessons to build a better future, organised over time various dialogue groups, seminars and educational trips for people of different ethnic and religious backgrounds. It worked with young people from Foča and Goražde, Milići, Srebrenica, and Bratunac, to name a few areas, and engaged in international gatherings such as the Regional Youth Conference (Belgrade, 2008), the Belgrade Youth Summit (Belgrade, 2009) and mutual tours of Serbs and Croats to the destroyed city of Vukovar (2012). More than 15,000 young people took part in various programs in Croatia, Bosnia and Herzegovina, Kosovo,

---

[13] Youth Initiative for Human Rights/Inicijativa Mladih za Ljudska Prava: www.yihr.org/.

Macedonia and Serbia with the aim of meeting peers from other former Yugoslav republics.[14]

Many other NGOs were established after the end of the wars in Bosnia and Croatia. Some eventually disappeared, but others developed into important infrastructures of human rights and the peace industry, such as Dokumenta – the Centre for Dealing with the Past; Peace Net; the Humanitarian Law Centre; the Miramide Training Centre, Peace School Mrkopalj; PeaceNexus; the Society Civil Forum; the Regional Commission (RECOM);[15] and the Regional Youth Cooperation Office (RYCO).[16] The list is almost endless. Most of the activities were financed on a project basis by institutions such as the Swedish Helsinki Committee; the British Foreign and Commonwealth Office; the Balkan Trust for Democracy; the German, Norwegian, Swedish, Swiss, American and other embassies; ERSTE Bank; USAID; the Open Society Foundation; the European Commission; and many other EU, private and corporate funds (McKone 2015).[17]

Other projects, based on the 'facing the past' and victim-centred agenda were developed as well, mixing and merging previous knowledge of dialogue groups, and embracing the combination of activities that were less structured (although often facilitated) with a more cognitive and emotional experience. Whereas the practice of going to places of suffering was much less common in Israeli–Palestinian face-to-face encounters (for various reasons), in the Western Balkans countries almost every face-to-face encounter includes these emotionally charged

---

[14] Youth Initiative for Human Rights, Regional youth exchange program in the Western Balkans countries: www.yihr.rs/en/regional-youth-exchange-program-in-the-western-balkans-countries/.

[15] RECOM stands for Regional Commission Tasked with Establishing the Facts about All Victims of War Crimes and Other Serious Human Rights Violations Committed on the Territory of the Former Yugoslavia from 1 January 1991 to 31 December 2001. RECOM began as a grassroots project in 2008 and sought to provide more victim-oriented transitional justice projects; it focused on the local needs of victims and their families as they sought to cope with past mass atrocities committed during 1991 and 2001. This regional fact-finding movement was an attempt to democratize international humanitarian law – and globalized human rights concepts more generally – in local post-conflict settings.

[16] YIHR was founded in Serbia in 2003, and subsequently opened additional offices in BiH, Croatia, Kosovo and Montenegro. Since 2003, YIHR been organizing encounter journeys for young people from Kosovo and Serbia. Since 2009, it has also gathered together adolescents from all countries of the region in the context of the Sarajevo Film Festival.

[17] According the US Institute for Peace Community, and based on the sample of 277 projects used in this research, drawn from approximately forty-six conflicts across the globe, dialogue projects were the most numerous, accounting for 26 per cent of all projects. For more, see McKone 2015: 7.

'education trips'. In the Balkans, this marriage of psychologised, structured, face-to-face encounters behind closed doors with emotional pilgrimages to the places of suffering appears in one form or another in almost every project that is dedicated to the human rights memorialisation agenda. Thus, the line between the dialogue-based projects and many other types of projects is practically non-existent. Important insights can also be obtained by analysing less structured face-to-face encounters and the impact they succeed in producing in the value system in the long run – such as Fighters for Peace, Zochrot, Israeli–Palestinian Bereaved Parents for Peace (for Israel and Palestine), various victim groups initiatives and the Regional Youth Cooperation Office (RYCO; for the Western Balkans countries), some of which will be addressed later in this chapter.[18]

Methodological Issues

Now to some methodological points. First, it is important to mention that the logic of the encounter groups developed independently of the human rights agenda and has its own roots in social psychology and peace studies. With the development of moral remembrance from the late 1980s onwards, through the organisational and ideological power of human rights, those practices became adopted as a useful tool meant to re-humanise the 'other' in post-conflict settings across the globe. Face-to-face encounters served to promote the 'dealing with the past' agenda, and they became deeply embedded into human rights institutions, discourses and practices as a guiding principle for a proper remembrance.

Regardless of their theoretical and/or methodological approach, all face-to-face groups aim to achieve two goals: an individual transformation that will further produce a spill-over effect, and a change in the wider society. Hence, I focus on encounter groups where face-to-face contact between the participants is not just a random, one-time encounter, but the encounters also include a temporal dimension which is important for micro-solidarity attachment. Also, those encounters are intense and purposely built to flood the participants with emotions, which can potentially increase the level of emotional energy between participants. Strong emotional energy, paired with feelings of attachment to group members, brings a certain moral justification to recruiting

---

[18] There are many other organizations that are important, but I will not discuss those because they either do not deal with 'facing the past' per se or do not include protracted face-to-face encounters.

people into action. Thus, it is important to stress that my focus is not on assessing the work of any particular NGO or any particular project.

What interests me is whether such emotionally intense and prolonged encounters, which are performed within and framed by the human rights memorialisation agenda, can lead to human rights in the long run. In other words, do the people who participate in intense small-group encounters that are framed and facilitated through the agenda of moral remembrance actually internalise human rights values so that they can become a part of the macro-solidarity of human rights ideology? As this is a comparative study not just of the countries in one region but of two very different geo-political contexts, and as I wish to gain from these micro encounters a wider macro perspective on the ways in which the human rights memorialisation agenda is internalised (or not) on the ground, I do not intend to focus on one particular NGO or project (though that has clear merits and advantages of its own), nor will I analyse one-time encounters (such as conferences, documentation or oral history projects, or any other activities that bring random people into sporadic encounters).[19]

I use here a wide variety of materials to bring to the fore the main rituals shaped by the emotional energy of the participants, the main symbols developed in those encounters and the potential that this emotional energy has to push people into action that translates the micro-solidarity of a small group into the macro-solidarity of human rights. The available materials are different for the Israeli–Palestinian context and for the Western Balkans context. In Israel and Palestine, the tradition of face-to-face encounters is a long-standing one, and there has been an impressive amount of research both on particular cases and on the long-term processes. Both in-depth analyses and partial transcriptions are available that give a pretty clear picture on the aspects of interest to me – in particular, in relation to the ritualisation of historical narratives and emotional energy. Some practices relevant for my research also received extensive TV coverage, such as the communal commemoration by the Israeli–Palestinian Bereaved Parents for Peace.[20] In contrast, in the context of the Western Balkans, research with concrete examples is nascent due to the Europeanisation process and the demand for transparency; there is a rich documentation (made by the NGOs that facilitate those projects or by external professionals/agencies or independent

---

[19] This is why I choose not to use ethnography or Garfinkel-like ethnomethodology; these methodologies are more suitable for singular case studies.
[20] Media coverage of the activities carried out by the Israeli–Palestinian Bereaved Parents for Peace is available at http://theparentscircle.org/en/media_eng/.

researchers) of project reports and evaluation statements and research articles that give (relatively) correct indicators of the success and failures of multi-ethnic face-to-face projects. These projects are followed by intense reporting that offers some precious insights from the participants themselves.[21] In addition, a large number of surveys are available on a variety of topics including 'dealing with the past'. Likewise, several documentary movies give some important insights on what happens to the participants during and after participating in the projects.[22]

Micro-Solidarity Rituals

The rules governing the production and interpretation of historical narratives serve as scripts that regulate and inform people's actions and identity and that are deeply connected with people's primeval need for knowing who they are and how their knowledge of the past influences their present and future lives (Manojlović 2016). The connection between memory and identity highlights two important issues. First, it emphasises the political value of collective memory because past representations are preserved through social and ideological practices. Furthermore, the connection between memory and identity is relational; that is, memory is constructed in particular social and political contexts that encourage certain visions of national identity (Bekerman and Zembylas 2012: 83–84). Hence, the ways in which historical narratives are shaped and ritualised in multi-ethnic face-to-face encounters are always a product of social practices as well as the wider geo-political context.

Rituals here are not to be understood as mere celebrations of collective representations that predate them, in the sense that Lloyd Warner and many of the mainstream anthropologists analysed them, but instead as social practices, through which such collective representations are created, renewed or replaced by alternative representations. In other words, rituals are performances that not only create ideal images of self-negotiating social ties, but also require certain material resources and cultural skills. Hence, we will see that, for example, with the face-to-face project in the Israeli–Palestinian context inside Israel (where the formal

---

[21] Though they also appear in the evaluation reports, they are often framed in such a way as to promote the goals of the NGO that sponsored the project.

[22] *Albanian–Macedonian Simulated Dialogue*, 2015; *Not a Bird to Be Heard* (Bosniak–Croat simulated dialogue), 2007; *All Wish to Cast a Stone* (Serb–Croat simulated dialogue), 2006; *It Cannot Last Forever* (Serb–Bosniak simulated dialogue), 2006; *Traces* (former combatants), 2004; *War-Veterans Visits*, 2009 – all these are produced by the Center for Nonviolent Action (CNA). *Reunion: Ten Years after the War* (Norwegian–Serbian coproduction), 2011; *Ženski sud – Feministički pristup pravdi/Women in Black* (2015).

language is Hebrew), language skills are a clear marker of power relations between the groups. These skills enlarge the space for manoeuvring and negotiating by the Jewish group whilst simultaneously shrinking the Palestinian space. In both Goffman's and Collins's sense, the performance taking place in face-to-face encounters sets up a stratification between different people. As pointed out in Collins's interaction ritual chain theory, it is really the excitement caused by this mutual presence that furnishes a potential emotional weight which, bit by bit, is reinforced as the gathered people begin to gain a mutual rhythm in a coordinated and synchronised manner, as they follow repertoires of action regulated by a whole set of explicit and implicit prescriptions. These prescriptions are crucial for setting the tone of both the action and the emotion. The excitement rises as it is expressed, and transports those who participate in the ritual to a different world, away from the daily routine, transmitting to them the sensation of being in contact with something 'sacred' that they themselves are helping to create (Sterchele 2007: 214).

But what happens in those face-to-face societal pockets when the logic of moral remembrance is being followed? Two distinctive legacies have become a motor and a logic behind the human rights memorialisation agenda, setting the stage for performative action in those face-to-face encounters. The first, which has an overreaching effect on the ground, embodies the political character of human rights. The main and unreplaceable matrix for all inter-ethnic encounters has religiously adopted and promoted the 'balance formula', wherein the encounters are seen as representing a micro cosmos of the outside conflictual reality, so that the participants need to be recruited and balanced according to ethnic/religious lines. The development of the Franco–German model was a handy solution for post–World War II German and French realities. It yielded some positive results, and was later adopted into the human rights memorialisation canon as a blueprint for ethnic (or religious) reconciliations across the globe. Second, these encounters, fuelled by the 'facing the past' agenda, rely on psychological notions of healing through transformation. The idea is that the healing comes once those ethnic identities become transformed, producing a spill-over effect that leads to the slow pacification of the entire society. The main presumption, that hearing other narratives will help reduce intergroup fear and break down stereotypes and misconceptions, is a bedrock of the human rights reconciliation agenda. Hence, face-to-face encounters are often viewed as 'the jewel of reconciliation work' (McKone 2015: 23). However, both the Israeli–Palestinian case and the former Yugoslav countries, with their striking differences, suggest significantly different outcomes from those envisioned by human rights promoters.

Here is what happens on the ground. Among the dozens of dialogue projects that promote a structured form of dealing with the past, while each has its own methodology (often very different from one another), all have in common the use of the 'balance formula'. In all face-to-face dialogue projects, in both the Israeli–Palestinian context and in the former Yugoslav context, participants are recruited based on their ethnic/religious affiliations. This is crucial if we want to understand the creation of interaction rituals. Bringing participants together in face-to-face encounters in which they already have ascribed roles has an immediate impact on the ways in which they start forming and negotiating rituals among themselves. From the very beginning, it works as a primary set of references; in turn, the interactional rituals that evolve during the process are all seen through the prism of this structured division. In practice, this means that even those participants who have an ambiguous relationship with their ethnic/religious identity prior to the meetings are likely to become *more* attached to their ethnic/religious identity.

One of the main products that results from these encounters is how historical narratives become ritualised in such a way as to form clear stratifications between the groups. From the beginning, the participants are encouraged to freely express their views on the past or the ongoing conflicts. However, under the pretence of a 'safe space', they are also guided to do it in a particular way. For example, the Nansen Dialogue Network organisation, just like other face-to-face encounter projects, emphasises this point, saying that those encounters 'provide opportunities for young people to discuss BiH's history and to tell their side of the story and listen to others in a neutral and "safe" environment, if necessary with the presence of a person skilled in post-conflict reconciliation and dialogue' (Nansen 2012: 6).[23] This is important because it is how facilitators, who are also recruited along ethnic lines,[24] dictate the dynamics of the historical narrative ritualisation. For example, in the former Yugoslav context, there is an unwritten rule between NGOs that forbids dealing explicitly with the 'crimes of others'. There seems to be a consensus that if I am an ethnic Serb, I am expected to criticize only acts

---

[23] Nansen (2012). The idea for this research came from a study carried out by Saferworld and Nansen Dialogue Center in Sarajevo in 2009–2010, which looked at communities' perceptions of conflict and security in BiH – in the Federation of BiH: Drvar, Sanski Most, Novi Travnik, Sarajevo and Mostar; in Republika Srpska: Trebinje, Srebrenica, Bratunac, Doboj and Banja Luka; age sixteen to thirty years. In parallel, Saferworld (2010) carried out interviews with selected key informants (eighty in total).

[24] For the Israeli–Palestinian encounters, the facilitators always include one Jewish facilitator and one Palestinian facilitator. For the Serb–Bosniak–Croat encounters, the same logic apples.

on the Serbian side; I should not deal with acts of Croats or Bosniaks but rather leave this to others, meaning, 'they should clean their own house' (Franović 2008). Palestinian and Israeli moderators seeking to question issues pertaining to more collective aspects of the situation – such as the war of 1948 and the disastrous demise of the Palestinian community in what became the state of Israel, the pre-1948 chapters of Palestinian history, or the desire of Palestinians to redefine their place as second-class Israelis – have been discouraged and, if necessary, ousted (Rabinowitz 2001). Other topics deemed off the table are the status of the Palestine Liberation Organization (PLO) or the 'Jewishness' of the state (Abu-Nimer 1999). This fine-tuning of the direction that the discussion takes occurs within two main frameworks: (1) the Goffmanian 'front-stage' and 'backstage' scenario, meaning a threshold regarding what can and should be said when negotiating self-interests, and (2) the degree to which the participants control or are controlled by their rituals.

Thrown into their ethnic identities, all participants are pushed into a role-playing that enables them to embrace their own ethnic narratives, moving from the 'I' to the 'we'. It is fascinating because, although many of the participants have, to some degree, blurred perceptions of their ethnic identities, those identities get more pronounced over the course of the meetings. In other words, those meetings bring together people who are assigned their ethnic or religious identities, lessening the importance of other possible identities, such as their gender, class, rural/urban location, profession or differences based on generational gaps, which become just a side effect of their ascribed ethnic identities. The transition from 'I' to 'we' is contextual and works as a marker for the ritualisation of their historical narratives. In the Israeli–Palestinian context, the shift from an individual to a collective ethnic identity is the locus of the encounter and happens almost instantly, once participants feel a threat to their assigned role as 'representor of their own group' belonging. I cite here an example of a Jewish male student, addressing a Palestinian participant, who participated in a year-long face-to-face dialogue encounter:

May *I* ask *you*[25] a question? *You* are telling *me* that *you* are discriminated against and *I* believe *you*, *I* agree with *you*. ... *They* show *me* the Palestinian Covenant and the different things [Palestinian] instigators have written and said, and *I* am sure that *you* have relatives that do not really like *us* [the Jews]. And the question *I* ask is: What would have happened to *us* [the Jews] if, in 1948, an Arab state had been

---

[25] The distinction here is between 'you' that implies singularity and 'you' that implies plurality. In both Hebrew and Arabic there are different words for singular, as opposed to plural, speech; thus, during the conversation, it is perfectly clear whether the conversation is about individuals or about the groups they represent.

established here? What would have happened if *we* were the minority and *you* the majority? ... Do *you* think that *we* could live in peace, and *I* could be a student at one of *your* universities? (Helman 2002: 331)

Or, as a Palestinian female participant put it: 'Everyone has their own problems. *You* have *yours*, *we* have *ours*' (Bekerman and Zembylas 2012: 80). Or as another Palestinian interlocutor pointed out: '...but in the end *you* are all Jews. The bottom line is that *Jews are Jews*, and *Palestinians are Palestinians*' (Bekerman 2009: 216). Ethnic identities, liberated by the discourse of culture and hybridity, return to their primordial meaning and assert again their hegemonic power (Bekerman 2009: 216).

This is precisely how the shift from ambiguous, individual self-narrating to a socially formed (and often ossified) and patterned collective identity enables the ethnically based ritualisation of the past, while dismissing variety in favour of essentialisation (Helman 2002). The participants demonstrate an inclination towards simplified and/or invalid (but often useful) inductive reasoning in the form of analogism (Rydgern 2007: 225). This on and off between using 'I' and 'we', where particular essentialised ethnic identities are, employed to justify and help negotiate one's own position in the group as a whole, as well as in one's own ethnic group, is easily traceable in the use of personal names. The use of personal names affirms the individual character of the relationship through which what one thinks of that person as an individual, with their own biography and history is communicated (Collins 2004: 84). However, both individual names and narratives of those individuals become charged with significance through the accumulation of the general capital of each ethnic group. An individual positioning in the group becomes a subject of 'the publicly available symbolic forms through which people experience meaning' (Swidler 1986: 273). In other words, it matters greatly whether the group participants chose to address each other by names or through ethnicised categories such as Jews, Palestinians, Serbs, Croats or Bosniaks. The switch from singular to plural participation of the self is not only a matter of placement within the group, but more importantly an appeal for a collective action. It is a (performative) recruitment to a display of power between 'us' and 'them'.[26] From the interaction ritual chains' point of view, the shift to 'we' is contagious. Once this becomes an available option in the repertoire of communication, it does not take long to see that participants in these structured face-to-face encounters start internalising their ascribed roles, pushing for the homogenisation of their ethnic groups. This is fascinating,

---

[26] As brilliantly illustrated in Bergholz's (2016) *Violence as a Generative Force*.

because, at the beginning, they all tend to display their differences and their individual points of view.

This is more pronounced within the Israeli–Palestinian encounters, where initial differences soon become part of a power negotiation centred on ritualising their historical narratives. On the one hand, Jewish participants channel their desire to be seen as liberal, egalitarian, progressive and humane individuals. However, this suddenly clashes with their position of control, a position that gives rise to feelings of superiority and to patronising attitudes towards the Arabs (Halabi and Sonnenschein 2004). On the other hand, Palestinian participants often feel less comfortable than their Jewish counterparts in expressing their views due to requirements or expectations to speak Hebrew during the encounter. Thus, while aspiring to full equality, the Palestinians in the encounter come face-to-face with the degree to which they have internalised their oppression, resulting in differences between them largely fading away, and their constructed and suddenly available similarities homogenising them into a seemingly unified group of suffering people.

Interestingly, the division between 'us' and 'them' in post-Yugoslav spaces has its own route. The initial point of differentiation tends to be not along ethnic lines, but along generational ones. One of dialogue participants' first concerns is the gap they feel between themselves and their parents in relation to their national past. Their understanding of the past, though ethnicised through the educational system and stories of their parents and relatives, is much messier and incoherent. They often stress that 'young people are being manipulated by adults (politicians, media, parents and teachers), and I'm concerned that another cycle of conflict might occur in the next 20 years' (Nansen 2012: 35).[27] They also struggle to develop their own worldview, independent of their parents:

> I disagree with my dad in many things when we talk about the war. He had terrible problems during the war. Now my father is poisoned by hatred, does not like anyone from other ethnic groups, and does not even want to have any contact with 'them. ... I understand why people do not enter into inter-ethnic marriages, but it is necessary to socialize and co-operate between different ethnic groups.[28]
> (Nansen 2012: 36)

Serb, Croat and Bosniak youths often seem generally uninterested in facing a past that is both distant and still very present: 'we, the youth, do not care who believes in which God, we are interested in travelling. We meet with each other regardless of what religion we practise and

---

[27] Key informant interview, Youth Initiative for Human Rights, 12 May 2011, Sarajevo.
[28] Focus-group discussions participant, female, age twenty-eight, Bosniak, unemployed, Sanski Most.

regardless of our ethnic background. We celebrate holidays together. We all face the same problems, and live with our parents because we do not have enough money to rent or buy apartments for ourselves' (Nansen 2012: 36).[29] In many ways, they feel that the past is keeping them from moving forward: 'There are cases where parents teach their children from an early stage not to socialize with members of another ethnic group ... it is easier to work with children than with their parents' (Nansen 2012: 36).[30] Or: 'there are cases where parents teach their children from an early stage not to socialize with members of other ethnicities' (Nansen 2012).[31] Or: 'we are constantly being poisoned by hate, listening to our parents' stories about the war. We are trying to overcome this situation, but we are not strong enough, because we live in a mono-ethnic environment and are influenced by our parents' (Nansen 2012).[32] 'We learn from older people, our parents ... we cannot recall the last war. We are all born into war, some of us in exile. Our parents share their experiences from the war with us, they tell us that 'the others' are not good and that we should not mix with them' (Nansen 2012).[33] 'The older generation, who went through the horrors of war and survived, are trying to instil in the younger generation a certain distance towards members of other ethnic groups. It causes a lot of problems. So, the comments from the parents are: do you really have to socialize with them (members of other ethnic groups)? Or they say: it is okay to socialize, but do not go falling in love with him/her' (Nansen 2012: 34).[34]

The generational axis brings to the fore the profound difference between these two conflicts – one that ended and the other that is still ongoing. For the generation born after 1990 in Serbia, Croatia or BiH, the wars belong to the generation of their parents, and their memories are mediated and shaped for them both by their nationalist surroundings and by the stories of their local communities. For the Jews, whereas this is the case with the Holocaust, the ongoing Israeli–Palestinian conflict has real effects on the course of their life, a fact that become more pronounced once they begin their army (IDF) service. For Palestinians, the Nakba is an ongoing reality and not just a distant past, and one that affects their

---

[29] Focus-group discussions participant, male, age thirty, Sanski Most.
[30] Focus-group discussions participant, female, age eighteen, Bosniak, high school student, Bratunac.
[31] Focus-group discussions participant, female, age eighteen, Bosniak, high school student, Bratunac.
[32] Focus-group discussions participant, female, age seventeen, Bosnian Serb, high school student, Trebinje.
[33] Focus-group discussions participant, female, age seventeen, Sanski Most.
[34] Focus-group discussions participant, female, age eighteen, Bosnian Serb, high school student, Doboj.

lives on a daily basis. Gazans have been trapped in a ghetto for decades now, Palestinians from the occupied territories are restricted and monitored in every aspect of their lives, and the Palestinians in Israel are subject to discrimination on almost every level. Hence, the ways in which their historical ethno-centric narratives become ritualised in face-to-face encounters correlate with the shift from their daily reality to this multi-cultural laboratory that aims at transforming national sentiments into universal, human rights–based values.

The triggers that ascribe power to national narratives and generate emotional energy around them, as a pattern for micro-solidarity in the Israeli–Palestinian case, take place in response to liberal Jewish showing off. Once the Palestinians ask to re-balance the power, they are usually interested in focusing on politics, resulting in a Jewish attempt at 'restoration of power' (Halabi and Sonnenschein 2004). Essentialism is at its strongest once the Jewish side becomes defensive: all culturally embedded stereotypes come out regarding each other's religious beliefs, cultural norms and societal values. Essentialising discourses of culture and identity are geared towards the naturalisation of inequality and domination, and thereby disguise the context of their production and reproduction (Scott 1995). Once this box is opened, it almost instantly polarises the groups. In the following example of a Jewish participant, we see this clearly: 'if the Arabs were to be in control, they would massacre the Jews and throw them into the sea, since Arab values and their moral level are beneath Jewish values; or in the society where women are killed for the sake of honour, what kind of values can we expect … ?' A Jewish female participant continued with this essentialisation: 'we think that Arab culture values human life less, they kill women to restore the family's honour' (Helman 2002).

This essentialisation immediately triggers the Palestinians to enter the 'forbidden ground' of comparing Israeli behaviours towards Palestinians to those of the Nazis towards the Jews. Once a comparison is made, everything that takes place afterwards is an accumulative process of emotional energy that only adds to the value of their clashing perceptions of the past. Facts are occasionally brought up to establish authority, stories of suffering are told to claim moral victory. Villains and victims appear.

Consider the words of a female Palestinian student:

I don't know what would have happened after 1948, but there were Jews in Spain under Moslem rule. That period was one of the greatest periods in Jewish history, the Golden Age. And we are Arabs, I don't want to say Moslems. They treated the Jews with respect, and even you present it as such. We are told that the Jews were rich, that they reached important positions and some of them were ministers. And after the Arabs left, and the Christians came, the Jews were expelled from Spain. I am going back in history to say that there is a chance that it might have been possible [to respect you as a minority if a Palestinian state was established instead of a Jewish one]. But I want to ask you: you were victims of the Holocaust, of the Nazis and it was hard, I know it was hard. And after all that [suffering] you came here, and established a state, and despite all your suffering, you treated the Arabs the same way... well not the same, but almost the same ... and you always get furious when people say that you treated the Arabs the same way the Nazis treated you. You went through a terrible time, you did not have a state, you did not have a home, you had nothing, and you came here and treated us the same. That is my question. (Helman 2002: 332)

In a furious response to her, a Jewish female student said: 'you really hurt me. It hurts even more that you [pointing to the Jewish male student] agreed with her and you feel ashamed. Because it is not the same as they [the Nazis] did to us' (Helman 2002: 332).

Comparison between the plight of the Palestinians and that of the Jews in the Holocaust is the biggest no-go issue in the Israeli–Palestinian conflict discourse in general, and in the laboratory of face-to-face encounters, it is an 'exploding point'. This immediately ratifies the legitimacy of both narratives and is a one-way street to further homogenisation of participants' narrow, ethnically bound identities. As detailed in Chapter 4, the retrieval of basic, nationalised patterns of collective memories reflects more than anything else the tenacity of the memory infrastructures in the societies from which they come and to which they are going back. A Jewish female participant explained: 'I identify with the weak side. With the difficulty of defending my home... when they lined them up [in Majd al Krum, to be executed] against the wall and shot them, in pain, in humiliation, it reminded me of the Holocaust' (Bekerman and Zembylas 2012: 80). Another Jewish female protested: 'it was strange to hear her saying it [bringing up the Holocaust in the 1948 context]'. The first Jewish participant self-corrected herself: 'I apologize. There is no comparison'. A Jewish male participant joins the conversation: 'I am not ready to allow any comparison between the Holocaust and the Nakba' (Bekerman and Zembylas 2012: 81). A Palestinian male participant protested: 'for us, it is a catastrophe [the Nakba]. I know that the Holocaust is a sensitive subject for Jews. But instead of enabling me to identify with that, the Jews treat it as taboo and tell me not to come near it. Suddenly, I discover there is no place for [Palestinian memories]'.

Attempts are often made to find a common ground. A Palestinian female student suggested: 'I always wanted to make a common ceremony, focusing on the pain in both people. In war, nobody wins, everybody loses. Those who lose family ... to neutralize it politically and to focus on human pain' (Bekerman and Zembylas 2012: 91). A Palestinian male participant continued: 'I have no problem with a common ceremony. I have a problem with Nakba and Memorial Day together, where the only common thing is the pain ... if I think of Memorial Day, I think of soldiers, who are also people but they went out and killed people who died in the Nakba' (Bekerman and Zembylas 2012).

As Brubaker and Cooper (2000), Malešević (2006b) and Bergholz (2016) rightly pointed out, national identities are not living things in the world but a perspective of the world. The ritualisation of historical narratives points to the co-constructed nature of categories, which are always in need of a differential to be sustained. This difference might be hidden or visible, but without it, the clarity of national/ethnic identity would not be possible. Hence, those ascribed and internalised identities are co-dependent, coupled and constrained by the available resources and the power boundaries of the stage on which they are enacted. Intergroup dialogue between Israeli Jewish and Palestinian students shows that dialogic encounters between groups in a situation of domination and structural inequality do not inevitably crack the code of essentialism. Instead, as Helman (2002: 346) rightly pointed out, they often reproduce monologic discourses of culture and identity and solidify them, further legitimising power differentials and structural inequality. This monologic discourse and essentialisation are nicely captured by a Palestinian who had been a moderator ten years earlier: 'What I wanted to achieve at the time was that Jews should understand that the national identity of an Arab does not necessarily manifest itself in threats towards Jews. It does not contradict their civil identity as an Israeli. On the contrary, it can be integrated into it. In this way I hoped to do away with the threat that Jews so often feel from Arabs' (Rabinowitz 2001).

On both sides, participants were recruited based on their national identification; thus, from the very beginning it was not 'people' who came to embrace differences among group members, but Jews and Palestinians who came to establish clear ethnic boundaries. Even when embracing an image of Palestinians 'which Israelis can identify as PLU (Person Like Us): rational and eloquent, and possessing positive characteristics' (Rabinowitz 2001: 76), and an image of Jewish Israelis as understanding and empathetic, both groups often ascribed exceptionalism to the participants in that particular face-to-face encounter. In other words, even in this categorical key of ethnicity, group members did not come to think of the opposite group much differently just because they presumably met a nice person belonging to that group. Instead of humanising group as a whole, the micro-solidarity formed in face-to-face encounters enabled further ethnicisation, making the category of ethnicity a focal point of reference.

The Western Balkans context where, in fact, nationalism became deeply institutionalised after the wars of the 1990s, offers a different picture. Just as in Israel and Palestine, the educational systems of all three countries (Croatia, Serbia and BiH) left little or no space to include different perspectives of their own historical narratives or of narratives of other ethnic groups. However, in Croatia, Serbia and BiH, at the bottom-up level, though those narratives provided general guidelines for the binary positions of victims and perpetrators, they also left much ambiguity because they only loosely corresponded to the personal stories of the participants. What all sides held in common was how little, in fact, they knew about what happened in areas other than their own. In Croatia, the majority of the population is familiar with the destruction of Vukovar and the bombardment of Dubrovnik, yet most of them have never heard of Petrinja or the killing of Croats in Erdut, Sisak or Gospić, or the killing of Serbs in Dvor, to mention just a few events. There is a similar situation in Bosnia. Whereas Srebrenica became a symbol of Bosniak suffering, both nationally and internationally, as well as the siege of Sarajevo (to a lesser extent), other massacres and killings are often mostly commemorated and narrated locally and only by the victim side. In practice, this means that the general public rarely knows (or is willing to know) about the dozens of massacres committed during the wars of the 1990s. In Serbia, the ignorance is even more extensive, because the official position was and remains that Serbia never participated in those wars. Because the wars did not take place on Serbia's territory, and despite the fact that the veteran population who participated at some point in the wars of the 1990s numbered between 400,000 and 700,000 (David 2015a), and even though there was a massive influx of refugees from Bosnia and Croatia, the general population was not immediately affected by those wars. They were, however, deeply affected by their economic situation, inflation, the media blockage and sanctions, which also allowed the regime to distract people from expressing a real interest in those wars. However, the poor distribution of information, the fact that the conflict was triangular (meaning between the Serbs and the Croats in Croatia and parts of southern parts of Bosnia, between the Serbs and Bosniaks across Bosnia, and between the Croats and the Bosniaks in the self-proclaimed Croatian Republic of Herzeg-Bosnia) and their mutual Yugoslav past made ethnic identities the most pronounced category of collective identity, but with many gaps between the officially narrated and locally narrated histories. Thus, though the general narrative of the Bosniaks sees the Serbian side as the main villain, for the Bosniaks in, for example, the Mostar area, the perpetrators were the Croats, and vice versa.

This is important for two reasons. People who participate in face-to-face encounters are in many ways just like the general population: though highly impacted by official nationalist narratives, they are very much rooted in the narratives of their local communities. Hence, once brought together to face their contested past, the dynamic of ritualising historical narratives will depend on to what extent their local narratives are clashing. Bringing together a Serb refugee from Zadar with a Bosniak from Mostar, or a Bosniak from Sarajevo with a Croat from Bihać, or a Serb from Banja Luka with a Bosniak from Foča, or a Serb from Belgrade with a Croat from Dubrovnik, may lead to significantly different positioning regarding the victim–perpetrator scenario. In face-to-face structured encounters that bring two ethnic groups together, as in the cases of Croatia (Serbs and Croats), or Serbia (Serbs and Kosovars), or Bosnia, and in a similar way to Israeli–Palestinian dialogue groups, the themes of patriotism, victimhood and ingroup reconciliation will serve to operationalise morality and the legitimacy of the past action as well as ingroup identity (Manojlović 2016).

As opposed to Israeli–Palestinian encounters, in which the route to the ritualisation of their historical narratives is almost known in advance, the Balkans case often produces more ambiguities. Whereas the Jewish participants are invested in putting on a display of their liberal views, the perceptions of normality and mutual understanding in the Balkans case appear through narratives of tolerance and hospitality. The participants often share the stories of some segment of their life in which they engage with the other side. For example, an eighteen-year-old female Bosnian Serb said: 'in my class there are two Bosniaks and everything is okay. They bring cakes [baklava] to us during Eid. Also, we bring cakes during our religious holidays' (Nansen 2012: 29).[35] Another Bosnian Serb said in a similar vein: 'I have two friends, Bosniaks, from Kotorsko [about 10 km from Doboj] and we socialize. Their parents receive me well, as well as mine them. There are a lot more prejudices among older people than [among] the youth. For us, the most important [thing] is to socialize' (Nansen 2012).[36]

For older participants, those who grew up in Yugoslavia, there is a clear distinction between the good relations that existed then (largely narrated in the same way, through the prism of clear ethnic boundaries but with good neighbouring relations) and post-war realities. An elderly Croat, participating in a dialogue group in Zadar explains:

---

[35] Focus group discussions participant, female, 18, Bosnian Serb, high school student, Doboj.
[36] Focus group discussions participant, female, 18, Bosnian Serb, high school student, Doboj.

[In] Benkovac, ... the few years while I was [there] I gained friends ... and even our village was half-national, one half Serbs, half Croats, we used to say Orthodox and Catholic, during those times we were doing OK. And even during WWII, trust me. Not a single house got destroyed, not a single man, either theirs or ours, the village was peaceful ...what happened in the war [World War II], OK, but not even a single house was burnt down, in those days the Italians were the ones who burned down the houses. (Orlić 2017: 170–171)

Narrating the Yugoslav past is a common trope for those who experienced first-hand, or participated in, the wars.

It was better ... more hanging out together regardless of nation [national belonging]. And now? Well, now, there is less hanging out together, those that were here, they fled ... I mean Serbians ... I do not hate anybody. I love everybody; this is how I was raised. In the army [Yugoslav People's Army (JNA)] we were taught to respect everybody, if he is a good man, that there is no need to hate anyone. Eh, and what happened then? You know, the managers [the term interlocutors used for the political leaders] are guilty, always like that. The managers who are up there are guiltier than us below. People always manage to find their way together. Here, if you listen, in our parts of the land, we always were good together, we never argued, we managed to communicate, but somebody else seduced us. (Orlić 2017: 172)

Encounters between older participants, from different sides, show the sharp contrast between 'I never experienced any hatred before the war' (CNA 2007) and a 'sudden and unexpected outburst of hatred' (CNA 2006a). There is also a significant difference in the ways in which those who actively participated in or experienced the war address the internalisation of their ethnic identities. Their stories[37] show an important variance – from those who felt an immediate identification with their ethnic identity to those who were motivated to defend Yugoslavia and, later on, had to shift to a narrow ethnically bound identity.

Similar ambivalence is even more pronounced in the younger generation, who often relate to their ethnicities both as burdens and as their safety zone. Reports of the burden of being negatively labelled and the obstacle to socialisation are often heard: 'it is important to me to have the freedom to introduce myself by my name without having others

---

[37] See the films *It Cannot Last Forever* (CNA 2006b), *All Wish to Cast a Stone* (CNA 2006a) and *Not a Bird to Be Heard* (CNA 2007). This series of films aims to create 'a conversation about questions that we didn't get a chance to ask each other'. The team tried to 'find "ordinary people", not representatives of politics or the media ... just people who have questions for people of the other side about the war and the post-war period and are ready to answer questions'. The three documentaries simulate dialogue between people from two sides: Bosniaks and Serbs in the first film, Serbs and Croats in the second, and Croats and Bosniaks in the third. See https://nenasilje.org/en/category/film_en/.

humiliate me' (Nansen 2012: 38).[38] To most, this can be an obstacle to their daily life: 'when there was a football match between Borac [a football team in Banja Luka] and Sarajevo [the football team in Sarajevo], a lot of us Bosniaks supported Borac on Facebook ... however, a number of other Bosniaks sent us bad feedback because they perceive Borac as a Serbian team' (Nansen 2012: 39).[39] Or: 'I go to school in Prijedor [a town in Republika Srpska that is inhabited by a majority Bosnian Serb population], and when I introduce myself by saying my name, they change their attitude towards me. The reason is simply because my name immediately gives me ethnic and religious identity as Bosniak and Muslim' (Nansen 2012).[40] Often their ethnicity is understood as a shield, and youngsters feel safe and secure in 'their' part of town, but less so in 'the other' part: 'I'm from Novi Grad (in the municipality of Sarajevo). I feel physically safe in the local community where I live, while in other parts of the city I do not feel [safe]' (Nansen 2012).[41] 'I feel unsafe because, in our city, there are invisible boundaries between the lower [Bosnian Croat] and upper [Bosniak] part of the city' (Nansen 2012)[42] 'Since Mostar is a divided city, I feel safe on the side where we belong' (Nansen 2012: 39).[43]

In cases where people mix and interact with each other, they have developed certain coping mechanisms and ways of behaviour to avoid getting into difficult situations. For example, they avoid saying their names if this might give away their ethnic identity, or they avoid conversations that touch upon any potentially contentious topics, such as religion, ethnicity, politics or the past. Koruna educators explained: 'when the safety of the group feels threatened by too much denial or collusion, anger or blame, we shift the focus to their roles as educators where they can temporarily be on safer terrain' (Green 2000: 446).

Their personal stories are fragmented and similar to the stories of the Palestinians, and they often include the motives for their exile. Their stories reflect their family legacies. This is best seen in the ways they narrate their life stories. They address people they know/knew by their names or simply as neighbours, for example, but then move to more

---

[38] Focus-group discussions participant, male, age twenty-nine, Bosniak, unemployed, Novi Travnik.
[39] Focus-group discussions participant, female, age seventeen, Bosniak, high school student, Sanski Most.
[40] Focus-group discussions participant, female, age seventeen, Bosniak, high school student, Sanski Most.
[41] Focus-group discussions participant, female, age twenty-two, student, Sarajevo.
[42] Focus-group discussions participant, female, age seventeen, high school student, Novi Travnik.
[43] Focus-group discussions participant, male, age twenty, student, Bosniak, Mostar.

distant speech, switching to the general categories of Serbs, Croats or Bosniaks or their pejorative and stereotypic name of Ustashe, Chetnik or Balija: 'Serbs bombed us' or 'all of a sudden they started singing Ustashe songs' (CNA 2006a). However, whereas in the Israeli–Palestinian context, the ritualisation of their historical narratives is, in a way, inevitable, in the Balkans context, the participants often find much more common ground. The availability of a common language means that they can build different bonds unrelated to the 'facing the past' agenda. They can sing together, tell jokes, share cultural features. In the Bosnian case, they also face similar financial issues, unemployment and corruption.

The asymmetry is more visible in Croatia, where the relationship between the majority and the minority, as well as between urban and rural, plays a significant part and pushes the sides back to their ethnic identities. Both the Croats and Serbs have well-canonised narratives that, once put in face-to-face interaction, almost immediately surface. For the Croatian side, 'we have always wanted our independent state, but our dreams were always frustrated by them [Serbs]'; 'they [Serbs] started the aggression against us ... Milosevic sent his troops to attack and kill us'; and 'we fought bravely, lost many of our soldiers and won even though the other side was better armed'. For the Serbs, 'we wanted to stay in Yugoslavia where we felt safer and where our rights could be protected ... the Yugoslav army was protecting the borders of Yugoslavia'; 'they started to arm themselves, kill and dismiss our people. Everything they did reminded us of 1941 ... Serbia came to our defense'; and 'when troops from Serbia withdrew, we were left without protection and betrayed – our people were killed, exiled and destroyed' (Manojlović 2016). Bergholz (2013: 694) rightly pointed out that high levels of antagonistic 'groupness' often rapidly crystallise in response to incidents that are perceived to be based on 'ethnic conflict'. At such moments, some group members experience an abrupt shift, quickly interpreting the cause of an incident as being rooted in a participant's nationality, and especially the war-time associations they attach to whole nationalities. These interpretations do not merely describe such incidents as 'ethnically based'; they actually constitute them in such terms. As a result, incidents between individuals are rapidly transformed into conflicts between collectivities, between an 'us' and a 'them'.

Up to this point, I have shown how assigned ethnic identities help the ritualising of historical narratives in structured face-to-face encounters that promote the 'facing the past' agenda as a path to peace and reconciliation. With significant differences regarding their past and present, in both the Israeli–Palestinian and the Balkans cases, those face-to-face encounters lead to the past being seen as something dangerous that has to be dismantled for the sake of a peaceful future and the implementation of human rights. However, what is happening instead is a gradual process of ritualisation and sacralisation of the past.

Emotional Energy

Emotional energy is the key. Sharing personal stories entwined in historical narratives is not nearly enough to produce micro-solidarity among the participants, let alone to engage them in a common moral action. According to Collins's interaction ritual chains model, emotional energy is carried across situations by symbols that have been changed by emotional situations (Collins 2004: 107). The participants focus attention on the same thing; when aware of each other's focus, they become caught up in each other's emotions. The predicted outcome of a successful emotional coordination is feelings of solidarity. Hence, emotional experience is a significant trigger for moral actions.

Emotional energy in everyday life is dictated by the context. Some situations will not result in any significant emotional energy even when people have face-to-face encounters – travelling on the morning train to work or shopping in a department store, for example. Emotional energy will rise if, for example, the train becomes stuck and people need to spend several hours together co-depending on each other. Some situations will lead to short-term solidarity; others may produce strong micro-solidarity between the group members that can last a lifetime.

However, structured face-to-face encounters are artificial environments that need to stage and, in many ways, manipulate participants' feelings. Generally speaking, two major methods are used in all memorialisation projects to provoke a particular emotional state of mind as a way of re-humanising each other. The first method, used in peacebuilding and reconciliation training, envisions the mental and emotional transformation of the participants and is a technique widely used in all kinds of group dynamics sessions. It includes approaches such as role playing, sharing stories in a particular manner, mapping life stories, association games, problem solving in conflictual situations and working in groups or in pairs. Each of those techniques is designed to provoke not only a cognitive reaction but also an emotional one. When a participant is sitting in the middle, alone and surrounded by other participants, the staging produces a particular framing through which the story will be told.

Veterans from Bosnia, Serbia and Croatia, who toured across the Balkans telling their war stories, describe the meetings where they tell their personal life stories as very powerful. Not only did they get to hear 'those who they've met only through their shotgun', which in itself is an emotional statement, but they were also put under the spotlight on the stage to share their story with the wider audience. Coming from the frustration of not being appreciated for their huge sacrifice for a society and having a deep feeling of marginalisation (David 2015b), suddenly getting all that attention had a true impact on them. Indeed, participation in public forums was a major motivation for the former combatants to take part in the project. It was of personal importance to them to tell their story and address the public (CNA 2004: 23).

A very similar 'staging' format can be found in the Parents Circle–Families Forum (PCFF) dialogue meetings, which bring bereaved parents and family members from both the Israeli and Palestinian sides into a dialogue. This group organises meetings that last ninety minutes, and include the facilitators' personal story and their deeply emotional journey towards reconciliation.

The performativity of the stories of sufferings matters because it is how the audience is recruited both emotionally and cognitively. It is an invitation to empathy but also to a conflict. After hearing a story of a Palestinian who got shot during the First Intifada in 1987, a Jewish high school[44] student said: 'I think there cannot be peace because there are so many fanatic people. In particular on the Palestinian side. What is the purpose of the State of Israel? To be a home to Jewish people. What is the purpose of Hamas? To destroy Israel'.[45] A debate continued between the Jewish student and a Palestinian facilitator, and in the sudden change of rhythm, a Jewish student said, 'Why don't *you* [switch from singular to plural speech] move to Jarden? There is no place for both of *us* [our people] here!'[46] The tempo of those sessions is intense and leaves participants uneasy. Though the emotional energy produced in the clash between the sides is directed to produce an eye-opening moment, the effect is often quite the opposite. The rhythmic coordination of gestures transforms participants' feelings into collective sentiments and makes it possible for the members of the group gathered together to feel part of the same community of belonging.

The staging is crucial for emotional energy because it also dictates the content. For example, when the Jewish teachers sit in the inner circle with their backs to the Palestinian teachers, they almost instantly start talking more openly and with less political correctness. The role reversal, which takes place when the otherwise silent underdog assumes a voice

---

[44] Itzhak Rabin High School, Nesher, Israel.
[45] PCFF. Israeli–Palestinian Bereaved Parents for Peace – dialogue meetings video: http://theparentscircle.org/en/pcff-activities_eng/dialogue_meetings_eng/.
[46] Ibid.

and becomes a raconteur, was expected to infuse the moment with emotional significance. The counter-intuitive situation in which a person stereotypically perceived as belonging to a hostile and potentially violent group surfaces as an articulate victim was designed to create a cathartic impact, which it often did (Rabinowitz 2001: 70).

The members of the community of belonging come together, share a certain level of excitement and begin to act together, each seeking to adapt their own individual rhythms to the collective rhythm, and by doing so, increase their level of emotional involvement. Once the process of ritualisation of historical narratives starts to unfold, it becomes fuelled with emotional energy. In both contexts, addressing the past is a central theme around which the emotional build-up and the division to ethnic categories takes place.

For example, Palestinians, in their sustained silence throughout the exchange with their Jewish counterparts, seem at no point to be ready to allow any social sphere, formal or other, to be considered free of inter-ethnic tension (Bekerman 2009: 210): 'You said it angers you if a Palestinian does not condemn terrorist attacks. What angers you? I am not a saint. I am dying of fear. What should I apologize for?' (Bekerman and Zembylas 2012: 79). Sentences like those often fill the group with tension. Once such references are made, participants start using the third-person plural in their ongoing attempts to categorise the group. The discourse becomes full of self-reparations, overtly strong comments and multiple pauses, all pointing to the difficulty encountered by the interlocutor while attempting to prevent confusion and maintain a mutual orientation. In the words of the Koruna NGO facilitator in Bosnia, this emotional tension is transformational where they (the facilitators) try to allow the participants a 'modicum of vulnerability, self-reflection and personal insight as they feel trust' (Green 2000: 445). However, those fluctuations in emotional energy are significant because they are used to regroup solidarities among the group participants.

The second method to produce emotional energy goes even further. It takes people from their controlled environments and pushes them to have a real emotional and bodily experience. The degree of the intensity of the experience varies and will produce different degrees of micro-solidarity. Almost every such face-to-face encounter has a component of an outdoor experience. It can be a light and even enjoyable experience such as an 'educational tour', an emotionally difficult and painful journey such as visiting Srebrenica, or a highly emotionally contested and engaging event in which both pain and fear are present, such as in the Israeli–Palestinian Memorial Day Ceremony. For example, the most notable event held by the YIHR took place in late 2012. when

YIHR Croatia and YIHR Serbia brought together youths from Croatia and Serbia to Vukovar, a town in eastern Croatia that was largely destroyed during the 1990s war and where young Croats and Serbs live separately and go through different educational curricula, in particular in history. During this activity, youths from Croatia and Serbia attended a history class delivered at the town's main square by Croatian and Serbian history teachers and participated in a partial reconstruction of the yard of Vukovar's Europe House, thus promoting an attitude of a generation willing to work together for a common peaceful future (YIHR 2015). As another example, the Initiative for Human Rights in BiH held a summer camp in Kozarac in August 2010. Activists from Serbia (Novi Sad, Niš and Prijepolje), Bosnia and Herzegovina, Montenegro, and two guests from Iraq stayed in the 'Srcem do Mira' (Reaching Peace by Heart) House. The summer camp's theme was 'Dealing with the Past'. Participants also visited the memorial and the museum in Mrakovica, as well as concentration camps from the last war in Omarska, Trnopolje and Keraterm.

Of course, different participants will react differently to those experiences. Nevertheless, Collins's (2004: 125) argument that short-term emotions are derived against the backdrop of an ongoing flow of emotional energy developed between group participants seems to be right. Whether the Israeli and Palestinian participants are taken to Deir Yassin or to see the Palestinian village ruins from 1948, and the participants from Serbia, Croatia and Bosnia visit commemorative sites in Vukovar, Ovčara, Srebrenica, Bratunac or elsewhere, their previous experiences will affect them in a very particular way. They might feel anger, anxiety, humbleness, pain, sorrow, empathy or something else. However, those emotions are filtered through the processes of ritualisation in which their assigned ethnic identities position them either as the victim or the perpetrator in the event. For example, the Southeast Europe Initiative of the French–German Youth Office (FGYO),[47] as part of its dialogue curricula, organised visits to Srebrenica. Participants from Serbia, once in Srebrenica, internalised their ethnic legacy (though they were not even born at the time of the event) and started crying and apologising. Their Serbian colleagues from Republika Srpska felt differently. They complained that no one was interested in seeing what happened to the Serbs

---

[47] A group of twenty participants in all: five from Serbia, five from BiH (three from the Federation of Bosnia and Herzegovina and two from Republic of Srpska), five from France and five from Germany. The information is based on a conversation I had on 3 July 2018 with Cecille Blaser, who conducted ethnographic research done between 2014 and 2016. I was looking at projects of the Southeast Europe Initiative FGYO, including a pilot RYCO project. RYCO officially started to operate in 2017.

just a few kilometres from there. Young people who come from places that have a symbolic association with atrocities and war crimes, such as Srebrenica, feel burdened with this 'legacy' of their own perceptions about others' identity. They find it hard to stand up for where they came from out of fear of stigmatisation (Nansen 2012: 39). Having said that, this instant role play is a direct product of the ritualisation of historical narratives.

This essentialisation and ethnic homogenisation stand in sharp contrast to the ways in which they talk about their participation: 'When I think of my own environment, I realize that nationality is a very stressful issue. It's something that everyone seems to worry about. But in this space, over the 10 days, national differences have been irrelevant' (Fischer 2001: 31). Or: 'At the forums, a lot of people can come and listen, see three different nations, who were at war and hear personal experiences. The participants of the forums are there as persons and individuals. That's important: I want people to understand that they have individuals in front of them, with names and surnames. It's an opportunity for people not to blame all the nation' (CNA 2004: 21). This gap between their feelings and ethnical detachment in fact testifies to just the opposite – how deep the internalisation of their ethnicity becomes during their face-to-face encounters.

Emotional energy is crucial for interpersonal attachments. Anger, fear and frustration play a major role in this process. A veteran from Bosnia wrote about his experience when his dialogue partner, from the other Bosnian entity against which he was fighting in the war, unexpectedly brought with him some unfamiliar people. The anxiety and fear that the meeting might develop into a conflict left a strong emotional impact on him:

We met and if I remember correctly, I think that one was named P., and the other B. I saw they were carrying officers' purses and cameras. I thought 'Fuck Lj., who did you bring along!' They did not seem to me like people who came to see something and evoke some memories. At that moment, I was angry with Lj., for not telling me in advance who was coming. Perhaps he was afraid that in that case I would turn him down ... All that time, I felt confused. Thousands of questions were building up in my mind, I was looking for answers: who were they, did they belong to some security forces, what were they really interested in? The only thing that encouraged me was that I recognized some signs of their discomfort, too. (Delić 2010: 78–80)

Fear has huge potential to engage people in feelings of solidarity. In the face-to-face meetings between the Serbs and the Albanians from Kosovo, organised by the YIHR, the border crossing appeared to be a major source of fear. An Albanian participant testified:

On the border, we saw the police, they reminded us of when we last saw the police in our streets ... at that time I was scared ... I have strong memories of the Serbian police in Priština ... I was ten years old when the police came to our house and ordered us to go out ... we then had to leave to the train station and on our way [to Macedonia] they were maltreating us ... the police, uniforms and flags of Serbia, all make me feel unsafe. (Fridman 2013: 151)

Probably the most intense emotional energy is produced once two high-intensity emotions collide. The Israeli–Palestinian Memorial Day Ceremony is organised by peace activists, and in full collaboration with the PCFF and the Combatants for Peace (CFP) movement. Apart from ongoing dialogue meetings, they organise annual commemorations for the fallen Jewish and Palestinian people. This is a highly intense gathering, with a high volume of media coverage, that each year brings more and more people to the ceremony, but also a significant opposition. Because this event is highly contested, the police forces are spread around the commemorative grounds, separating the bereaved parents from the Jewish right-wing protestors. While the sorrow, the pain and the togetherness of the participants are intensified through the testimonials of the bereaved parents and the sad songs of peace and loss played on the main stage, the shouting of the protestors just behind the police cordon, their physical closeness, their extensive use of Israeli flags, their raw emotions of hatred and inability to understand a collective Jewish and Palestinian grief, all come together to produce a strong emotional energy that brings the participants closer together. The pronounced feeling of danger, of the forbidden, of the mutual grief, and the emotional and threatening cries of the protestors – 'Traitors! Traitors! How much do you get paid for the betrayal? Nazis! Death to the terrorists!'[48] – create an extraordinary emotional and bodily experience that leads to strong emotional ties and solidarity attachments among the participants.

Hence, through the process of ritualising the past, and despite the homogenisation of their ethnic identities, face-to-face encounters shape emotional energy that produces micro-solidarities on the ground. The short-term impact of these encounters is well reported in both the Israeli–Palestinian context and the Balkan context. Participants often report that they have gone through a significant emotional experience:

It was a completely new experience. I think it was the trainers' skills and sensitivity in presenting the issues and then leading the group which encouraged the participants to open up so much. There were many things

[48] 'Israel: Tensions Flare at Israeli–Palestinian Memorial Day ceremony in Tel Aviv' (2017), video: www.youtube.com/watch?v=LoRFgsEQYxk.

I had never really thought about, and I was suddenly guided towards them in a way which clarified a lot of issues for me. They were quite simple everyday situations. (Fischer 2001: 31)

The training changed my life. In the small town where I live, I have very few opportunities for the kind of encounters I experienced at the seminar. (Fischer 2001: 34)

I gained a lot more than I expected. The whole training was magic. I learned to listen, I'm able to perceive things I did not perceive before and I became a lot more active in the centre. (CNA 2004: 14)

Similarly, the typical reaction to those encounters amongst the Jewish participants is described as earth-shaking, a significant experience in which they confronted, for the first time, their roles in the Jewish–Arab conflict (Ron, Maoz and Bekerman 2010: 574). The excitement and feeling of collective effervescence are empowering, and the vast majority of participants feel strong bonds with most of the group members. The time spent together over several months, the mutual educational trips, the intensive emotional ups and downs, and the time spent together during breaks or bus rides – in a Goffmanian sense, backstage moments – all produce real feelings in a group. As one Bosnian war veteran explained: 'The unofficial part of the training was very important to me. Former soldiers were eating together, even played football in a team. The normal political situation does not allow normal people to come together' (CNA 2004).

Whether we talk about the prolonged, tense and often emotionally difficult encounters of Israeli and Palestinian students or teachers, war veterans from the wars in the 1990s in the Balkans, Israeli and the Palestinian ex-combatants, bereaved parents from both sides, or pupils and students from different ethnic backgrounds in the Balkans, we see that the participants report that the emotional impact was significant. Paradoxically, even though the main outcome of those face-to-face meetings is further strengthening of their ethnic identities, the overall feeling of the excitement over a significant meaning-making process masks those stratifications and enables sweet feelings of group solidarity.

This, however, is a deception. Those warm feelings will soon either evaporate or become hijacked by the state apparatus. Make no mistake, though: those feelings are real and true. Nevertheless, what stays in the long run is the ritualised nature of their historical past, while the group solidarity is destined to fade away. The evaluation of such face-to-face encounters shows very limited and narrow transformations in the long run. In practice, this means that the ethnic categories of the groups have just gained additional weight, not the other way around.

The Inability to Sustain Solidarity Based on Human Rights Values: Two Reasons for the Failure

So far, we have seen that all participants in dialogue projects testify to a great impact on the personal level, with some even speaking of a 'life-changing experience' (CNA 2008). Now, the main question becomes: is this solidarity sustained in the long run, and is it capable of pushing distant people into a moral action? In other words, can those human rights pockets of solidarity lead to the wider appreciation of human rights values? It is my argument that the evidence from both settings (Israeli–Palestinian and the Western Balkan context) suggests that we end up with those solidarities either crumbling apart or being hijacked by the state. This, I argue, is a consequence of two unrelated factors. First, once the participants leave those largely artificial environments, they immediately face a lack of the basic infrastructure needed to successfully endure the acquired emotional energy to keep the human rights vision alive. Moreover, they instantly encounter nationalist infrastructures instead. Second, the understanding and promotion by human rights organisations of the practice of memorialisation, embedded in moral remembrance, brings about a series of unfortunate misconceptions. Paradoxically, even when the participants continue to promote human rights values, these misconceptions end up enforcing nationalist sentiments even further. Those two processes are discussed in the remainder of this chapter.

Infrastructures

Conceptualising human rights as an ideology is not only beneficial but also necessary if we wish to understand what happens with human rights values on the ground. The successes of different ideologies, as discussed at length so far, can be traced and measured through three parameters: (1) institutionalisation of their organisational powers, which points to the institutional infrastructures; (2) institutionalisation of their ideological power, which points to the infrastructures of the content; and (3) micro-solidarity produced in small-group encounters that are recruited and sustained through content, instructions, practices and discourses. In other words, for micro-solidarity to be effective in a broader community, it has to be widely supported by the existing infrastructures.

Human rights within the nation-state, however, are in the foreign territory. Whereas they are deeply and widely embedded at the world polity level, within nation-states, human rights cannot compete with nationalist infrastructures.[49] That is not to say that all nationalisms are the same or negative, but rather is intended to point to the ideological modus operandi of nationalism. Even in cases in which nationalism has absorbed and adopted human rights as its impression management agenda, such as in the case of Denmark in the 1990s, the inclusion of human rights will appear only as long as it serves the nationalist project. Human rights and nationalism are, at the same time, both competing and complementary projects. In other words, once the participants are outside the dialogue setting, the emotional energy formed in those face-to-face encounters has to be pushed not only against a stream of nationalist infrastructures but also as individuals (rather than as a group). The difficulty with human rights memorialisation discourses, at least in part, comes down to the lack of official ritual forms (consisting of rules, ceremonial idioms and symbols) designed to unite and integrate the human rights–based meta-group formed into wider communities. In other words, other than the ethnicised narratives of their historical past, interaction rituals produced during the face-to-face encounters do not translate into symbols capable of bringing an imagined community of human rights supporters together.

But apparently, not all is lost. Some evidence suggests certain impacts of face-to-face encounters lead to a moral, human rights–based action. However, it seems that, in the Palestinian–Israeli case, the only segment that goes through a lasting transformation and that is working actively to promote human rights values is the Jewish side. Not the Jewish participants, though – only the Jewish facilitators. An examination (Ron, Maoz and Bekerman 2010)[50] of the extent to which the continuous involvement of Israeli Jewish group facilitators brought about an ideological shift showed that the vast majority of Jewish Israeli group facilitators described their continued encounters with Arab citizens of Israel as leading them to an increased detachment from Zionist ideology and to a significant decrease in their support of the definition of Israel as a Jewish state. Even during the Second Intifada, there was an increase in commitment among

---

[49] States, having the power to implement the meta-narrative as a basis for national memory in society, create as part of the national identity 'the state-sponsored memory of a national past' or 'national memory'. This includes commemorations, museums, monuments, national calendars, history textbooks and other vehicles. These are essentially memories which serve the state's need for control, unity, legitimization and discipline.

[50] A thematic content analysis of thirteen in-depth interviews, seven women and six men, aged twenty-four to fifty-eight, conducted by Yiftach Ron, Ifat Maoz and Zvi Bekerman. It was based on an empirical study conducted between 1992 and 1998, which investigated six encounter programs, and on a series of interviews with Arab and Jewish facilitators conducted in 2001.

the facilitators associated with long-term co-existence activities. The relationships built among members of such groups survived the Intifada events and even helped renew trust in each other's responses and attitudes (Abu-Nimer 2004: 417). More generally speaking, the Jews readily report on changes that they undergo during the encounter. Maoz (2000) showed that, after participating in the workshops, both Jews and Palestinians viewed each other as more 'considerate of others', 'tolerant' and 'good-hearted' than they did before. The Jewish participants are often proud of these changes and see them as a courageous act deserving of recognition on the part of the Arab group. The Palestinian group tends not to report on the changes it undergoes. In fact, the Palestinians may even report a complete absence of change (Halabi and Sonnenschein 2004: 380). Palestinian interviewees[51] did not voluntarily come up with accounts of their influence on Palestinian youths. For them, these interactions clearly failed to constitute a category of real significance (Rabinowitz 2001: 72).

The results from Serbia, Croatia and BiH present, to some extent, a similar picture.[52] Whereas there is no evidence that one particular side becomes more prone to human rights actions, we clearly see that those who succeed in maintaining the activity are mostly those who were human rights promoters to start with, or those who find a way to make a living out if it. For example, research on NGOs in Bosnia that promote face-to-face encounters for dealing with the past as a means to achieving peacebuilding points out that donors unintentionally undermined reconciliation by creating a class of professionalised young activists from elite, urban backgrounds who already agreed with the donor agenda. NGO 'frequent flyers' are individuals who were repeatedly recruited to attend workshops, who moved from programme to programme within and between organisations, monopolising opportunities in civil society (Micinski 2016). Just as with the Jewish participants, and especially the Palestinian participants, opportunities to travel abroad, interact with international facilitators and practise foreign languages were bigger motivators then the actual promotion of human rights. This is evident in particular in face-to-face projects that are internationally based, such as those promoted by the RYCO and Nansen organisations in the Balkans, as well as projects conducted by Yad BeYad, Abraham's Vision or Seeds of Peace in the Israeli–Palestinian context. The engagement in moral issues of human rights gave additional value and incentives. This meant that the true targets of reconciliation projects – the nationalist

---

[51] Interviews conducted by Dan Rabinowitz in 2000.
[52] We do lack systematic research on that issue for the Balkans context.

youth and their families who do not support the liberal peacebuilding agenda – stayed out of reach (Djipa and Fazlić 2012: 102–103). This is precisely how those encounters ended up gathering 'all people who agree with each other' (Micinski 2016: 102).

These structural issues related to the recruitment politics of NGOs play a role but are not the reason why people rarely continue to engage with the moral actions of human rights. It is what they encounter in the real world. Unsurprisingly, their real environments, to which they inevitably return, become even more hostile. Filled with feelings of familiarity, a certain level of intimacy, loyalty and enthusiasm from their interactions with the participants in the encounter, they come back to their local communities to face deeply embedded structures of nationalism. They encounter them every day not only through the educational system and the media, but also in everyday conversations, encounters with the family members, neighbours and even random passers-by. The gap they experience can range from confusion and frustration to fear and intimidation. The founder and the facilitator of the CNA, Nenad Vukosavljević, explains:

> The main challenge lies in the stirring of this 'local' pro-peace energy into constructive action and attitude and in making it visible. We have noticed 'negative impacts' in this sense in several cases. Participants from the Training for Trainers programme, for instance, tried to change structures within their organisations. They wanted to introduce more participatory decision-making processes and principles to share responsibility, thereby undermining existent hierarchies. They failed and finally had to leave the organization. They now face the problem of how to find a new way to act, which is very difficult as they have lost motivation. Another negative development, which I have observed in my closest environment, is that people who put much energy into peace and conflict transformation suffer from burn-out and get ill. And yes, the question poses itself: why should you expect to stay healthy if the whole society is ill? (Vukosavljević 2011: 280)

According to Vukosavljević (2011: 281), some have had the experience that, due to their increased level of empathy and tolerance, they are considered 'traitors' who act against the 'collective national interests', especially when they express a view that seems to diverge from what is defined as mainstream by ethnopolitical discourses. The inability to transform micro-solidarity into a wider network of solidarity is often evident at the very end of the project: 'Unfortunately, not all the contacts were maintained with everyone in the group. With some of them, the link broke off immediately. With others, there are intensive contacts and ideas for possible projects. But there are no firm plans as yet. This may be because we live on different sides of the border' (Fischer 2001: 41).

The general population is neither very keen nor ready to resist the comfort of existing ethnic boundaries. In Croatia, for example, the 'facing the past' process has a negative connotation for 60 per cent of the Serbs from the war-torn parts of Croatia (Dokumenta 2006). This has to do with deeply embedded ethno-centric perceptions of victimhood. The perceptions of who were the main victims are firm. On the one hand, 80 per cent of the Serbs in Croatia say that the Serbs were more the victims than were the Croats (with 10 per cent saying that the Serbs were exclusive victims). On the other hand, almost 50 per cent of Croats say that only Croats were the victims (Dokumenta 2006). Additionally, a public opinion study in Serbia revealed that a general scepticism towards NGOs contributes to a lack of trust in initiatives on 'facing the past'. The 'image problem' of NGOs in societies in the former Yugoslavia is evident on the ground. In all societies, but most pronounced in Bosnia, there is a highly negative public image of NGOs or civil society organisations, which are frequently seen to be foreign-donor driven, working for their own rather than society's good (CNA 2008: 16). The general public position is that, while abstract arguments such as 'facing the past processes benefit the whole of society' are accepted in international discourses on transitional justice, they are seldom believable to people on the ground (Obradović-Wochnik 2013). Moreover, people often respond negatively to efforts to face the past, out of a fear that their identity is being threatened, that the image of Serbs will be further tainted. These fears indicate a clear link between their personal and national identities (Yerkes 2004). In BiH, which is divided into two different entities, there is no willingness to engage in breaking down the ethnic identities that come in particularly handy to the political elites. Just as elsewhere in the Balkans, those ethnic identities are the main force behind the ruling political elites.

The lack of structures and motivation that would enable alternatives to nationalist infrastructures is evident. Neither the Federation of BiH nor the Republika Srpska has any political parties that explicitly address dealing with the past, peacebuilding or reconciliation in their programme (Fischer and Petrović-Ziemer 2013: 99). Also, positions of power are unavailable to the younger generation, which immediately reflects on their motivation to act. We see that young people have no influence or trust in their political structures and their local communities. In 2008, 90 per cent of those surveyed[53] stated that they did not think they could

---

[53] The survey was conducted in 2011–2012 and had 2,360 respondents, aged 15–30, in the general population in BiH and 352 respondents categorized as belonging to vulnerable groups in BiH. See United Nations Country Team (2013) Common County Assessment

influence or trust their political organisations or NGOs; 87 per cent felt the same way about their local communities. In 2011–2012, this number increased to a staggering 99 per cent who distrusted their political organisations and NGOs and 97 per cent who were wary of their local community. People are generally discouraged to engage (Djipa and Fizlić 2012). Particularly in rural areas, the NGOs' presence is very limited.

One activist reported: 'The experience from CNA trainings was amazing, but I finished them, nothing new happened' (CNA 2008). This apathy affects not just inter-ethnic and inter-regional interaction, but almost all aspects of young people's lives. According to Nansen (2012: 52), this situation is 'both a blessing and a curse for peace and conflict dynamics. Young people are less likely to become radicalized and manipulated by others for ethno-nationalist and confrontational ends, but they are also unlikely to become a driving force for positive change without considerable support and encouragement'.

Similar reflections are shared by Jewish and Palestinian trainers. In describing major problems with programs, a Jewish facilitator stated: 'We send people home more confused, and we say it is good to be confused and raise questions regarding the reality of the conflict. But we do not know what will happen to them when they settle back in their home environment' (Abu-Nimer 2004). A Palestinian said: 'I still think it did something to the children who took part. The problem was it had no continuity. It is hard to keep in touch, hundreds of kilometers away. We moderators tried to keep in touch, to come to the schools, to do simulation games, whatever. But then one father says something to his daughter about one of us being "a dirty Arab" and that spoils everything' (Rabinowitz 2001: 71). Encounters between Arabs and Jews end without assigning a common task, or even a long- or short-term plan, for the future (Abu-Nimer 2004: 413). Several facilitators noted that the lack of institutional and structural connections to the advocacy and protest movements in Israel continues to stymie development in the field, arguing against the substantial lack of formal and institutional links between encounter programs (Abu-Nimer 2004: 417). In fact, some models of face-to-face encounters[54] include explicit mechanisms that are directly geared towards mobilising collective action aimed at changing the non-egalitarian distribution of resources between Jewish and Palestinian citizens of Israel. The role of mobilising collective action and attempting to

---

Bosnia Herzegovina – a survey conducted by the Prism Research commissioned by the Office of the UN Resident Coordinator in BiH.

[54] The co-existence model, the joint project model, the confrontational model and the narrative-telling model.

produce social change is mostly left to other agencies and organisations that are explicitly self-defined as politically activist groups (Maoz 2011: 122). To put it even more bluntly, according to Bar, Bargal and Asaqla (1995), most of the effects of the encounters are lost or forgotten within a few months, prompting encounter program participants to return to their previous negative or stereotypical attitudes. One evaluation report discloses this tendency to go 'back to normal' in the Balkans as well. Only eight out of thirty participants were willing to answer the CNA's request to participate in the survey three years after their training (CNA 2001: 14) or to engage in some more meaningful action.

Hence, face-to face encounters within the human rights memorialisation agenda, in a way, become a substitute for meaningful human rights actions. From the point of view of the nation-state, it even brings benefits to nationalist projects. It further ethnically homogenises people, leaving them without sufficient rituals to push their micro-solidarities into macro actions based on universal human rights moralities. However, this is not to claim that more human rights, as often argued, would bring a solution and the necessary infrastructure to further promote human rights globally. The real challenge lies in the false assumptions adopted and promoted through moral remembrance worldwide. Those, as we will see, under the pretence of human rights, actually reproduce ethnic sentiments and solidarities along ethnic lines.

The Dangers of Moral Remembrance

So far, I have used Collins's interaction ritual chain theory to explain what happens in face-to-face encounters that are based on the human rights memorialisation agenda and why the established micro-solidarity fails to translate into a wide promotion and adoption of human rights values. Here, I want to go beyond the strength and tenacity of existing nationalist infrastructures and address some far-reaching effects of the human rights memorialisation agenda. I wish to demonstrate that the pillar principles of moral remembrance described at length in Chapter 3 – 'facing the past', 'duty to remember' and 'justice for victims' – have troubling effects on the ground. Moral remembrance is an outcome of the accumulative process of the standardisation of human rights–sponsored memorialisation practices. But is it even remotely possible to generate and standardise memorialisation processes across the globe? And what are the possible outcomes on the ground?

The 'Facing the Past' Agenda: What's Wrong with That?

The rationale for placing the notion of 'facing the past' at the heart of post-conflict processes and remembrance of massive human rights abuses has been generated on the assumption that working through the past is necessary for healing, forgiveness and reconciliation. The first problem with this approach is the presumption that nations are like individuals and need to face the past to 'heal' or 'work through' their traumatic experiences. As described in Chapter 3, this presumption seems to rest on an unfortunate congruence of 1960s psychoanalytical theory and the need to show that Nazism was not simply a modern political phenomenon but rather a manifestation of German national psychosis, which needed to be (and could be) cured.

This overtly psychological approach, which became the foundation for the 'facing the past' approach, makes no real distinction between the ways in which individuals reckon with their traumatic memories and the ways in which collectives engage with their painful past. It defines only one set of events of the national past as being critical: nothing else can be mentioned and everything else must, ironically, be repressed. In his well-known article 'Schindler's Fate: Genocide, Ethnic Cleansing, and Population Transfers', Robert Hayden (1996) defined this reductionism in the spirit of Milan Kundera's notion, saying that shrinking the past to a single set of events 'reduces (and teaches others to reduce) the life of a hated society to the simple listing of its crimes'. In practice, this means that for Bosniaks, for example, their identity is perceived through the Srebrenica massacre, as well as that they see Serbs through that frozen segment of the past. Serbs, for their part, reduce their identity to the Jasenovac concentration camp, perceiving all Croats as Ustashe and ultimately ignoring other segments of the past. Croats see themselves through the justified war of independence, ignoring atrocities committed on their behalf. Thus, a particular narrow framing of a particular past that has to be dealt with does, in fact, strengthen the bonds between individuals and their imagined ethnic community. Dan Stone (2006) rightly pointed out that all atrocities are bound up with memory. However, on an individual level, they are bound up with trauma, whereas on a collective level, they instigate a (re)production of stereotypes, prejudice and post-genocide politics.

Individual and collective reckonings with the past are far from being identical. In fact, the very concept of social memory presupposes that individual memory and collective memory are not the same. Through a series of empirical investigations into social suffering around the globe, Jeffrey Alexander (2004) outlined a model of trauma work that relates the interests of carrier groups, competing narrative identifications of victim and perpetrator, utopian and dystopian proposals for trauma resolution, the performative power of constructed events and the distribution of organisational resources. He shows that every collective trauma is a social construct and not an inherited quality of an event. For that matter, a traumatic element of the past is often hijacked by a state elite and (re)constructed to serve that elite's own needs. Meticulous analysis by Robert Hayden (2017) on the ways in which Holocaust imagery was used to promote genocide claims in Bosnia during the wars of the 1990s, and Jackie Feldman's (2010) accounts of Israeli Jewish students' voyages to Poland and the precise framing of their sentiments regarding the Holocaust, and Joanna Bourke's (2004: 473) comparative study on remembering different wars across the globe, which showed that certain wars such as the Korean war were simply 'ignored', are just some examples that prove Alexander's point.

Similarly, Hamber and Wilson (2002) have shown that nations are not like individuals in that they do not have collective psyches, that nation-building discourses on reconciliation often neglect individual needs, and that individual and collective processes of healing work on different timelines. They convincingly demonstrate that 'this act of "psychologizing the nation" mistakenly implies that the pursuit of national unity is a unitary and coherent process, and that individual and national processes of dealing with the past are largely concurrent and equivalent' (Hamber and Wilson 2002: 36). The image of a nation as an organic body that is hurt/ill, and thus also may be healed, becomes a way of understanding how different memorialisation agendas are motivated and promoted. States – or, more precisely, their political elites – implement the metanarrative as a basis for a national memory in society, and create, as part of their national identity, 'the state-sponsored memory of a national past' or 'national memory' (Young 1993).

The 'facing the past' approach also makes the false presumption that Freudian-derived individual psychology is based on universal human needs, and thus obscures ideological roots deeply embedded in Western(ised) cultures, persistently ignoring cultural, religious and societal differences. This deficient approach based on clinical psychoanalysis, whose main potency lies in its catchy metaphor of 'an ill nation contaminated with its contested past', became the bedrock of the 'facing the past' agenda. It not only erroneously assumed that individuals and collectives act similarly upon their traumatic past, but also applied medical diagnostic categories of mental illness, which universalise culturally specific meaning systems and frame how one interprets and practices the suffering self (Lambek and Antze 1996). These complex meaning systems are shaped by psychological explanatory models and therapeutic discourses of treatment and recovery (Herman 1992). Thus, once those Western, Freudian-derived psychological explanatory models are applied to a nation as a whole, 'facing the past' is encoded as a therapeutic remedy that has beneficial psychological consequences for 'healing the nation'.

The falsity of psychologising the processes of human rights memorialisation is presented with clarity in the works of anthropologist Carol Kidron, based on her extensive field work among Cambodian Canadian and Jewish Israeli descendants of the survivors of the mass murders by Pol Pot's regime and of the Holocaust, respectively. Studying moral modes of being as well as descendants' living experiences of memory and forgetting, Kidron (2012) showed that both case studies deviate in similar ways from the reductionist 'descendant profile' of the pathological, publicly enlisted witness in search of a redemptive testimonial voice. The Khmers refer to Buddhist forward-looking modes of being and the corresponding valourisation of 'forgetting' to explain emotional wellness through *not* recalling trauma, while the Jewish descendants' emotive scar is subjectively interpreted as a Jewish Israeli culturally valourised form of commemorative remembering and as such not experienced as univocally distressing (Kidron 2012: 739). Kidron convincingly demonstrates that those very different culturally specific approaches to achieving psychological wellness after trauma challenge key universalising axioms in trauma theory, Holocaust and genocide scholarship and humanitarian practice, thereby demonstrating an empirically grounded disproof of the supposed universality of Euro-Western semiotics of suffering, even in individual psychology.

When discussing dealing with contested pasts, explanations rooted in cultural differences are generally avoided. However, to paraphrase a famous anthropologist, Marshall Sahlins (2013), the difference is not just a historical circumstance, but also a positive value. Differentiation is not so much a natural process but a cultural intention; thus, to understand the effects on the ground of moral remembrance, based on human rights notions of universalism, cultural differences must be addressed and analysed. Cultural conflict theorists have shown that remembering comes into view as a control system, revealing not what can be remembered but what should be remembered (Schwartz, Fukuoka and Takita-Ishii 2005: 256). Hochschild (2012 [1983]), for instance, discusses the customs and rituals that engender and regulate not only the meaning and display of particular emotions, but also our social and political attitudes. The anthropologist Unni Wikan (1988), for example, compared expressions of grief and mourning in Egypt and Bali, both Islamic cultures. She found that Bali women were strongly discouraged from crying, while Egyptian women were considered abnormal if they did not incapacitate themselves in demonstrative weeping.

Culturally embedded differences regarding the perception and expression of suffering, pain, illness, memory and forgetting may often result in silence that is likely to be far more effectively therapeutic than 'working it through' could be. While the implicit assumption in the transitional justice discourse is that silence is detrimental to collective and individual healing in countries emerging from violent conflict, and this view is grounded in the psycho-medical discourse on war trauma, Eastmond and Mannergren-Selimović (2012: 524) have discussed silence as a form of communication, as multifaceted as speech and conveying a broad range of contextually situated social meanings. They demonstrate that, in the case of Bosnia, given the circumstances of highly polarised and hostile ethnic communities, silence communicates caution, respect and recognition; thus, it can be seen as a pragmatic and successful strategy for co-existence. Similarly, Obradović-Wochnik (2013: 328) conceptualises silence in post-conflict Serbia not in terms of denial of the past, but rather in terms of 'sites of silent knowledge' that include 'shared knowledge, secret practices and inability to discuss violence' which differ drastically from the purposely top-down strategic silencing that is aimed at disabling any open public debate on the past (David 2013). Kidron (2009: 6), in her fascinating research on Holocaust survivors, deconstructs the erroneous foundations of silence as 'repression'. Silence, she argues, 'as a negatively marked absence, is all the more problematic [to psychologists and psychoanalysts] because it deviates from the Eurocentric psychosocial norm of voice. The absence of voice is understood as signaling psychopathologised processes of avoidance and repression, socially-suspect processes of personal secrecy, or collective processes of political subjugation'. Similarly, Priscilla Hayner (1996: 176), author of *Unspeakable Truths: Transitional Justice and the Challenge of Truth Commissions*, questions whether a 'right to the truth' should be turned into an unbending obligation. Based on a Mozambique case study, she suggests that 'for a number of reasons, victims sometimes show no interest in focusing on their past suffering'. In other words, the human rights–sponsored 'facing the past' agenda not only reduces all pasts to a singular remembrance framework while psychologising memorialisation discourses and practices with therapeutic constructs of 'healing', 'health' and 'illness', but also disables other cultural recourses to provide a meaning-making process of the past.

The Victim-Centred Agenda: What's Wrong with That?

Standardisation of memory may actually be harmful. The schematic conceptualisation of past human rights abuses, based on simplified and purified categories of victims/perpetrators/bystanders, creates a universal pattern as the only framework through which memorialisation should take place. While most scholars agree that those are social categories, and these roles are complex and often not clear-cut, the victim/perpetrator/bystander triangle has become the ultimate prism through which human rights ideology conceptualises memorialisation processes in the aftermath of (and during) massive abuses of human rights. This, again, has to do with the fact that most psychological research on genocide and its aftermath addresses these distinct social roles, shaping them as real things in the world, not as constructs (Vollhardt and Bilewicz 2013).

Every remembrance always assumes a particular memory-frame of recollection. The importance of critical reflection on the framing of memory cannot be overstated, as it reveals an investigation's guiding assumptions (Kobalek 2016: 177). It is precisely this memory-frame that serves as a setting in which the specific content of a memory may be situated and, when situated in a certain way, is imposed through the normative schemes of standardisation of memory.

If so, what is the memory-frame that the human rights memorialisation agenda imposes? As all practices and discourses included in the moral remembrance corpus are crafted through the prism of universalism, standardisation of memory requires a shift from concrete memories to the abstract remembrance of barbarous acts (David 2015a). This, however, always occurs at the expense of complexities and moral ambiguities. It means that, to apply certain memorialisation standards, one has to erase complexities from categories of victim/perpetrator/bystander and keep them purified and normative. In 1985, the United Nations General Assembly[55] adopted the following definition of victims: 'victims are persons who individually or collectively suffered harm, including physical or mental injury, emotional suffering, economic loss or substantial impairment of their fundamental rights, through acts or omissions that constitute gross violations of international human rights law, or serious violations of international humanitarian law'. Such a definition reflects the humanistic universalism of the victim as an embodiment of pure humanity. It is particularly this great achievement of human rights activists, putting the spotlight on victims, that has, unfortunately, ascribed moral virtues and glory to victims, turning them into new heroes.

Even participants in the face-to-face groups pointed out that, in mixed seminar groups, the narratives of victims can cause discomfort for other participants because it leaves them with the impression that victims claim some form of moral superiority, and this blocks the flow of

---

[55] The Declaration of Basic Principles of Justice for Victims of Crime and Abuse.

communication (Fischer and Petrović-Ziemer 2013: 68). The legitimising stamp of human rights, in giving justice to the innocent victims, has also reduced victims to a simplified logic: if I am a victim, I cannot be responsible for anything, and no one can argue with me because it would be showing a lack of respect for a victim (Franović 2008: 5). Hence, this position of victimhood, which was (and still is) used to recruit nationalist sentiment, became the ultimate position that both individuals and nations aspire to achieve. Tzveran Todorov (2003: 143) describes this succinctly: 'What pleasure is to be found in being a victim? None; but if no one wants to be a victim, everyone wants to have been one ... having been a victim gives you the right to complain, protest, and make demands ... your privileges are permanent.'

This tendency to universalise victims as a special kind of people serves the human rights agenda in depoliticising victims and defining them as ahistorical, universal humanitarian subjects. Liisa Malkki (1996: 378) similarly analysed the issues of purification and classification of phenomena regarding the category of refugees, showing that civil society and agencies of the international community often depoliticise the category of refugee, portraying refugees as 'pure victims' rather than specific persons. The same logic is applied in standardisation of memory, where the vast differences and idiosyncrasies present in any victim community are forgotten, and it is generally assumed that all who were affected by the same kind of violations constitute a homogenous group that has identical needs, motives and aspirations. This universalist, purified and ahistorical logic thus ignores the specific histories, political and economic conditions, and contexts of individual victims. However, *victim* as a categorical order has an impact on the historical transformation of social and political identities.

In human rights discourses, victims and perpetrators are usually referred to as two completely separate and homogenous sets of people. In reality, not all victims are the same, nor are all perpetrators the same, and some victims are also perpetrators (Borer 2003). For example, in Croatia, the war veterans have been homogenised and placed under the patronage of their national leadership; in contrast, in Serbia, where the veteran population that participated in the wars of the 1990s is estimated at approximately 15 percent of Serbia's male population (Baera, Miljanović and Popov 2004: 47), that is not the case. While the human rights sector silently kept promoting the vision of Serbian war veterans as a homogenised group of 'Milošević's people', the diversity among the veteran groups is actually enormous. However, instead of engaging with those groups in which different positioning means, first and foremost, a different veteran perception of what transpired in the wars of the 1990s, human rights organisations either widely ignored them or tried to mobilise veterans under a particular key – as perpetrators who are deserving of their support only when they are willing to be publicly transformed into peacebuilders.

As discussed previously, several projects organised by the CNA in Sarajevo and Belgrade brought veterans from all sides together, with the participants allegedly showing 'great motivation to meet people from the other side they fought against' (Franović 2008: 44). This is misleading, as the number of those willing to participate in such projects was extremely small.[56] However, even those who participated were conditioned by the situational setting. Within the CNA project, which was aimed at bringing war veterans from different ethnic sides together, their participation was framed through performative and transformative sentiments of moral regret. To frame it in Collins's terms, to fit the human rights memorialisation agenda, the participants were pushed into deducting the complexities of their positioning, which consequently reduced their profit in emotional energy. Thus, even in Serbia, where the war veterans were fragmentised and marginalised, the vast majority of them realised that obtaining state recognition was far more beneficial than any human rights framework (David 2015b).

In fact, this schematic and reductionist labelling of victims as pure and deserving, of perpetrators as brutal and cunning, and of bystanders as morally obliged to intervene (a position often hijacked by human rights institutions) is generally present in all human rights organisations that deal with past legacies. For example, the most important initiative in the Western Balkans – the Regional Commission for Establishing the Facts about War Crimes and Other Gross Violations of Human Rights Committed on the Territory of the Former Yugoslavia (RECOM) – originally aimed to include families of victims, prisoners and veterans. Ultimately, though, it ended up almost entirely excluding all veterans groups,[57] as victims' groups were unwilling to include them and acknowledge more complex and ambivalent representations of a contested past (Kurze and Vukušić 2013).

Such a victim-centred approach also erroneously shifts our attention to remembering victims because of what has happened to them, rather than because of who they were. This partially forced homogenisation, according to the human rights memorialisation key, is also apparent within the victim category, where different victim groups need to frame

---

[56] All war veterans I interviewed during 2019–2012 refused the very idea of participating in such events.
[57] Six veteran groups and more than one hundred victim organizations.

and unify their voices to fit the purified category of innocent and apolitical victim. Although the human rights memorialisation agenda speaks loudly of the need to place violations into context, this context is applied in a predetermined pattern that draws clear lines between the opposing categories of victims/perpetrators/bystanders. Once this categorical division, based on the nominal human rights rejection of the hierarchy of victims, is applied, precisely the absence of the hierarchy is what de-contextualises and de-historicises the actual deeds of past injustice (Levy and Sznaider 2010: 131). For the vast number of associations of families of victims, ex-detainees in concentration camps, victims of sexual abuse, and refugees across the region – where all victims are allegedly encouraged to speak up – 'this categorical framework forces them to adapt their stories and to actually filter and de-contextualize certain memory contents' (David 2015a: 103) to fit the situational context and obtain recognition.

The ongoing competition of suffering across the region, enabled through hidden economies of victimhood, and promoted and legitimised simultaneously by human rights and nationalist ideologies, creates a polarised context in which it is difficult for people in the victim category to be approached as distinct historical actors. This testifies to the reality that the pre-constellation of victim–perpetrator, in which morality is understood in semiotic binary terms, allows group participants to gain their emotional energy both by identifying themselves as sacred and by polluting others as profane (Alexander 2014: 307). Such a framing of past human rights violations, constructed from the moral position of the bystander as a party who has a moral obligation to intervene and possibly set things right, further promotes societal division across binary categories of victims and perpetrators, neglecting temporal and spatial dimensions and bleaching all grey areas to fit the opposed categories. For example, rape victims in Bosnia need to frame their stories in a particular way to keep the image of the ideal-type victims and gain acknowledgement and (mostly symbolic) benefits. They are forced to live their lives backwards, with a feeling that their validity rests on their victimhood, and are strongly discouraged from sharing happy moments of their lives.[58]

Even within those societal pockets, such as victim groups, that were probably the biggest 'consumers' of the human rights agenda through the

---

[58] In a conversation with Dr Nena Močnik, who worked for several years with rape victims, this reduction of their value as victims is evident. She told me a story of a rape victim who, fifteen years after she was raped repeatedly by Serbian soldiers, was finally getting married. However, she was not willing to talk about her marriage outside her inner circle because she said she needed to maintain her status as a victim.

funding schemes, international volunteers and other human rights efforts, it seems as if they do not internalise human rights values. Interestingly, as documented in post-war Bosnia, 'there is also a lack of acknowledgment of the suffering of the members of the other associations, having a competition about who is the greater victim' (Franović 2008: 42). Furthermore, victim groups from different sides, while all subscribing to the same victim-centred 'facing the past' principles, often act to prevent other groups from reaching their goals. In practice, this means that the adoption and promotion of a moral remembrance framework bring justice for some victims but render many other victim groups invisible, reducing human rights values to nationalist sentiment. It sets the stage for a competition not only for nominal recognition and particular rights, but also for the supremacy to determine who gets to be perceived as an ultimate victim, creating competing hierarchies of suffering (David 2017a) instead of global communities of solidarity.

However, besides silently promoting the politics and hierarchies of victimhood, silencing and de-politicising victims and de-contextualising the past, the biggest 'sin' of them all, in my opinion, is the generational transmission of the categorical orders of victims and perpetrators. I have already demonstrated that, in human rights–sponsored face-to-face encounters, what happens is a process of ritualisation of the historical past. Brubaker (2004) convincingly showed that no group has fixed and inherently stable properties. Nevertheless, this is precisely how those properties come together to mark clear ethnic boundaries. The encounters in groups that promote human rights memorialisation agendas always underpin the ontological security of the groups that force them to retreat to their safe, ethnically bounded identities. The ritualisation of historical narratives, in fact, may promote ethnic hostilities between the group participants, where ethnicity trumps class as the main form of social stratification, in the process 'capturing' and 'channelling' class-like sentiments towards ethno-nationalism. For example, in the Israeli–Palestinian context of face-to-face encounters, this meant that the groups' ethnic categories just gained additional value, adding to ethnically centred feelings of morality. Interestingly, though starting as allegedly apolitical human rights–oriented encounter groups, the dialogues soon became catalysts of ethnically bound competing histories: for the Jews, it cemented their existence in the Holocaust experience; for the Palestinians, the centrality of the Holocaust legacy served as an antidote for their prolonged experience of Nakba, a fundamental issue in their seven-decades-long conflict. The process of appropriating the Holocaust memory, which travels through generations and becomes internalised even among Jewish participants whose families moved to

Israel from places that never experienced the Holocaust (such as Iraq, Iran, Yemen and elsewhere), sets the stage for the Palestinian students' attempts to constitute themselves into a 'community of suffering' (Helman 2002) along temporal and spatial lines.

The generational transmission of the simplified and purified categories of victim and perpetrator is a direct result of the human rights moral remembrance framework. For example, members of the third generation of Hutu in Belgium are still marked as perpetrators even though many of them have never even been in Rwanda. Not just the descendants of Holocaust survivors are still regarded as victims: practically all Jews, regardless of their geography or age, are regarded and treated as victims. Moral remembrance assumes German or French twenty-year-old youngsters (recruited for RYCO and dozens of other 'facing the past' projects regularly organised across Europe) should encapsulate the guilt and responsibility of their nations, or retrospective victimhood, on behalf of their national/ethnic identities. Hence, from the very start, it was not 'people' who came to embrace differences among group members, but rather Jews, Palestinians, Serbs, Croats, Bosniaks and other participants who came to establish clear ethnic boundaries through the narration of their collective histories.

This is the core logic embedded in human rights–sponsored moral remembrance. In other words, even in this categorical key of ethnicity, group members did not come to think of the opposite group much differently just because they presumably met a nice person belonging to that group. Contrary to human rights presumption, instead of humanising the group as a whole, the micro-solidarity formed in face-to-face encounters enabled the further ethnicisation of each party and the forming of 'essentialist identities' (Bashir and Goldberg 2014), making ethnicity, based on constructed shared histories and competing victimhood, a focal point of reference. It is the schematic conceptualisation and purity of the categories that actually disables moving beyond the contested past, transmitting the legacies of the past far into the future. Such a classificatory system perpetuates a fixed status based on purified and simplified categories of victim/perpetrator/bystander. Not only are those fixed categories being transmitted through generations, but they also inevitably bind individuals to their ethnic and religious ethnicities.

This logic is truly troubling because it reinforces the importance of ethnic and national boundaries. The starting point is the perception of selfhood in terms of Serb/Croat/Bosniak/German/Palestinian, rather than 'I, as a human being'. If there was a consistency and purity in the logic of human rights, the rational definition of selfhood should comprise (and not just nominally) 'I, as a human being'. Humans should care what happens to humans. When Serbs care for Croats or Bosniaks, or Jews for Palestinians, and vice versa, that is not proof of a triumph for human right values: it is instead a victory of essentialist, narrow, national identities.

The 'Duty to Remember' Agenda: What's Wrong with That?

Finally, the false logic of the necessity of 'facing the past', which shifted an awareness-oriented 'duty to remember' as a promoter of public debate on contested pasts to a policy-oriented 'proper way of remembrance', was meant to prevent a recurrence of violence. Forgetting is seen as a pathology, as the biggest enemy that is, true to say, often employed by nation-states to erase contested elements of their past. According to the human rights memorialisation agenda, the only way not to slip back into the abyss of violence is to remember the past.

Significant proof showing, unambiguously, that once the past has been faced and remembered, the result will be 'the non-recurrence of violence' and the adoption of human rights values, is, however, lacking. There are at least two separate problems with this assumption. First, it would need to be tested. But what is an appropriate time frame for such a test? Ten years? A generation? A century? Further, not only are memory constructions long-term processes, but remembrance is also always dynamic, in flux and changing. Second, once conflict emerges, it is hardly possible to isolate processes of facing the past from wider geo-political, economic and societal contexts to test their relationship with the outbreak of conflict. Simply put, the notion of facing the past for the sake of the non-recurrence of violence is just a wishful ideological construct based on false premises.[59]

Even so, this remains one of the major pillars of human rights memorialisation efforts across the globe. The shift to policy-oriented 'proper ways of remembering' (David 2017a) is often translated into pushing states to remember atrocities they committed in the past. Through different types of pressures, and with different degrees of success, international human rights bodies (such as the European Parliament, the Human Rights Committee in the United Nations, Amnesty International, Human Rights Watch and many others), try to dictate the content of a 'proper memory'. As explained in Chapters 3, 4 and 5, the human rights memorialisation agenda frames what should be remembered and how, and it is pushed, through various memorialisation policies, resolutions and decrees.[60]

---

[59] The example often used to justify this logic is post–World War II Germany. However, Germany is rather different from most of other places in conflict because it suffered a total defeat. In most of the conflicts, that is not the case.

[60] Chapter 3 provides more information on memorialization policies.

This, policy-oriented pressure to engage in moral remembrance leads to two deeply entwined reactions on the ground. First, and contrary to what is expected, it does not bring justice to the victims, but rather deepens feelings of injustice. Even the Srebrenica resolution did not bring justice to the survivors of the genocide because it was instantly hijacked by the Bosniak political and religious leadership. By raising the Srebrenica event to the level of national Bosniak suffering, the needs and multiple feelings of the survivors are put aside and effectively silenced. It also instantly deepens the feelings of marginalisation of other Bosniak victims across Bosnia who become 'the second-best' victims, leaving practically very little or no space for Serbian or Croatian victims, for example (David 2017b). Moreover, it brings to the fore old historical injustices – first and foremost, that of Jasenovac concentration camp and the lack of recognition for Serbian suffering. Similar effects are also produced by policing and the enforcement of the Holocaust memory. Holocaust remembrance, as managed through the International Holocaust Remembrance Alliance (IHRA), operates as a technocratic-like manual for a proper way to remember the Holocaust. In the Israeli–Palestinian context, where the experience of Palestinians has been overshadowed by the Holocaust remembrance, it results in strong feelings of resentment and injustice. And again, while the Holocaust memory is synonymous with the State of Israel, many of the Holocaust survivors live in disturbing poverty, marginalised and largely forgotten.

The second, related, problem with the obligation to remember is that it is widely presented as an oppressive external force, which often reads as a new colonialism. One Serbian interviewee summarised this perception, saying that many people were facing strong international pressure and have the feeling 'that they are held collectively responsible for what has happened … and then there is a reaction that people do not want to acknowledge' (Yerkes 2004). This 'remembrance by proxy', contrary to expectations, provides legitimacy to the rise of nationalist sentiments, where these sentiments become viewed as an oppressed, authentic, autochthonic truth that is under attack. In the attempt to force remembrance so as to prevent future violence, human rights ideology comes to a dead-end street, putting human helplessness on display as a means to come to terms with its own messy politics. In fact, with its organisational and ideological power in place to establish a global human rights memorialisation regime, human rights ideology acts as a destabilising force that further strengthens nationalist sentiment, potentially adding fuel to the very same nationalist fires that it is supposed to extinguish.

Conclusion

In this chapter, I have tried to demonstrate that the human rights understanding of memorialisation processes is not capable of translating solidarities produced in small-group encounters into large-scale human rights values. Not only can moral remembrance not compete with nationalist infrastructures that are in place, but the three core pillar principles of moral remembrance – facing the past; justice for victims and duty to remember – actually generate and legitimise national sentiments and produce new inequalities on the ground. In the end, we find that implementation of the human rights memorialisation agenda rarely (and only sporadically) leads to the actual adoption of the values of human rights.

7 Mandating Memory, Mandating Conflicts

Introduction

The impact of the human rights memorialisation agenda is enormous and far-reaching. Many groups that suffered injustice and mass human rights violations became visible, first and foremost, as victim groups. This is, in a way, the real triumph of human rights. However, while the majority of the current research focuses on those successes, we can only truly appreciate the impact of the human rights memorialisation agenda if we also take a closer look at the 'side effects' that arise as an outcome of such an agenda. I wish to address here three aspects of the worldwide implementation of moral remembrance that are often ignored and obfuscated. First, when and how does the human rights memorialisation agenda translate into nationalistic sentiments? Second, what inequalities are produced as a result of the human rights memorialisation agenda? Finally, do people and communities, whose suffering is disclosed and framed in terms of the human rights' vision of morality, become true believers in human rights?

I do not suggest that 'we' as collectives would be better off if 'we' forget past human rights violations, as claimed by David Rieff (2017) in his recent book *In Praise of Forgetting*. Framing this question in terms of 'we' as ethnically or nationally bound collectives just reinforces categorical divisions based on selective categorical orders that human rights wanted to extinguish in the first place. At least nominally, the human rights agenda aspires to offer a different, category-free understanding of collectiveness, pushing for solidarities that are not based on those ossified and historically constructed categories of ethnicity and nationhood. Furthermore, both remembering and forgetting are active processes that cannot be fully controlled. Rather, they are products of structures and agency that are already in place.

However, as argued throughout this book, to understand how effective human rights are in re-shaping human beliefs and behaviours, it is highly beneficial to understand and analyse human rights as an ideology. Once we comprehend how its organisational and ideological power becomes a normative force globally (but unevenly), we can understand how local communities shape feelings of micro-solidarity and group attachment. Do people accept and adjust to human rights values? Do those values push them into a human rights–based moral action and if so, how? In other words, does human rights remain only a poster ideology, with a selective impact on governments, or do those values truly penetrate beyond into small societal pockets that can bring change from the bottom up?

Moral Remembrance and Nationalism

To be clear, the human rights memorialisation agenda always lands on particular historical settings. Hence, the way in which it will be accepted, rejected (fully or partially) or modified inevitably depends on the already deeply developed and rooted relationship that exists with certain segments of the national past, as well as current political realities. Human rights, with the centre of their power in the world polity, are always unavoidably filtered through the needs of a state. This means that, in practice, states will welcome some rights but reject other rights, perceiving those as damaging to their own interests. To complicate this issue even further, the power of moral remembrance, as a concrete set of practices and discourses forced upon states, is dispersed and divided into numerous bodies, committees and institutions. Hence, it is often perceived by states as having a certain degree of ambiguity. This tension between the external powers and state interests often results in the only smallest common denominator being accepted with regard to the adoption of human rights.

The human rights memorialisation agenda is, in that sense, particularly subject to potential clashes. The believed truth regarding the past, sponsored by the state, often exhibits sharp dissonance with the truth mandated in the name of human rights. The clash here is obvious, expected and well documented. We are well aware of the 'paradox of empty promises' wherein governments often adopt human rights norms of behaviours as a matter of window dressing, radically decoupling policy from practice and, at times, exacerbating negative human rights practices (Hafner-Burton and Tsutsui 2005). In regard to the human rights memorialisation agenda, governments, if not conditioned otherwise, are likely to ignore it. Big powers, such as United States and even the EU,[1] will not

---

[1] For example, there is an ongoing fierce debate between the ICC and some African countries that rightly asks why, to date, all of the cases dealt with by the ICC involve only Africans, especially in a world awash with impunity in Iraqi, Afghanistan, Colombia, Palestine, Israel and elsewhere. Indeed, the selective action suggests that the African countries are being strategically targeted.

adhere – to the same degree – to the standards they themselves set. Yet again, through their power positions in international bodies, they will push for other, weaker states to comply with the human rights memorialisation agenda as a means of pacifying and even policing those entities.

That is, of course, not new. When it comes to human rights, Hopgood (2013: 14) rightly argued that 'there is a clear double standard at work' that needs to be acknowledged and addressed. There is an ongoing criticism of human rights in general, which argues that the West, via human rights, is seeking to impose its categories onto the rest of the world. David Kennedy (2002: 21) noted that the human rights movement was launched in the 1970s and early 1980s 'just as the pendulum swung for a generation toward Thatcher, Reagan and the politics of neoliberalism'. Kennedy (2012) gave probably the most elaborate critique of human rights, sharply pointing to the failures in its logic and structure. Immanuel Wallerstein (2004), who conceptualised a 'world-system' based on US hegemony, regards human rights as part of an ideology which obfuscates underlying capitalist economic relationships shaped by colonialism. This line of thinking is followed by other 'radical' thinkers such as Chomsky, Herman, Peterson and Žižek. Human rights are understood as politics as in the 'political economy of human rights' (Herman and Peterson 2010), a conspiracy-like theory in which powerful states – first and foremost the United States – use human rights ideology for personal gain (Goodale 2006). Žižek (2005) goes even further in his criticism, stating that human rights often provide an alibi for militarist interventions, sacralisation for the tyranny of the market and an ideological foundation for the fundamentalism of the politically correct.

Different states have different strategies, to the extent they are willing to be supportive of human rights in general and the human rights memorialisation agenda in particular. States with contested pasts are less likely to willingly embrace the human rights memorialisation agenda. As Gordy (2013) rightly pointed out, it should come as no surprise that, generally speaking, confrontations with uncomfortable facts about the past do not happen in such societies, or happen only after an extended period of time. However, states are often forced to comply with the standards as part of their attempt to improve their status in the international arena. This, again, is a mere reflection of the tension between the importance of narrating their histories for the domestic electorate and these states' impression management for the international audience.

States deal with the contested elements of their national past in a great variety of ways. First, a society may prove its moral righteousness by publicly addressing the past (Levy and Sznaider 2002; Olick 2007) and may even exploit its culpability through war tourism (Tunbridge and

Ashworth 1996). Second, various memory agents may produce multivocal and fragmented spaces and commemorations which are constructed in a way that allows for multiple readings (Vinitzky-Seroussi 2002; Wagner-Pacifici and Schwartz 1991). Finally, for numerous reasons, some nation-states may put significant effort into concealing and obfuscating contested elements of the past (Aguilar 1999; David 2014a; Giesen 2004; Rivera 2008). How states choose to address human rights mass violations, committed in their name, is always subject to both internal and international affairs. It also reflects the amount of pressure they face from the international community. Hence, weak and post-conflict states, which are largely dependent on international funding to rehabilitate their sovereignties, are most likely to be in a position to nominally present alterations in the ways they treat their past to satisfy the international community (which is also a key donor stakeholder). However, at the local level, those alterations are often tailored in such way so as to reinforce their own narrow nationalist narratives.

Here, I want to point out that the external mandating of memory often produces a backlash and, contrary to the expected outcome, reinforces nationalist infrastructures. While significant research has been dedicated to how governments worldwide instrumentalise those processes and what the damaging effects on the transformative process of 'facing the past' are, little has been said about how such instrumentalisation gives rise to what is widely known as 'new nationalism'. As shown in previous chapters, governments often nominally adopt, and even sponsor, the human rights memorialisation agenda, including a vast variety of isomorphic practices and processes based on the human rights agenda of 'duty to remember', 'facing the past' and 'justice for the victims'. They proclaim their commitment to those goals, introduce human rights in their history books, open museums dedicated to the better appreciation of human rights, officially prescribe Holocaust education and remembrance, perform public apologies, sponsor 'facing the past' dialogue groups and even erect inclusive monuments that are for all of the victims. Three of those distinctive human rights memorialisation attempts are briefly discussed here to establish the logic through which nationalist infrastructures and sentiments become reinforced by attempts to mandate memory in the name of human rights: Holocaust education, public apologies, and memorialisation laws.

Holocaust Remembrance as a Transformational Remedy for Human Rights Values

Educational projects that redirect attention from narrow nationalist interpretations of the past to a wide, universal understanding of mass human rights abuses are the bedrock of the transformative human rights memorialisation agenda. The best example of this strategy involves Holocaust remembrance. Over the past three decades, Holocaust remembrance, as one of the key templates within the human rights/moral remembrance toolkit, has become enforced through various mechanisms and has been globally accepted as an important measurement for the appreciation of human rights. In the European context in particular, the 'Europeanisation of the Holocaust' process was meant to serve as a glue to unify the European past. Vast research has been conducted on the ways in which different countries adopted, adjusted and modified the Holocaust remembrance to serve their own political agendas. The results are disturbing, yet largely ignored. For the countries joining the EU, Holocaust remembrance was understood as a necessary toll paid to join the European free market and enjoy the delights of democracy (Russou 2007). With different strategic approaches in place, governments nominally adopted and included Holocaust education and remembrance in their official agendas (to various degrees), yet the Holocaust is always read though their national struggles and utilised and conceptualised in new idiosyncrasies with a view towards framing their nationalist histories in a particular way.

In places in which states perceive their participation in World War II through victimhood terms, with strong feelings of being victims themselves, such as in Serbia or Poland, the adoption and inclusion of the Holocaust remembrance serves to (1) homogenise narratives of victimhood, while ignoring their own culpability (Milerski 2010; Subotić 2019), and (2) act as a background for equating their own suffering with that of the Jews (David 2013). For the states that had a major role in contributing to the Nazi occupation – such as Croatia's Ustashe regime, which systematically killed thousands of Jews and Serbs, or Marshall Ion Antonescu's decision to cleanse Romania of all Jews (Misco 2008) – the Holocaust has been used to reduce and minimise their own culpability. In Serbia's history textbooks, this has led to an inflation of the number of victims. In contrast, in Croatia's history textbooks, the Jasenovac concentration camp – in which an estimated 100,000 Serbs, Jews and Roma were executed by the Ustashe regime – is mentioned only in passing, with the texts re-labelling it as a 'labour camp' and focusing on how Croat anti-fascists lost their lives (Pavasović-Trošt 2013). In Ukraine, just as in Serbia, the Holocaust is used as a template for understanding genocide (Carrier, Fuchs and Messinger 2015) and has been applied to the Soviet-imposed 1932–1933 famine in the Ukraine, known as the Holodomor, making the Ukrainians the central victims (Dietsch 2012).

Within Eastern Europe, societies have generally strived to release their conceptions of the past from the burden of the officially mandated Soviet interpretations of World War II (Malksoo 2009: 658), in which the Holocaust was never understood as their prime 'issue'. For example, in the current self-reflections in Estonia, Latvia, Lithuania and Poland, one can see that the intensity of the presence of the past six decades reverberates with archetypical outbursts of suppressed memories, a delayed affirmation of the 'right to memory'. During the Soviet occupation, these countries' educational systems rarely addressed the topic of the Holocaust. Once liberated from the Soviet regime, however, they all had to re-examine the monochromatic Communist interpretation of the past while pushing the Holocaust further to the margins. Such processes of reformulation of the past are linked to problems of restitution, political rehabilitation, legal problems relating to Communist party assets, the role of the former *nomenklatura* as privatisation proceeds and the treatment of former Communist functionaries and state security services (Welsh 1996). All post-Communist countries, whether already accepted or still waiting to become EU members, have had to face ignorance and non-recognition by the core EU countries, in which their historical memories were largely overlooked (David 2014c). The post-war realities in Eastern Europe have generally been concealed in the Western public's consciousness and have been marginalised; hence the pressures to implement Holocaust education was met with animosity and resistance.

However, while East European countries that have already joined the EU have tried to expand their memory agendas by moving away from the Holocaust memory (Russou 2007), nation-states still waiting (or hoping) to enter the EU, such as Serbia, Bosnia and Macedonia, and until recently, Croatia, have promoted Holocaust discourse (with different degrees of success) as a precious signifier of their moral boundaries. This is important since Holocaust memory has become globally understood as 'a unit of measurement' (Levy and Sznaider 2002) in relation to the human rights regime. This dual use of the Holocaust to reduce pressure at both the domestic and international levels is possible since, as cosmopolitanised memory, it is simultaneously constitutive of a European outlook and of a more nationalistic perspective (Levy and Sznaider 2010). Regardless of the difference in these countries' national histories, Holocaust remembrance regularly functions as a model, paradigm or measure for representing other atrocities in accordance with one of several processes.

The demand to present and shape local histories through the lens of the Holocaust requires, to a certain extent, marginalising local narratives of victimhood and bravery, and has been perceived by many as an attack on national sovereignty and integrity. Even when the Holocaust, which is perceived to be a legacy for all parties involved in World War II, becomes adopted in a top-down manner, it lands on nationalist infrastructures that are already in place. Once again, it is the power relations between these structures and the hierarchies of 'otherness' that clearly dictate the supremacy of memory contents, which in turn just serve to cement narrow nationalist perceptions on the ground. Hence, at the local level, the Holocaust becomes a template for reproducing and reinforcing nationalist narratives. Once the Holocaust is domesticated and glocalised, it is put back in the service of the state. The outcome is that, at the top-down level, ethnic nationalism is reinforced and strengthened rather than dissolved, while at the bottom-up level, a multitude of contradictory and competing narratives are created, which are preserved and held on the side-lines, waiting to burst out (David 2014b). Consequently, the big hope of transforming national realities into human rights values actually strengthens nationalist narratives that are perceived as being under attack. This is important because the hijacking of the language of human rights for nationalist purposes is not, by any means, evident only in what we understand as weak democracies. In fact, even countries that have strong democracies and protections for human rights – such as Austria (Bastel, Matzka and Miklas 2010), Germany (Ozyurek 2018) and South Korea (Carranza Ko 2018) – often tailor their approaches to past human rights abuses in such a way so as to nominally condemn them while at the same time relativising them, thereby reducing the culpability of the state and the nation.

To substantiate my claim that moral remembrance enforces nationalist sentiment, it is necessary to move beyond the Holocaust remembrance, which, through history textbooks, the erection of monuments, museums of solidarity and tolerance, and other practices, is used as window dressing for putting human (in particular, minority) rights on display.

Public Apologies as a Psychological Remedy for Human Rights Values

We have witnessed an avalanche of collective apologies – an apology from one community to another for historical wrongdoings (Edwards 2010) – over recent decades. For example, American presidents Ronald Reagan and George H. W. Bush apologised to Japanese Americans for their internment during World War II. In 1997, British Prime Minister Tony Blair spoke of the British government's remorse in not doing enough to help the Irish during the potato famine (Marrus 2007). Danish Prime Minister Poul Nyrum Rasmussen offered an apology for the forced relocation of Inuit people in 1953. Palestinian leader Mahmoud Abbas issued an apology to the Kuwaitis for Palestinian support for former Iraqi dictator Saddam Hussein's invasion during the 1990–1991 Gulf War. In 1996, Frederik Willem de Klerk, the last South African leader of the apartheid era, went before the country's Truth and Reconciliation Commission to apologise for forty-six years of oppression, saying the racist policy was 'deeply mistaken'. The Prime Minister of Australia, Kevin Rudd, speaking before Parliament in 2008, apologised for policies that have inflicted profound grief, suffering and loss on fellow Australians. In 2010, British Prime Minister David Cameron apologised for the 'Bloody Sunday' massacre, saying it was unjustified and unjustifiable. The German government issued an apology for the colonial-era massacre by German soldiers of tens of thousands of ethnic Herero people in Namibia.

Israeli President Reuven Rivlin, at a memorial ceremony to mark the fifty-eighth anniversary of the Kfar Kassem massacre, condemned this 'terrible crime'. Serbian President Boris Tadic broadcast an apology to the Croatian people in 2007 during an interview with Croatian television; in 2010, he also issued an apology for the crimes Serbs committed in Vukovar in 1991. His Croatian counterpart Ivo Josipovic laid a wreath at the graveyard of eighteen Serbs killed by Croats in 1991 in the village of Paulin Dvor, saying that 'those victims deserve our apology'.

In 2008, both the Canadian and Australian prime ministers apologised to their indigenous populations for the forced removal of children from their families. In 2018, the Norwegian government apologised for the mistreatment of those known as the 'German girls'. Other examples of these collective apologies include those made by political leaders from Japan (Cunningham 2004), Australia (Power 2000) and Belgium (Barkan and Karn 2006).

The success of these (and many other) apologies is questionable. Those who support government redress for historical harm argue that it is a moral imperative (Thompson 2008) and fulfils important psychological goals in coming to terms with the past.

Often, the public apologies are perceived as not expressing 'real' remorse. They are frequently orchestrated to avoid litigation that might result from an admission of guilt or responsibility. The federal apology for slavery finalised by Barack Obama's government, on 29 July 2009, explicitly said the writ could not be used as a legal rationale for reparations. The expression 'mistakes were made' is commonly used as a rhetorical device within apology speeches, whereby a speaker acknowledges a situation was handled poorly or inappropriately but seeks to evade any direct admission or accusation of responsibility by using the passive voice, avoiding any possibility of the apology being used as evidence of liability.

Transitional justice scholars, aligned with the normative logic of moral remembrance, stress that acknowledgement, accountability, non-recurrence, financial compensation and access to support services are essential to the process of the alleged societal 'healing'. Broadly speaking, public apologies can offer a sense of validation and vindication to victims/survivors, as their suffering becomes formally and finally acknowledged. The research team at Queen's University Belfast[2] identified five features of meaningful public apologies: acknowledgement of the wrong; acceptance of responsibility; expression of regret; assurance of non-repetition; and an offer of repair or corrective action. They suggested that, for the apology to be taken seriously, the offender (or a representative of the institutions that committed the offence) must address the public in a timely manner, have a performative ability to express sincere emotions and be ready to offer meaningful repair (in terms of changing a legal system, offering a resignation and/or providing institutional support and reparations). However, such an approach, where contextual knowledge is transformed into a policy-oriented schematic blueprint, poses the danger of becoming a damage control manual for the offending party, which could be easily manipulated and used to better impression management. Opponents of public apologies address a number of dangers that come with redress, saying that (1) it is illogical to apologise for the actions of others, (2) it is unfair to ask current generations to pay compensation for injustices they did not commit and (3) members of the previously victimised group regard the offer as inadequate (Blatz, Day and Schryer 2014).

However, going beyond these important insights into the problematic nature of public apologies, the impact of such instrumentalisation should be evaluated in relation to not only the victims' groups that are primary recipients of those expressions of regret, but also the people in whose name such apologies are being issued. For that matter, public apologies issued to address historical injustice claims are like no other public apologies, and they differ significantly from apologies for institutional abuse such as child abuse or sexual misconduct. Public apologies that are delivered in the name of an entire ethnic/religious group or nation, by placing responsibility on all group members, make the group boundaries more significant and clearer. Public apologies issued in the name of the entire nation or ethnic group may produce a wide range of emotions and create instant new solidarities on the ground. Some may see it as a moral and righteous act, or as an irrelevant political manoeuvre; others may be

---

[2] See more on the project website: Apologies, Abuses and Dealing with The Past: A Socio-Legal Analysis, https://pure.qub.ac.uk/portal/en/projects/apologies-abuses-and-dealing-with-the-past-a-sociolegal-analysis(2f76e9d0-dbbd-4c5c-80f8-1726c20a5bff).html

puzzled and aggravated, asking why they should apologise for something they didn't do; and still others may be enraged, perceiving such apologies as a negation of their own cultural and national narration of history. Often, the people in whose name regrets are expressed find this measure insulting and perceive it as clashing with their own personal and culturally acquired knowledge on what has transpired in the past.

My point here is that we rarely pay sufficient attention to those groups who see such acts as a revisionist act and an attack on their own personal grievances. Those groups may re-emerge as ultimate defenders of their national narratives, in a similar fashion to that described by Bergholtz (2016) as 'sudden nationalism', when dormant attachments to national symbols and histories become awakened.

The processes through which these groups' ethnicity becomes a substitute for their identity is largely overlooked and generally underestimated. Drawing a line from Estonia to Greece, and in many other postcolonial contexts worldwide, we find an abundance of examples of peoples who, for significant periods of their history, were subordinate to empires. All of these countries fought continuously to free themselves from the imperial pressure, whether it was exerted through cultural assimilation (as in the case of Czechs and Slovenians), imperial conquest and partition (Poland), imperial conquest tout court (the Baltics and the Balkans), temporary inclusion as a second-tier ruling nation (Hungary) or any other way. Their histories are practically nothing but unending struggles for national and religious emancipation (Milanović 2017). This is crucial because their histories provide the key to why they all (or at least in large numbers) become sensitive, aggravated and even enraged by attempts (perceived or real) by external actors to shape their historical knowledge and notions of freedom.

This points exactly to the intersection of the organisational and ideological power of nationalism that comes into play. Memory projects sponsored by the state, such as commemorative practices, national calendars, history textbooks, and museums and monuments, even if they nominally adopt the human rights memorialisation agenda, filter this content in such way as to (directly or indirectly) give additional weight to the category of ethnicity and belonging, clearly marking group attachment boundaries. Whether someone apologises in your name, or when you pay your respects to the suffering of an 'other', 'you' is always addressed and treated as a limited collective of people who belong together due to their origin and their collective past. Hence, public apologies for historical wrongdoings are always an invitation to reinforce the boundaries of the national group. What gains additional weight is precisely the socially shared histories of one particular group, which consequently reinforces the significance of the nation (or ethnic group). Thus, the implementation of human rights content into state-sponsored memorialisation projects provides further organisational power to cement the category of belonging to one's nationalist sentiment. At the ideological level of nationalism, the message is the same: you belong to this group and we need to stick together.

Memorialisation Laws as a Legal Remedy to Human Rights Values

The institutionalisation of a selective memory as a means of homogenising peoples under one governmental system can be traced to the Treaty of Westphalia (1648), which was a stepping-stone in the development of modern international law. The Treaty of Westphalia obliged states to enforce amnesties and pardons for all war-time wrongdoings. The French Revolution replaced this model with 'zealous remembrance' (Belavusau 2014: 6) through its new republican calendar, which became an efficient means of structuring attachments to the state. Throughout the eighteenth century, museums were transformed into 'sites of glory and podiums of state achievements' (Belavusau 2014: 7). Museums and national calendars gradually evolved into instruments of republican citizenship and social management, engineering national unity and cultural homogeneity, along with encouraging active political participation and issuing a strong invitation to commemorate and remember the heroes and victims (Bennett 1995).

Later, in the realm of law, the Treaty of Versailles (1919) stipulated a specific 'War Guilt Clause', assigning full responsibility for all losses and damages incurred during World War I to Germany. However, only after World War II did a coupling of the accountability for human rights abuses and their remembrance emerge within the legal framework, as a means of restoring moral cosmologies within international arenas.

From that point onwards, two often contradicting sets of memorialisation laws started operating simultaneously. On the one hand, memorialisation laws in international arenas became coupled with both the Declaration of Human Rights (1948) as an ideological guidance and the Convention on the Prevention and Punishment of the Crime of Genocide (1948) as a legally binding document. On the other hand, memorialisation laws within nation-states did not cease to exist, but were further conceptualised as a means of legitimising the socio-political reality and homogenising a group within the nation-state setting (Meral 2012).

In practice, this meant that both human rights and nation-state–led memorialisation laws were vastly invested in securitisation of memory, offering different visions of the future. Securitisation of memory refers to the process in which, by means of law, certain historical remembrances are secured while others are completely delegitimised and criminalised (Malskoo 2015; Subotić 2019). All memory laws, regardless of their ideological source, became central to the politics of memory – that is, to the political means by which events are classified, commemorated or discarded in an effort to influence community values and attitudes (Malskoo 2009). Securitisation of memory by means of law is a fascinating phenomenon, as it clearly distinguishes between nationalist, as opposed to human rights, understanding of memory. Once human rights–sponsored laws and resolutions were introduced in international arenas to mark the boundaries of an imagined collective, based on an abstract notion of humanity as a whole, states responded in a very similar manner. They simultaneously adopted the laws that protect the universality of human equality, while at the same time, in their local settings, they pushed for the adoption of discriminatory laws to safeguard their narrowly understood ethnic boundaries.

Nation-state memory laws use and contextualise certain memory contents tailored in such a way as to secure national, exclusive boundaries of belonging. In contrast, human rights–sponsored memory laws are utilised to deal with difficult and violent histories and focus on two central categories: one that bans and criminalises a positive perception of an atrocious past such as genocide or mass violence, and as second that bans a negative perception of a violent past (Gutman 2016: 576). Those attitudes are also reflected in militant democracy (Belavusau 2014), referring to the prohibition of hatred exhibited through constitutionally protected rights of free expression in an effort to preserve liberal democracy. For example, in 2005, the European Union considered enacting common rules banning or restricting the use of Nazi symbols and the promotion of Nazi ideology, including Holocaust denial. Holocaust denial laws and legislation criminalising the Nazi message, which are the best-known human rights–led memory laws, are currently in place in Austria, Belgium, the Czech Republic, France, Germany, Liechtenstein, Lithuania, the Netherlands, Poland, Romania, Slovakia, Spain, Switzerland and Israel. It is important to stress that those laws are empowered by the International Covenant on Civil and Political Rights, a multilateral human rights treaty to which 160 countries are parties, and which obliges member nations to pass domestic legislation prohibiting advocacy of national, racial or religious hatred. Those memory laws have proved instrumental to the politics of coming to terms with the past (*Vergangenheitsbewältigung*) in Germany and other countries (Belavusau and Gliszczyńska-Grabias 2017: 11); as such, they are now perceived as a necessary tool of moral remembrance.

In that sense, the international community has been capitalising on a moral commitment to the past as a promise of a better future by pushing forward the development of common identity sentiments based on recognised common values, history and culture. In other words, human rights–sponsored memory laws, while establishing the moral measurements by which states become accountable for their past mass human rights violations, criminalise certain visions of the past to pacify and stabilise international relations.

However, though memory laws have become a standard practice within the human rights memorialisation rapporteur, the very same logics of morality that are used to advocate human rights values and norms have become a paravane for the very opposite view – for dictating narrow nationalist interests and their exclusivist views of their national past and for enshrining state-approved interpretations of crucial historical events. Examples of those practices are abundant: the French 'Colonialism Law' (2005), which aims to 'recognize in particular the positive role of the French presence overseas, notably in North Africa'; Russia's 'Law against the Rehabilitation of Nazi Criminals' (2014), which bans views different from the verdict of the Nuremberg Tribunal or distributing false facts about the actions of the USSR during World War II; the Israeli 'Nakba Law' (2011), which bans the commemoration of Israel's Independence Day as a day of mourning for Palestinian people (Nakba); Croatia's 'Declaration on the Homeland War' (2000), which officially prescribes the nature of the 1991–1995 war as 'just and legitimate, defensive and liberating, and neither aggressive nor conquering' and as such prevents the voice of the Serbian minority from being heard; the Turkish article that, in 2008, became 'The Turkish Penal Code', a law making it illegal to insult Turkey, the Turkish nation or Turkish government institutions; and the Polish Law (2017), which makes it a crime – punishable with up to three years in jail – to accuse the Polish nation or state 'publicly and against the facts' of being 'responsible or complicit in Nazi crimes'. All those laws, articles and resolutions reflect the various ways in which nation-states push back to retain their coercive power by safeguarding their nationalist interests. Once memory laws are consolidated and human rights discourses become perceived as a threat to nationalist attachments because they de-stabilise the power of the state, nation-state memory laws are issued and set in motion.

A phenomenon that goes hand in hand with memory laws is historical revisionism. Historical revisionism is not a novel phenomenon. On the contrary, it appears as evidence of ideological cracks in an otherwise unified public front. It aims to re-interpret historical records and is widely understood in negative terms as a distortion or denial of history for nefarious purposes. An abrupt rise of historical revisionism can be seen in the meaning of the anti-fascist struggle in Hungary, Poland, Serbia, Croatia, Italy, Ukraine and elsewhere across Europe; Germany's revisionism both after World War I and World War II; revisionism in post-Soviet spaces; Israeli revisionist histories starting from the late 1970s; Japan's historical revisionism regarding the Asia-Pacific War – the list is virtually endless. Those clashes should be understood in terms of colliding ideologies, especially in regard to the historical revisionism in post-Communist or post-colonial states. Collisions between the ideology of human rights – promoted externally – and that of nationalism – promoted internally – are often seen as attempts to re-colonialise people whose national freedom has just been regained. Hence, it is the nationalist community that comes under attack, and historical revisionism and memory laws become the means to secure the moral boundaries of a limited group of people, a nation, by safeguarding the majorities at the expense of the nation's minorities.

However, historical revisionism is a slippery concept. Not only does our knowledge need revisions to progress, but most of the crucial paradigms of recent centuries, such as feminism and historical justice movements, started as revisionist projects. Different historical revisionist movements are guided by different moral premises, and their success is defined by their ability to acquire resources and support for their struggle. Human rights ideology, with its organisational and ideological capacity, provided legitimacy for the rise of revisionist historical movements globally. Historical justice movements – such as the anti-apartheid movement, the indigenous movement in the Americas, Brazil's indigenous land rights movement, Colombia's Campesino Movement, the Zapatistas in southern Mexico, the Maya movements in Guatemala, the indigenous and peasant movements in the Andean countries (Bolivia, Peru and Ecuador), the Landless Movement in Brazil, the indigenous people's movement in Australia, and slavery and the African American quest for reparations – though all deeply embedded in local histories, were pushed forward by the power and legitimacy of moral remembrance to redress historical wrongs. Their causes are generally perceived as just; however, that status has been acquired through time, by successfully linking their agendas with the global human rights network. This achievement should not lead us to believe that the 'right causes' are guaranteed to be instantly recognised and promoted as such. Clifford Bob (2005; 2015) brilliantly demonstrated the importance of adjusting (and at times re-adjusting) one's agenda to that of human rights to achieve visibility, showing why Tibet's quest for self-determination has roused people around the world, while pushing aside and making other minorities invisible, such as Mongols, Zhuang, Yi, Hui and Uighurs, all of whom suffer similar conditions to that of the Tibetans.

Thus, the clashing notions of moralities sponsored by different ideologies result in a variety of practices and discourses. On the one hand, they often lead to a strengthening of nationalist sentiments, through the adoption of discriminatory memory laws and state-promoted historical revisionism that undermines historical facts for the sake of valorising and sacralising deeds committed in the name of the nation. On the other hand, they seemingly enable wide-network solidarities that are meant to right the wrongs of the past. However, the real (yet largely hidden) impact of those clashing systems of moralities is, in fact, the production of new social inequalities on the ground.

New Inequalities and Social Division

Evidence from around the globe shows that the normative pressures of human rights have made a difference for millions of people worldwide. From social equality issues to gender, political and cultural rights with a focus on housing, health, sex trafficking and climate change, the list of topics addressed by human rights is gargantuan, and the impact is self-evident. Over the last sixty years, human rights advocates have embodied their ideas in laws and institutions, pushing governments to improve and recognise gender rights, along with the rights of minorities and refugees, including the rights of various marginalised groups. It would be an understatement to say that human rights have changed the world in which we live. In many ways, this change has been profound, affecting, on a global scale, the conventional and normative aspects of the way we perceive, remember, make distinctions, notice and ignore things, assign meaning and construct our identities. Having said that, the impact of human rights is also troubling, pointing to the wider intersections of power and societal structures that, contrary to what is desired, contribute to the furthering of inequality, often creating new societal margins on account of identity politics.

When it comes to the human rights memorialisation agenda, the formation of new inequalities is rarely mentioned and is overwhelmingly under-researched. So far, I have shown that every state filters the human rights memorialisation agenda and includes it in its repertoire only to the point where it benefits the (re)production of nationalist ideology and the petrification of the imagined community, based on ethnicity or religion. Yet it is also necessary to further unpack the dynamics of the magic triangle – that between the groups who have suffered human rights abuses, advocates and NGOs that promote human rights, and the state apparatus.

Victim groups oscillate between slow and controversial processes of limited justice and widespread denial by their opponents in the conflict. In their constant pursuit of justice, victim groups are crucified between two opposing poles. On the one hand, their suffering is (fully or partially) recognised by human rights promoters both locally and globally. Human rights promoters target victim groups, offering them not only much needed (financial or psychological) support that is denied by the state (for all sorts of reasons), but also a framework through which the victims can frame their sufferings and their memories and consequently their rights. This recognition plays an important role in their individual and communal recovery, but it often lacks any institutional long-term support. Moreover, the 'protection' offered by human rights NGOs always comes with an expiration date. Ten to fifteen years after a conflict, their support (including human and financial resources) inevitably becomes relocated to other 'fresh' conflicts.[3] On the other hand, victims are seemingly remembered by politicians only when their support is needed to defend national identity and homogeneity or to gain political advantages (Baćirbašić 2011). In the long run, for all victim groups, state support – both financial and symbolic – is actually far more important than that of human rights actors, as it institutionalises the victims' nationwide recognition. This serves a double purpose: their own revalidation within their ethnic group and a revalidation of the nation as the most significant category of reference.

The problem is that victim groups' inclusion into and recognition within infrastructures of their own nation-states is not guaranteed and comes with great costs. The way to 'earn' recognition often proceeds through 'activism of victimhood' that 'compels the survivors to constantly reassess their victim status' (Barkan and Baćirbašić 2015: 100). The victims who carry the physical and mental scars, who remain in the moment of the atrocity even as decades pass, are often trapped in the role of victims (Langer 1996), trying constantly to navigate 'the moral truth in atrocity and the facts of the atrocity itself' (Hopgood 2013: 74). In practice, this means that, for both human rights groups and political elites, the suffering party can gain status only through the position of being the victim, a status that needs to be constantly reaffirmed.

It is precisely here, in the day-to-day politics of victimhood, that new social inequalities are produced. The process of reaffirming victim status has two direct implications. First, the need for the 'ideal-type victim' means that victim groups inevitably (and often very consciously) engage

---

[3] This period is regarded as sufficient to train and habilitate local stakeholders to further implement human rights values and norms.

in the homogenisation of their group members. Such a homogenisation process results in an unhappy side effect – an attempt to sanction any complexities or messiness that might jeopardise the group's victim position in the power struggle between two opposing camps, the human rights and nationalist-centred ideologies. Second, and even more importantly, the homogenisation and pressuring of the victim group into this framework of ideal victim means that other victim groups become understood as rivals and opponents in the struggle for scarce resources.

Victim groups are rarely interested in advancing goals that are not of benefit for their own good, even though a myriad different post-conflict groups try to achieve apparently similar goals – namely, to have their truth acknowledged (through various means). Consequently, as documented in post-war Bosnia, 'there is also a lack of acknowledgment of the suffering of the members of the other associations, having a competition about who is the greater victim' (Franović 2008: 42). Moreover, victim groups from different sides of the conflict often act to prevent these groups from reaching their goals. The management of the post-conflict order, as promoted by the human rights memorialisation agenda, 'operates through various bio-political strategies masked in the therapeutic paradigm of transitional justice' (Husanović 2015: 20). In practice, it means that the adoption and promotion of moral remembrance bring justice for some victims but render many other victim groups invisible. This sets a stage for a competition not only for nominal recognition and particular rights, but also to determine supremacy (i.e., who gets to be perceived as the ultimate victim), creating competing hierarchies of suffering (David 2017a). Such sectorial politics is often accompanied by ethnic and/or religious homogenisation. It further constructs hierarchies that immediately and inevitably translate into battles over recognition and resources.

For example, in Bosnia, such hierarchies are present in every aspect of political life. Srebrenica victims and the survivors of the cleansing/genocide are regarded both locally and internationally as the prototype for victims: their execution fits into a well-formed pattern based on the Holocaust experience, reflecting what the 'ideal-type victim' looks like. But if we zoom in on that case, we see that 200 victims executed and buried prior to the well-known genocide in Srebrenica are excluded from the major commemorative ceremony. Though subsumed into the Srebrenica victims to show Bosniak suffering on a larger scale, in practice they are left out. Other Bosniak victims throughout Bosnia-Herzegovina (BiH) are acknowledged locally – that is, mostly only by their own local communities. Croatian victims are denied by Bosniaks in the place where those two parties were in direct conflict, such as in Mostar. In places where Croats and Bosniaks fought together, such as in Odžak, Serbian victims are commemorated solely by Serbs. This immediate binding of victimhood with ethnicity translates into a zero-sum game in which one's victimhood is always understood at the expense of others. For example, all victims' associations in Republika Srpska campaigned heavily for the abolition of the Prosecutor's Office and the BiH court, effectively preventing truth-finding and justice efforts.

However, even within the same ethnic community, deeply immersed in sectarian politics of recognition, victim groups fight among themselves. The question that might seem logical to ask is why, within the same ethnic communities, those victim groups do not form a unified front to achieve their rights. I have previously discussed how nationalist infrastructures absorb human rights ideas to further promote nationalist ideologies. It is crucial here to stress that political elites, in charge of translating the human rights ideology into nationalist sentiments, rarely do that because of a deep consideration for the benefit of the members of their own national/ethnic/religious group. On the contrary, the nationalist prism simply provides a venue for mixing and merging political and economic power. In practice, this means that victim groups are 'regularly exploited by political elites to further their political and economic interests and to support corrupt practices by labelling corruption charges as a hostile act' (Barkan and Baćirbašić 2015: 105). In other words, all kinds of trade-offs occur between the political elite and victim groups, as leaders of victim groups often aim at 'privatising' the associations they represent for their own political and economic gains. While the financial burden of crucial services, such as psychological, health or legal support, is assumed by victim organisations that have succeeded in attracting human rights funding, those organisations are also well aware that, to ensure their survival, they need to gain support from their government by acting as guardians of their ethnic communities. In other words, new social inequalities are formed on the basis of a differential in access to state power, where the access to state bureaucracy is seen as a foundation for the emergence of a new social class.

Hence, the relationship between the human rights memorialisation agenda, the nationalist usage of memorialisation processes and new social inequalities needs to be viewed through the prism of economic corruption and competing authorities. Nationalist sentiments often act as a disguise for corruption, or at least economic privileges for certain groups within the political structures of the state.[4] However, apart from

---

[4] This is true for Israel, Serbia and Croatia but even more evident in the cases of Palestine and BiH.

this blatant merger of nationalism and corruption, human rights ideology contributes to the stratification of social groups. It is precisely the idea, gradually adopted into the human rights memorialisation agenda, that suffering can be, and should be, measured and translated into material means, that propels and ignites sectorial politics even further. This idea, subsumed under the slogan 'this is the least we can do' for those who suffered human rights abuses, is embedded in the International Bill of Rights as well as in the 60/147 Resolution on Basic Principles and Guidelines on the Right to a Remedy and Reparation for Victims of Gross Violations of International Human Rights Law and Serious Violations of International Humanitarian Law. It suggests that sufferings caused by mass political violence and historical injustice can be compensated through reparations. Reparations can be shaped in a variety of forms: as courts of justice, administrative compensation schemes or forms of community development and support (Roth-Arriaza 2004). Whether we speak of the 'atonement model' of reparations, which is premised on an apology and the necessity of monetary and other reparations to make that apology believable (Brooks 2004), or of the 'reparation as reconciliation' approach, which emphasises historical obligations to repair past wrongs, such as the theft of lands from indigenous people or the injustice of slavery (Thompson 2002), the argument is the same: reparations are much needed.

Reparations might sound appealing to both human rights defenders and the victim groups, but they are troubling on several grounds. Once the suffering becomes catalogised and monetarised, the battle for reparations becomes displaced from the normative, value-driven realm of human rights to the sectorial politics of the victims' and survivors' groups who compete for scarce resources. Consequently, dealing with compensation for very large numbers of victims of political violence or oppression imposes financial burdens and creates political snares in many transitional contexts where victim parties compete for limited resources. The competition crystallises the hierarchical orders between the victim groups which, in practice, results in strengthening the strong and marginalising the weakest of the weak. Ultimately, 'the monetization of the guilt', to use Zelizer's (1994_ words, replaces emotions of suffering and guilt with the monetary transaction, and the trade-off obscures the relationship between the sides, effectively translating human experience into a common signifier between the perpetrator and the victim.

The reparations transaction acts as a signifier of guilt/victimhood, but it also provides hush money intended to seal and suppress the categorical divisions of victims and perpetrators. Once the transaction is complete, it allegedly puts an end to historical injustice. Thus, it is particularly convenient for the guilty party. However, for the suffering side, though reparations may be beneficial in the short term, victims are left with the bitter feeling that their lives and the lives of their loved ones are tradeable and inexpensive. This practice also suggests that every crime and every suffering can be calculated and paid off. Further, only a narrow number of victim groups will be compensated under the reparations scheme, while many others will be left aside.

Hence, the victim groups are pushed both by human rights organisations, which pressure government, and by political elites, who try to maximise their political gain, into a sort of gladiator arena to fight each other and thereby increase their likelihood of getting any sort of recognition. In fact, moral remembrance sets the stage for the politics of opportunism, where those who are better off socially and culturally have better chances not only to gain recognition but also to improve their societal status. Inevitably, those who cannot afford the cost of this struggle are left out and pushed further out to the margins of society, where they become invisible.

From the Human Rights Memorialisation Agenda to Believing in Human Rights Values

Debates on the effectiveness and legitimacy of human rights laws, institutions and movements, both among human rights scholars, and between them and practitioners, are voluminous. Those two debates are interconnected and reflect deeply on the ways in which moral remembrance is understood at the bottom-up level.

The legitimacy debate is often centred on the historical origins of human rights in the Global North and their alleged coercive imposition on the Global South. In his book *The Last Utopia*, Samuel Moyn (2012) argued that debates over human rights emerged in the 1970s, during US President Jimmy Carter's government, rather than in the 1940s. Similarly, Aryeh Neier (2012), in his book *The International Human Rights Movement: A History*, focuses on the period from the 1970s onwards. He describes the growth of the human rights movement after the Helsinki Accords, the roles played by American presidential administrations, and the astonishing Arab revolutions of 2011, arguing that the contemporary human rights movement was, to a large extent, an outgrowth of the Cold War. However, Kathryn Sikkink (2017: 30). in her book *Evidence for Hope: Making Human Rights Work in the 21st Century*, points out that the historical origins of human rights are much more complicated and diverse, arguing that the 'powerful countries have never been a constant, or even a primary source of support for the international support of human rights'.

The debate over historical origins matters because it brings to the fore the hidden links among human rights, neoliberalism and the power of the Global North to silently colonialise and impose an ideological set of beliefs and values worldwide. Both Douzinas (2000) and Nolan (2011) stressed what seems to be the complementary forces of human rights and neoliberalism, and the ways in which those two agendas go hand in hand. However, Sikkink (2017: 30) rightly point out that this form of critique, in which human rights are seen as a colonialising project, 'echoes the discourse of many repressive governments in the Global South who try to discredit their local human rights activists by portraying them as foreign agents'.[5]

It seems to me that the intimate connection between human rights and neoliberalism has much wider implications because, as Stephen Hopgood (2013) noted, human rights emerged as a project of secular religiosity that was supposed to replace the decline of (the Judeo-Christian) religion. Hopgood (2013: 61) argued that 'it is humanism's aim, as the ideology of modernity, to transcend culture in the name of the secular, universal, and categorical'. Thus, the implementation of human rights, as a substitute project for secular religion and ideology, also facilitated the comeback of religion and other competing ideologies, often resulting in the promotion of narrow nationalist sentiments. Those clashes between different sets of values have real implications for the ways in which people on the ground perceive human rights in general and moral remembrance in particular. At the end, the question remains: what is the true impact of the human rights memorialisation agenda for the people in local communities who have suffered massive human rights abuses? Do they internalise human rights values and norms in the long run? Or do they choose human rights over state-sponsored infrastructures as long as it proves beneficial for their own personal status? The answers to those questions, I am afraid, are not straightforward.

Human rights scholars, practitioners, and activists use a variety of measures and indicators to describe advances and setbacks in the promotion and protection of human rights, to provide explanations for their overall global variation and to find solutions to guarantee their improved protection in the future. However, despite the growth and proliferation of legal instruments intended to protect human rights, there is a continuing disparity not only between the official proclamation and the actual

---

[5] This is true not only for the Latin American countries Sikkink is discussing at length in her book, but also for the Balkans countries as well as for Israel and Palestine.

implementation of human rights protections, but also between the implementation of human rights and the actual beliefs and actions of the people who are to benefit from it.

Social and political psychologists are well invested in their attempt to understand the attitudes and behaviours of different groups towards human rights so as to examine the structure and social anchoring of the organising principles of personal involvement when it comes to human rights (Cohrs et al. 2007; Crowson and DeBacker 2008; Moghaddam and Vuksanović 1990; Spini and Doise 1998). Using the three-factor model of human rights endorsement, commitment and restriction, psychologists report on individual differences that predict attitudes, arguing that empathy, education and global knowledge contribute to the endorsement of human rights ideals (McFarland and Mathews 2005). A huge amount of effort in cross-cultural studies has been devoted to the question of the effectiveness of human rights in implementing values and norms in the long run. Particular stress has been placed on the differences between authoritarian and democratic societies and the role of religiosity, so as to understand the psychological roots of positive and negative orientations towards human rights, including the role of human rights education (Cohrs et al. 2007; McFarland 2015). There is a significant difference in whether governments adopt and promote human rights values and whether those values are actually being internalised by groups and individuals on the ground. Sikkink (2017) is right to suggest that a clear distinction should be made between an empirical comparison and a comparison to the ideal when measuring the effectiveness of human rights; from that perspective, we can see the widespread implementation of human rights across the globe increasing over time.

The persistent difference between 'rights in principle' and 'rights in practice' gave rise to numerous forms of measurement, such as coding country participation in regional and international human rights regimes, coding national constitutions according to their rights provisions, qualitative reporting of rights violations, survey data on perceptions of rights conditions, quantitative summaries of rights violations, abstract scales of rights protection based on normative standards, and individual and aggregate measures that map the outcomes of government policies that have consequences for the enjoyment of rights (Landman 2004). Such mechanisms use qualitative and/or quantitative indicators to measure the current state and/or progress of particular human rights or to assess the impacts of policies/measures in a defined geographic area within a given time frame, often with the intention of promoting policies and determining further actions. The UN guide to measuring human rights, published in 2013,[6] introduces the structure–process–outcome model selected for use by the UN Office of the High Commissioner for Human Rights (OHCHR). This model is 'designed to measure the extent to which human rights dimensions respect, protect, fulfil and promote human rights standards in any given environment' (Starl et al. 2017).

Yet, little is known about how the concern for human rights develops and why people respond selectively to the same types of human rights violations. Even the most elaborate measurement mechanisms, such as that used by the OHCHR, can tell us nearly nothing about whether, and under what circumstances, people on the ground adopt human rights norms and values in the long run. We know so little about why some people who have suffered relate to some victims but stay indifferent to others who have suffered in a similar fashion. More strikingly, we lack any significant research on how those whose lives are heavily impacted by human rights infrastructures and values – such as refugees, internally displaced persons (IDPs) and victims of violence – understand human rights. Do they internalise human rights in the long run? How does their experience of solidarity, filtered through a particular interpretation of symbols and history, impact their attachment?

I argue that, to understand when and why people become motivated to act in the name of human rights, we need to look more closely at those small groups at the level of local communities and the ways they perceive selfhood in relation to their collective histories. As I demonstrated at length in Chapter 6, human rights ideology has very limited power to recruit people into a sustainable human rights action. Sceptics might rightly point out that those face-to-face dialogue groups, analysed in Chapter 6, can teach us little about human rights successes globally. However, I wish to argue just the opposite. I suggest that this analysis reveals bigger structural problems for human rights in general, and for the human rights memorialisation agenda in particular. Going beyond the damaging effects of standardisation of memory, on which I elaborated in the previous chapters, I will summarise my argument by showing the limited potential of human rights ideology to offer a viable alternative to collectiveness.

The Inability of Human Rights to Offer a Potent Alternative to Collectiveness

Generally speaking, most people see no harm, and even nominally support, people worldwide having the same rights as they do. Those

[6] International Justice Resource Center (2013).

neutral/positive attitudes change, however, when those rights are perceived (rightly or not) as coming at their own expense. Hopgood (2018) rightly pointed out: 'When it comes to a tradeoff between human rights and other things people hold dear – their material well-being, their security, their children's opportunities and accomplishments – people are reluctant to make sacrifices to realize other people's rights'. This should not be understood as evidence of inherited human egoism; on the contrary, many people who react in such ways are actually altruistic, capable of empathy and ready to help. What matters here is the scale of the community of belonging and the perception of who is deserving and on what grounds.

Feelings of belonging can vary in scope – from wider families and clans, to neighbourhoods, villages and cities, ethnic groups, nations or transnational religious communities. However, any imagined community is inherently limited in scope (Anderson 1983). It is imagined because the actuality of even the smallest group to which one belongs exceeds what is possible for a single person to know. It is limited because, regardless of size, it is never taken to be co-extensive with humanity itself. Every imagined community, regardless of its size, needs to have particular infrastructures that help produce feelings of mutual solidarity. In a world that is predominantly divided through national sovereignties, the main point of reference is a nation, which can be considered a community because it implies a deep horizontal comradeship which knits together distant people under one ideological roof. For the sake of creating the feeling of belonging and attachment to the community of a nation, nationalist ideology attempts to bridge the ongoing division between the 'state' part and the 'nation' part of the nation-state by depicting the nation as a community of close friends or a giant extended family (Malešević 2013a: 15). Solidarity lies at the heart of any nationalist project, and the nationalist ideology can work properly only when it is able to achieve full ideological penetration and tie the pockets of micro-solidarity around the existing bureaucratic scaffolding (Malešević 2013a).

However, solidarities in imagined communities are shaped by various features, such as a perception of a shared history (and destiny), shared beliefs and symbols, cultures, traditions and religions. For people to feel an attachment to and solidarity with their communities, infrastructures must be in place that promote and infiltrate a discursive repertoire, not only attuned to the intimate metaphors of family and friendship, simulating a closed cosy community (Gellner 1997: 74), but also stressing the difference between the 'us' group and the 'them' group. Hence, whether we are talking about ethnic communities, where 'the historic consciousness is an essential part of the definition of what we mean by the term ethnic community' (Smith 1981: 379), or nations, where nationalism promotes solidarity among the group's members and their need to preserve their cultural uniqueness (Malešević 1999), or religious communities that transcend the borders of the state through their religious infrastructures, what they all have in common is that they support the limited inclusion of their members. Of course, not all members are equally motivated to sacrifice for the fellow members of their imagined community. Indeed, people feel more obliged to intervene when injustice happens to the people with whom they have had prolonged face-to-face encounters. Plenty of evidence shows that, for example, the prime motivator for soldiers to fight and even sacrifice their lives is to save their fellow soldiers. For some, though, the ideological messages that transcend an immediate connection resonate deeply, and push them to sacrifice for the sake of the imagined community, often their nation, or their ethnic or religious group.

Despite the voluminous research, the relation between ideology and solidarity remains ambiguous. The only thing that is certain – even universal – is that all people, regardless of their race, ethnicity, class, gender or political views, are always affected by their personal experiences, the immediate group in which they live and their shared histories. The translation of the perceptions of their belonging impact the scale and the range of reference in their engagement with other people. The human rights memorialisation agenda, which frames personal and collective experience through the lenses of 'duty to remember', 'facing the past' and a 'victim-centred agenda', assumes a particular moral order in which there is no dispute about what is morally right and what is wrong. This assumption effectively enforces the idea that human rights norms must trump cultural norms and heritage. This view is deeply embedded in the discourse of human rights in general, and in the human rights memorialisation agenda in particular. Such views on human rights morality are succinctly expressed in the words of Geoffrey Robertson (cited in Hopgood 2013: 65), the first president of the Sierra Leone Special Court:

'We are beginning to call a savage a savage, whether he or she is black or white. We are becoming less respectful of old men with beards, be they mullahs or rabbis or patriarchs, who ordain cruelty in the name of religion. There is less mealy-mouthedness about intolerable behavior and fewer attempts to suggest that traditional practices are 'culturally relative' or that authoritarian governments are reflecting 'communitarian values'.

This position seems morally right, yet it is erroneous and even counterproductive on two grounds. First, in its attempt 'to normalize the universal, secular and categorical' (Hopgood 2013: 66) norms of human rights, it implies the hierarchical superiority of those who support such views. In religious and ideological terms, they are the ultimate truth owners and as such, are in charge of safeguarding it. For people who share other beliefs, such a position is oppressive and condescending.

Second, and most importantly, evil and morality are subjective constructs. People help or harm others (or themselves) because they genuinely feel that it's right. In that sense, violence, just like helping others, is an intentional moral action (Fiske and Rai 2014). Furthermore, when faced with significant threats, people will actually sacrifice a good deal of liberty – the liberty of others but eventually their own, too – to keep what they have safe from harm (Hopgood 2018). In turn, constructs of morality shrink, expand, change and adapt to fit the perceived realities on the ground. The key to understanding the ways in which people internalise human rights is to understand the notion of 'threat'. Threats, for the most part, are not immediate but rather are constructed and directly linked with the imagined experience of their collective past. In consequence, the perceptions of threat, which move the boundaries of people's ability to commit to human rights, are very much linked to, and constrained by, the effectiveness of certain (limited) groups based on ethnicity, nationality or religious belonging. The bigger and closer the alleged threat becomes, the more the scope of universalist human rights gets reduced. To put it bluntly, what people understand as 'good' and 'justice', as well as 'evil' and 'injustice', is not aligned with the morality of human rights. Instead, it is always subject to their own positionality and is filtered through their personal experiences, their shared histories and the perception of a 'threat'.

In other words, one can believe and act in the name of human rights as long as it comes at no cost. Human rights activists can promote human rights ideals (even at the cost of great personal sacrifice), but most will not jeopardise their societal positions, jobs, incomes, citizenships or their children's education for the sake of improving the lives of distant strangers. Jewish Israelis can go against the nationalist stream to fight for Palestinian rights, but not many would actually give up their own social benefits or their security to help the Palestinian cause.

To put it simply, human rights as an ideology are limited in their ability to transcend the boundaries of any imagined community, be it a nation or a religious or ethnic group. This might seem to be in contradiction with the fact that many anti-colonialist movements invoke human rights in their struggle to achieve historical justice, appealing for global solidarities to promote their goals framed in human rights garb. However, this is often done in the name of national liberation and self-determination, rather than as an outgrowth of a firm belief in human rights values and norms. What is more, to the extent that the different anti-colonial movements converge into a range of pan-nationalisms, they evoke a different mode of internationalism that is promoted in terms of the struggle for human rights. Understanding this point is crucial because efforts such as the Palestinian Boycott, Divestment and Sanctions (BDS) movement and the Israeli settlement movement outside the Green Line, while seemingly diametrically opposed to each other, both evoke human rights and historical justice to promote nationalist sentiments and territorial claims. While this comparison might sound odd, because their struggles are set on very different moral grounds, those movements share a commonality: they are not focused 'on classical liberties, or even social rights,' but on the right to the collective economic development of societies, in the absence of colonial intrusions, rather than that of individuals (Moyn 2012: 86). Human rights are situational, meaning that their effectiveness in changing people's beliefs expands or shrinks in relation to their socially constructed personal experiences, shared histories and perceptions of threats, real or imagined. In fact, they prove to be a useful outfit when fighting narrow nationalist struggles because they resonate with, and claim to affirm, global universal moralities.

The intertwining of human rights with national aspirations exposes further the limitations of the human rights memorialisation agenda, as the project of a globalising secular moral authority. Moral remembrance has very limited power to create an effective imagined community of human rights believers because people are not capable of narrating their own histories through disconnected struggles of distant communities. Instead, those struggles stay deeply grounded and limited by their own local context and histories, and by the attachment to their own imagined communities. Solidarities, based on pure humanity, are just rare temporal moments in which distant subjects elevate themselves from their socio-political and historical contexts, remembering for a second that we all breathe the same air – only to discover that even the air we breathe is not the same everywhere.

Conclusion

Belonging to the global community of humanity is yet another wishful destination – one that human rights, as desirable as they are, are not capable of delivering. Their organisational and doctrinal power crumbles apart once they land on the ground, where people, trapped within the particular boundaries their own local communities, assign meanings based on existing notions of selfhood and otherness. The human rights memorialisation agenda does not transform people into human rights believers, but rather reinforces the importance of their national, ethnic or religious belonging. Thus, moral remembrance captures the best and the worst of the humanity. It contours the dreams and aspirations of human morality, justice and equality, but ends up strengthening narrow nationalist sentiments, producing inequalities and perpetuating the animosities that it meant to extinguish in the first place.

Bibliography

Abu-Nimer, M. (1999). *Dialogue, conflict resolution, and change.* Albany: State University of New York Press.

——— (2004). Education for coexistence and Arab–Jewish encounters in Israel: Potential and challenges. *Journal of Social Issues, 60*(2), 405–422.

Achcar, G. (2010). *The Arabs and the Holocaust.* New York: Henry Holt and Company.

Ackermann, A. (1994). Reconciliation as a peace-building process in postwar Europe. *Peace and Change, 19*(3), 229–250.

Adorno, T. W. (1986 [1959]). What does coming to terms with the past mean? In: Geoffrey Hartman (ed.), *Bitburg in moral and political perspective.* Bloomington: Indiana University Press, pp. 114–129.

Aguilar, P. (1999). Agents of memory: Spanish Civil War veterans and disabled soldiers. In: J. Winter & E. Sivan (eds.), *War and remembrance in the twentieth century.* Cambridge: Cambridge University Press, pp. 84–103.

Agulhon, M. (1981). *Marianne into battle: Republican imagery and symbolism in France, 1789–1880.* Cambridge: Cambridge University Press.

Ahiram, E. (1995). *Whither EU–Israeli relations?* Frankfurt am Main: Lang.

Al-Daqaq, I., Abdel Karim, N., Ezbidi, B., Said, N., & Abu Fasha, W. (2004). *Palestine human development report 2004.* Birzeit: Birzeit University.

Al-Awda, T. (2003). FAQs about Palestinian refugees. Retrieved 19 May 2019, from http://al-awda.org/learn-more/faqs-about-palestinian-refugees/

Alexander, J. (2004). Toward a theory of cultural trauma. In: J. Alexander, R. Eyerman, B. Giesen, N. Smelser & P. Sztompka (eds.), *Cultural trauma and collective identity.* Berkeley: University of California Press, pp. 1–30.

——— (2014). Morality as a cultural system: On solidarity civil and uncivil. In: J. Vincent (ed.), *The Palgrave handbook of altruism, morality, and social solidarity: Formulating a field of study.* New York: Palgrave Macmillan, pp. 303–311.

Althusser, L. (1971). Ideology and ideological state apparatuses. In: B. Brewster, *Lenin and philosophy and other essays.* New York: Monthly Review Press, pp. 127–186.

American Anthropological Association. (1947). Executive Committee: Statement on human rights submitted to the Commission on Human Rights, United Nations. *American Anthropologist* 49(4), 539–543.

Ancelovici, M., & Jenson, J. (2013). Standardization for transnational diffusion: The case of truth commissions and conditional cash transfers. *International Political Sociology, 7*(3), 294–312.

Bibliography

Anderson, B. (1983). *Imagined communities: Reflections on the origin and spread of nationalism.* London: Verso.
Anheier, H., Glasius, M., & Kaldor, M. (2001). Introducing global civil society. In: H. Anheier, M. Glasius & M. Kaldor, *Global civil society yearbook.* Oxford: Oxford University Press, pp. 3–22.
Arendt, H. (1951). *The origins of totalitarianism.* Orlando: Harcourt Brace and Company.
Ariès, P. (1974). *Western attitudes toward death.* Baltimore: Johns Hopkins University Press.
Arthur, P. (2009). How 'transitions' reshaped human rights: A conceptual history of transitional justice. *Human Rights Quarterly, 31*(2), 321–367.
Assmann, A. (2007). Europe: A community of memory? *Bulletin of the German Historical Institute, 40,* 11–25.
Baćirbašić, B. (2011). *Tjelo, ženskost i moć: Upisivanja patrijarhalnog diskursa u tijelo.* Zagreb: Synopsis.
Baer, A., & Sznaider, N. (2017). *Memory and forgetting in the post-Holocaust era: The ethics of never again.* London and New York: Routledge.
Bajford, J. (2009). *Staro Sajmište: Mesto sećanja, zaborava i sporenja.* Beograd: Beogradski centar za ljudska prava.
Balfour, R., & Stratulat, C. (2011). *The Democratic transformation of the Balkans.* Epc Issue Paper No. 66: *European Policy Paper: European Politics and Institutions.*
Bar, H., Bargal, D., & Asaqla, J. (1995). *Living with conflict: Encounters between Jewish and Palestinian Israeli youth.* Jerusalem: Jerusalem Institute for Israel Studies. (In Hebrew).
Barkan, E., & Baćirbašić, B. (2015). The politics of memory, victimization and activism in post-conflict Bosnia and Herzegovina. In: K. Neumann & J. Thompson (eds.), *Historical justice and memory.* Madison: University of Wisconsin Press, pp. 95–113.
Barkan, E., & Karn, A. (2006). Group apology as an ethical imperative. In: E. Berkan & A. Karn, *Taking wrongs seriously: Apologies and reconciliation.* Stanford, CA: Stanford University Press, pp. 3–30.
Barsalou, J., & Baxter, V. (2007). *The urge to remember: The role of memorials in social reconstruction and transitional justice.* Washington, DC: United States Institute of Peace.
Bar-Tal, D. (1998). The rocky road toward peace: Beliefs on conflict in Israeli textbooks. *Journal of Peace Research, 35*(6), 723–742.
(2018). What Palestinians actually know about the Holocaust? *Haaretz.* Retrieved 19 May 2019 from www.haaretz.com/amp/middle-east-news/palestinians/.premium-what-palestinians-actually-know-about-the-holocaust-1.6075799?
Barthes, R. (1973). *Mythologies.* London: Granada.
Bartlett, F. (1932). *Remembering: A study in experimental and social psychology.* London: Cambridge University Press.
(2003). *Remembering.* Cambridge: Cambridge University Press.
Bartov, O. (1991). *Hitler's army: Soldiers, Nazis, and war in the Third Reich.* Oxford: Oxford University Press.

(2001). *The Eastern Front, 1941–1945: German troops and the barbarization of warfare*. London: Palgrave.
(2018). *Anatomy of a genocide: The life and death of a town called Buczacz*. New York: Simon and Schuster.
Bashir, B., & Goldberg, A. (2014). Deliberating the Holocaust and the Nakba: Disruptive empathy and binationalism in Israel/Palestine. *Journal of Genocide Research*, *16*(1), 77–99. doi: 10.1080/14623528.2014.878114
Bassiouni, M. (1996). Searching for peace and achieving justice: The need for accountability. *Law and Contemporary Problems*, *59*(4), 9–28.
Bastel, H., Matzka, C., & Miklas, H. (2010). Holocaust education in Austria: A (hi)story of complexity and ambivalence. *Prospects*, *40*(1), 57–73.
Bauman, Z. (1998). What prospects of morality in times of uncertainty? *Theory, Culture and Society*, *15*(1), 11–22.
Beara, V., Miljanović, P., & Popov, B. (2004). Zašto uopšte pomagati ratnim veteranima? Pojedinac̆ni projekti u vezi istine i pomirenja u bivšoj Jugoslaviji i svetu. *DoiSerbia*, *7*(4), 47–9.
Beckert, J. (2010). How do fields change? The interrelations of institutions, networks, and cognition in the dynamics of markets. *Organization Studies*, *31*(5), 605–627. doi: 10.1177/0170840610372184
Bekerman, Z. (2009). Identity work in Palestinian–Jewish intergroup encounters: A cultural rhetorical analysis. *Journal of Multicultural Discourses*, *4*(2), 205–219.
Bekerman, Z., & Zembylas, M. (2012). *Teaching contested narratives: Identity, memory, and reconciliation in peace education and beyond*. Cambridge: Cambridge University Press.
Belavusau, U. (2014). Hate speech and constitutional democracy in Eastern Europe: Transitional and militant? (Czech Republic, Hungary and Poland). *Israel Law Review*, *47*(1), 27–61.
Belavusau, U., & Gliszczyńska-Grabias, A. (2017). *Law and memory: Addressing historical injustice by legislation and trials*. Cambridge: Cambridge University Press.
Bell, C. (2009). Transitional justice, interdisciplinarity and the state of the 'field' or 'non-field'. *International Journal of Transitional Justice*, *3*(1), 5–27.
Ben-Amos, A., & Bet-El, I. (1999). Holocaust Day and Memorial Day in Israeli schools: Ceremonies, education and history. *Israel Studies*, *4*(1), 258–284.
Banjeglav, T. (2012). Sjećanje na rat ili rat sjećanja? Promjene u politikama sjećanja u Hrvatskoj od 1990 do danas. In: *Re:vizija prošlosti: politike sjećanja u Bosni i Hercegovini, Hrvatskoj i Srbiji od 1990 godine*. Sarajevo: ACIPS, pp. 91–154.
Bennett, T. (1995). *The birth of the museum*. London and New York: Routledge.
Bergholz, M. (2007). Među rodoljubima, kupusom, svinjama i varvarima: Spomenici i grobovi NOR 1947–1965. *Godišnjak za Društvenu Istoriju*, *1*(3), 61–82.
(2013). Sudden nationhood: The microdynamics of intercommunal relations in Bosnia-Herzegovina after World War II. *American Historical Review*, *118*(3), 679–707.
(2016). *Violence as a generative force: Identity, nationalism and memory in a Balkan community*. Ithaca, NY: Cornell University Press.

Berkovitch, N. (1999). *From motherhood to citizenship: Women's rights and international organizations*. Baltimore, MD: Johns Hopkins University Press.

Billig, M., Condor, S., Edwards, D., Gane, M., & Radley, A. (1988). *Ideological dilemmas: A social psychology of everyday thinking*. London: Sage.

Birnbaum, N. (1960). The sociological study of ideology (1940–60): A trend report and bibliography. *Current Sociology 9*(2): 91–172.

Bjelić, B. (2002). Propuštena katarza nakon Drugog svetskog rata. *Termida, 3*, 53–56.

Blatz, C., Day, M., & Schryer, E. (2014). Official public apology effects on victim group members' evaluations of the perpetrator group. *Canadian Journal of Behavioral Science/Revue Canadienne Des Sciences Du Comportement, 46*(3), 337–345.

Blau, J., & Moncada, A. (2007). *Freedoms and solidarities*. Lanham, MD: Rowman & Littlefield.

Blustein, J. (2012). Human rights and the internationalization of memory. *Journal of Social Philosophy, 43*(1), 19–32.

Bob, C. (2005). *The marketing of rebellion: Insurgencies, media and international activism*. New York: Cambridge University Press.

(2015). The quest for international affairs. In: J. Goodwin & J. Jasper (eds.), *The social movement reader: Cases and concepts*. 3rd ed. London: Blackwell, pp. 325–335.

Bogdanić, S. (2015). Hrvatska i BiH složne: U SFRJ se živjelo bolje. *Moje Vrijeme*. Retrieved 20 May 2019 from www.mojevrijeme.hr/magazin/2015/04/hrvatska-i-bih-slozne-u-sfrj-se-zivjelo-bolje/

Boli, J., & Thomas, G. (1997). World culture in the world polity: A century of international non-governmental organization. *American Sociological Review, 62*(2), 171. doi: 10.2307/2657298

(1999). *Constructing world culture*. Stanford, CA: Stanford University Press.

Borer, T. (2003). A taxonomy of victims and perpetrators: Human rights and reconciliation in South Africa. *Human Rights Quarterly, 25*(4), 1088–1116.

Börzel, T., & Risse, T. (2012). From Europeanisation to diffusion: Introduction. *West European Politics, 35*(1), 1–19.

Bourke, J. (2004). 'Remembering' war. *Journal of Contemporary History, 39*(4), 473–485.

Boutros-Ghali, B. (1992). An agenda for peace: Preventive diplomacy. *International Relations 11*(3): 201–218.

Boven, T. V. (1993). *Study concerning the right to restitution, compensation and rehabilitation for victims of gross violations of human rights and fundamental freedoms: final report*. UN Sub-Commission on the Promotion and Protection of Human Rights. E/CN.4/Sub.2/1993/8

Bowman, G. (2003). Constitutive violence and the nationalist imaginary. Antagonism and defensive solidarity in Palestine and former Yugoslavia. *Social Anthropology, 11*(3), 319–340.

Brett, S., Bickford, L., Ševčenko, L., & Rios, M. (2007). Memorialization and democracy: State policy and civic action. International Criminal Tribunal for the former Yugoslavia. Retrieved 19 May 2019 from www.ictj.org/publication/memorialization-and-democracy-state-policy-and-civic-action

Brooks, R. (2004). *Atonement and forgiveness: A new model for black reparations.* Berkeley and Los Angeles: University of California Press.
Browne, B. (2013). Commemoration in conflict. *Journal of Comparative Research in Anthropology and Sociology, 2,* 143–163.
——— (2016). Choreographed segregation: Irish Republican commemoration of the 1916 Easter Rising in 'post-conflict' Belfast. *Irish Political Studies, 31*(1), 101–121.
Brubaker, R. (1994). Nationhood and the national question in the Soviet Union and post-Soviet Eurasia: An institutionalist account. *Theory and Society, 23*(1), 47–78.
——— (2004). *Ethnicity without groups.* Cambridge, MA: Harvard University Press.
Brubaker, R., & Cooper, F. (2000). Beyond identity. *Theory and Society, 29*(1), 1–47.
Brubaker, R., & Laitin, D. (1998). Ethnic and nationalist violence. *Annual Review of Sociology, 24*(1), 423–452.
Brym, R., & Araj, B. (2006). Suicide bombing as strategy and interaction: The case of the Second Intifada. *Social Forces, 84*(4), 1969–1986.
Burke, P. (2002). Context in context. *Common Knowledge, 8*(1), 152–177.
Burns, H. W. (2019). Human rights. *Encyclopedia Britannica Online.* Retrieved 27 February 2020 from www.britannica.com/topic/human-rights
Byford, J. (2007). When I say 'the Holocaust' I mean 'Jasenovac': Remembrance of the Holocaust in contemporary Serbia. *East European Jewish Affairs, 37*(1), 51–74.
Caplan, R. (2000). Assessing the Dayton Accord: The structural weaknesses of the general framework agreement for peace in Bosnia and Herzegovina. *Diplomacy & Statecraft, 11*(2), 213–232.
Carranza Ko, Ñ. (2018). South Korea's collective memory of past human rights abuses. *Memory Studies.* https://doi.org/10.1177/1750698018806938
Carrier, P., Fuchs, E., & Messinger, T. (2015). A global mapping of the Holocaust in textbooks and curricula. In: Z. Gross & E. Stevick (eds.), *As the witnesses fall silent: 21st century Holocaust education in curriculum, policy and practice.* Paris and Braunschweig: Springer, pp. 245–262.
Casey, E. (2000). *Remembering: A phenomenological study* (2nd ed.). Bloomington: Indiana University Press.
Center for Nonviolent Action. (2001). *Evaluation report 1997–2001, internal report.* Belgrade: Center for Nonviolent Action.
——— (2004). *Traces* [Film].
——— (2006a). *All wish to cast a stone* [Film].
——— (2006b). *It cannot last forever* [Video].
——— (2007). *Not a bird to be heard* [Film].
——— (2008). *Developing linkages between peace education and peace promotion for increased impact in the region of former Yugoslavia.* Belgrade and Sarajevo: Report for the Centre for Nonviolent Action's Belgrade and Sarajevo Teams.
——— (2009). *War-veterans visits* [Film].
——— (2015). *Albanian–Macedonian simulated dialogue* [Film].
Chandler, D. (2005). From Dayton to Europe. *International Peacekeeping, 12*(3), 336–349.

Chomsky, N. (1999). *The umbrella of US power: The universal declaration of human rights and the contradictions of US policy*. New York: Seven Stories.

Chufrin, G., & Saunders, H. (1993). A public peace process. *Negotiation Journal*, 9(2), 155–177.

Cohrs, J., Maes, J., Moschner, B., & Kielmann, S. (2007). Determinants of human rights attitudes and behavior: A comparison and integration of psychological perspectives. *Political Psychology*, 28(4), 441–469.

Collins, R. (1993). Emotional energy as the common denominator of rational action. *Rationality and Society*, 5(2), 203–230.

——— (1994). *Four sociological traditions*. New York: Oxford University Press.

——— (2004). *Interaction ritual chains*. Princeton, NJ: Princeton University Press.

——— (2008). *Violence: Micro-sociological theory*. Princeton, NJ: Princeton University Press.

Committee on the Elimination of Discrimination against Women. (1994). Concluding comments of the Committee on the Elimination of Discrimination against Women: Bosnia and Herzegovina. *Women Watch*. Retrieved 20 May 2019 from www.un.org/womenwatch/daw/cedaw/cedaw25years/content/english/CONCLUDING_COMMENTS/Bosnia_and_Herzegovina/Bosnia_and_Herzegovina-Special_report.pdf

Coser, L. A. (1992). *Maurice Halbwachs on collective memory*. Chicago: University of Chicago Press.

Cox, M. (1999). The Dayton Agreement in Bosnia and Herzegovina: A study of implementation strategies. *British Yearbook of International Law*, 69(1), 201–244.

Crowe, D. (2013). *War crimes, genocide, and justice*. New York: Palgrave Macmillan.

Crowson, H., & DeBacker, T. (2008). Belief, motivational, and ideological correlates of human rights attitudes. *Journal of Social Psychology*, 148(3), 293–310.

Cunningham, M. (2004). Prisoners of the Japanese and the politics of apology: A battle over history and memory. *Journal of Contemporary History*, 39(4), 561–574.

Cvijić, S. (2008). Swinging the pendulum: World War II history, politics, national identity and difficulties of reconciliation in Croatia and Serbia. *Nationalities Papers*, 36(4), 713–740.

Datel, L. (2018). Despite the Polish law outrage the journeys to the concentration camps increased – and parents will pay. *The Marker* [in Hebrew]. www.themarker.com/news/education/1.5827250

David, L. (2013). The Holocaust discourse as a screen memory: The Serbian case. In: V. Stančetić & S. Janković, *(Mis)uses of history: History as a political tool in the Western Balkans*. Belgrade: CSDU, pp. 63–87.

——— (2014a). Impression management of a contested past: Serbia's evolving national calendar. *Memory Studies*, 7(4), 472–483.

——— (2014b). Mediating international and domestic demands: Mnemonic battles surrounding the Monument to the Fallen of the Wars of the 1990s in Belgrade. *Nationalities Papers*, 42(4), 655–673.

——— (2014c). Memory construction on the European Union's peripheries: East European and former Yugoslav countries. *Hagar: Studies in Culture, Polity and Identities*, 12, 144–147.

(2015a). Dealing with the contested past in Serbia: Decontextualisation of the war veterans memories. *Nations and Nationalism*, 21(1), 102–119.
(2015b). Fragmentation as a strategy of silencing: Serbian war veterans against the State of Serbia. *Contemporary Southeastern Europe*, 2(1), 55–73.
(2015c). Between Human rights and nationalism: Silencing as a mechanism of memory in the post-Yugoslav wars' Serbia. *Journal of Regional Security*, 10(1), 37–52.
(2017a). Against standardization of memory. *Human Rights Quarterly*, 39(2), 296–318.
(2017b). Holocaust and genocide memorialisation policies in the Western Balkans and Israel/Palestine. *Peacebuilding*, 5(1), 51–66.
Davis, M. (2005). Is Spain recovering its memory? Breaking the Pacto del Olvido. *Human Rights Quarterly* 27(3), 858–880.
(2000). *The Pinochet case*. London: Institute of Latin American Studies Research Papers.
De Baets, A. (2009a). The impact of the Universal Declaration of Human Rights on the study of history. *History and Theory*, 48(1), 20–43.
(2009b). *Responsible history*. New York: Berghahn Books.
Delić, A. (2010). Awakening: From a personal point of view: Veteran of Army of Bosnia and Herzegovina. *CNA Annual Report*, pp. 78–80.
Dembour, M. (2010). What are human rights? Four schools of thought. *Human Rights Quarterly*, 32(1), 1–20.
Dietsch, J. (2012). Textbooks and the Holocaust in ondependent Ukraine. *European Education*, 44(3), 67–94.
DiMaggio, P., & Powell, W. (1983). The Iron Cage revisited: Institutional isomorphism and collective rationality in organizational fields. *American Sociological Review*, 48(2), 147.
(1991). Introduction. In: P. DiMaggio & W. Powell, *The new institutionalism in organizational analysis*. Chicago: University of Chicago Press, pp. 1–38.
Dimitrijević, N. (2001). *Slučaj Jugoslavija: Socializam, ancionalizam i posledice*. Beograd: B92.
Djipa, D., & Fazlić, S. (2012). *Voices of youth: Survey of youth in BiH, quantitative research findings*. MDG Achievement Fund. Retrieved 27 February 2020 from http://mdgfund.org/publication/voices-youth-survey-youth-bih-quantitative-research-findings
Dokumenta, Centar za suočavanje s prošlošću. (2006). Istraživanje javnog mnijenja o suocavanju s prošlošću – sažetak rezultata – Zagreb. Retrieved 27 February 2020 from http://nenasilje.org/publikacije/ssp07/doc/06-istrazivanje.pdf
Donnelly, J. (1984). Cultural relativism and universal human rights. *Human Rights Quarterly*, 6(4), 400. doi: 10.2307/762182
(1999). The social construction of international human rights. In: T. Dunne & N. Wheeler, *Human rights in global politics*. Cambridge: Cambridge University Press, pp. 71–102.
(2007). The relative universality of human rights. *Human Rights Quarterly*, 29(2), 281–306. doi: 10.1353/hrq.2007.0016
Douzinas, C. (2000). *The end of human rights critical thought at the turn of the century*. Oxford: Hart Publishing.

Dragović-Soso, J. (2002). 'Saviors of the nation': Serbia's intellectual opposition and the revival of nationalism. London: Hurst.
  (2010). Conflict, memory, accountability: What does coming to terms with the past mean? In: W. Petritsch & V. Džihić, Conflict and memory: Bridging past and future in [South East] Europe. Baden-Baden: Nomos, pp. 163–179.
Durkheim, E. (1964 [1893])). The division of labor in society. New York: Free Press.
  (1997 [1893])). The division of labor in society. New York: Free Press.
Eastmond, M., & Mannergren-Selimović, J. (2012). Silence as possibility in postwar everyday life. International Journal of Transitional Justice, 6(3), 502–524.
Edwards, J. (2010). Apologizing for the past for a better future: Collective apologies in the United States, Australia, and Canada. Southern Communication Journal, 75(1), 57–75.
Eldar, A. (22 November 2001). Palestinian Minister of Information Yasser Abed Rabbo on the right of return: Brookings Institution debate with Yossi Beilin and Martin Indyk. Haaretz [in Hebrew]. Retrieved 27 February 2020 from www.haaretz.co.il/misc/1.750505
Elliott, M. (2014). The institutionalization of human rights and its discontents: A world cultural perspective. Cultural Sociology, 8(4), 407–425.
Evans-Pritchard, E. (1940). The nuer. London: Oxford University Press.
Falk, R. (2000). Human rights horizons: The pursuit of justice in a globalizing world. New York: Routledge.
Farah, R. (2009). Refugee camps in the Palestinian and Sahrawi national liberation movements: A comparative perspective. Journal of Palestine Studies, 38(2), 76–93.
Feldman, J. (2002). Marking the boundaries of the enclave: Defining the Israeli collective through the Poland 'experience'. Israel Studies, 7(2), 84–114.
  (2010). Above the death-pits, beneath the flag: Youth voyages to Poland and the performance of Israeli national identity. New York: Berghahn Books.
Finnemore, M. (1993). International organizations as teachers of norms: The United Nations Educational, Scientific, and Cutural Organization and science policy. International Organization, 47(4), 565.
  (1996). Norms, culture, and world politics: Insights from sociology's institutionalism. International Organization, 50(2), 325–347.
Fischer, M. (2001). Activities of the Centre for Nonviolent Action (Sarajevo): Conflict transformation in the Balkan Region Training in Nonviolent Action. Retrieved 21 May 2019 from www.nenasilje.org/publikacije/pdf/evaluacija/CNAEvaluE2001.pdf
  (2007). Confronting the past and involving war veterans for peace: Activities by the Centre for Nonviolent Action, Sarajevo, Belgrade. In: M. Fischer, Peacebuilding and civil society in Bosnia-Herzegovina: Ten years after Dayton. Münster, Hamburg andLondon: Lit-Verlag, pp. 387–416.
Fischer, M., & Petrović-Ziemer, Lj. (eds.). (2013). Dealing with the past in the Western Balkans: Initiatives for peacebuilding and transitional justice in Bosnia-Herzegovina, Serbia and Croatia. Berghof Report No. 18. Berlin: Berghof Foundation.

Fiske, A. (1991). *Structures of social life: The four elementary forms of social relations.* New York: Free Press.

Fiske, A., & Rai, T. (2014). *Virtuous violence: Hurting and killing to create, sustain, end, and honor social relationships.* Cambridge: Cambridge University Press.

Flere, S. (2007). The broken covenant of Tito's people: The problem of civil religion in Communist Yugoslavia. *East European Politics and Societies, 21*(4), 681–703.

Flesher Fominaya, C. (2014). *Social movements and globalization.* Basingstoke: Palgrave Macmillan.

Forsythe, D. (2018). *Human rights in international relations.* Cambridge: Cambridge University Press.

Foster, Z. J. (2011). *Arab historiography in mandatory Palestine, 1920–1948.* MA thesis: Georgetown University.

Franović, I. (2008). Dealing with the past in the context of ethnonationalism. Retrieved 19 May 2019 from https://nenasilje.org/en/2008/dealing-with-the-past-in-the-context-of-ethnonationalism/

Freeden, M. (1996). *Ideologies and political theory: A conceptual approach.* Oxford: Oxford University Press.

(2006). Ideology and political theory. *Journal of Political Ideologies, 11*(1), 3–22. doi: 10.1080/13569310500395834

(2008). *Ideologies and political theory.* Oxford: Clarendon Press.

Frezzo, M. (2011). Sociology and human rights in the post-development era. *Sociology Compass, 5*(3), 203–214.

Fridman, O. (2013). Structured encounters in post-conflict/post-Yugoslav days: Visiting Belgrade and Pristina. In: O. Simić & Z. Volčić, *Civil society and transitional justice in the Balkans.* New York: Springer Series in Transitional Justice, pp. 143–161.

Fronza, E. (2006). The punishment of negationism: The difficult dialogue between law and memory. *Vermont Law Review, 30,* 609–626.

Gabowitsch, M. (2017). Introduction. In: *Replicating atonement: Foreign models in the commemorations of atrocities.* Cham, Switzerland: Palgrave Macmillan, pp. 1–21.

Gagnon, V. (2010). Yugoslavia in 1989 and after. *Nationalities Papers, 38*(1), 23–39.

Galbraith, P. (1997). Washington, Erdut and Dayton: Negotiating and implementing peace in Croatia and Bosnia-Herzegovina. *Cornell International Law Journal, 30*(3), 643–649.

Galtung, J. (1976). Three approaches to peace: Peacekeeping, peacemaking, and peacebuilding. In: J. Galtung (ed.), *Peace, war and defense: Essays in peace research,* Vol. II, Copenhagen: Christian Ejlers, pp. 297–298.

Gardner Feldman, L. (1999). The principle and practice of 'reconciliation' in German foreign policy: Relations with France, Israel, Poland and the Czech Republic. *International Affairs, 75*(2), 333–356.

Gelber, Y. (2006). *Palestine, 1948.* Brighton: Sussex Academic Press.

Gellner, E. (1997). *Nationalism.* London: Phoenix.

Giesen, B. (2004). The trauma of perpetrators. In: J. Alexander, R. Eyerman, B. Giesen, et al. (eds.), *Cultural trauma and collective identity.* Berkeley: University of California Press, pp. 112–154.

Gillis, J. (1994). *Commemorations: The politics of national identity*. Princeton, NJ: Princeton University Press.
Goffman, E. (1983). The interaction order: American Sociological Association, 1982 Presidential Address. *American Sociological Review*, 48(1), 1–17.
Goldberg, A., & Hazan, H. (2015). *Marking evil*. Oxford: Berghahn Books.
Goodale, M. (2005). Empires of law: Discipline and resistance within the transnational system. *Social & Legal Studies*, 14(4), 553–583.
   (2006). Toward a critical anthropology of human rights. *Current Anthropology*, 47(3), 485–511.
Gordon, N., & Berkovitch, N. (2007). Human rights discourse in domestic settings: How does it emerge? *Political Studies* 55(1), 243–66.
Gordy, E. (2013). *Guilt, responsibility, and denial of the past at stake in post-Milošević Serbia*. Philadelphia: University of Pennsylvania Press.
Gramsci, A. (1971). The prison notebooks. In: Q. Hoare & G. Nowell-Smith, *Hegemony (civil society) and separation of power*. London: Lawrence and Wishart, pp. 506–508.
Green, P. (2000). For a future to be possible: Bosnian dialogue in the aftermath of war. *Medicine, Conflict And Survival*, 16(4), 441–450.
Guisan, C. (2011). From the European coal and steel community to Kosovo: Reconciliation and its discontents. *Journal of Common Market Studies*, 49(3), 541–562.
Gutman, Y. (2016). Memory laws: An escalation in minority exclusion or a testimony to the limits of state power?. *Law & Society Review*, 50(3), 575–607.
Haaretz. (2004). Joint Israeli–Palestinian expedition sets off for Antarctica. Retrieved 20 May 2019 from www.haaretz.com/1.5257423
Habermas, J. (1997). *A Berlin republic: Writing on Germany*. Lincoln: University of Nebraska Press.
Hafner-Burton, E., & Tsutsui, K. (2005). Human rights in a globalizing world: The paradox of empty promises. *American Journal of Sociology*, 110(5), 1373–1411.
Halabi, R., & Sonnenschein, N. (2004). The Jewish–Palestinian encounter in a time of crisis. *Journal of Social Issues*, 60(2), 373–387.
Halbwachs, M. (1992). *On collective memory*, L. A. Coser (ed.), Chicago: University of Chicago Press.
Hamber, B., & Wilson, R. (2002). Symbolic closure through memory reparation and revenge in post-conflict societies. *Journal of Human Rights*, 1(1), 35–53.
Hammel, E. (2000). Lessons from the Yugoslav labyrinth. In: Y. Halpern & D. Kideckel (eds.), *Neighbors at war: Anthropological perspectives on Yugoslav ethnicity, culture and history*. University Park: Pennsylvania University Press, pp. 19–39.
Hamilton, M. (1987). The elements of the concept of ideology. *Political Studies*, 35(1), 18–38.
Hamilton, W. (1964). The genetic evolution of social behavior. *Journal of Theoretical Biology*, 7, 1–52.
Handwerker, W. (1997). Universal human rights and the problem of unbounded cultural meanings. *American Anthropologist*, 99(4), 799–809.

Hayden, R. (1996). Schindler's fate: Genocide, ethnic cleansing, and population transfers. *Slavic Review, 55*(4), 727–748.

(2017). Mass killings and images of genocide in Bosnia in 1941–45 and 1992–95. In: D. Stone, *The historiography of genocide*. New York: Palgrave Macmillan, pp. 487–516.

Hayner, P. (1996). International guidelines for the creation and operation of truth commissions: A preliminary proposal. *Law and Contemporary Problems, 59*(4), 173–180.

Hazan, P. (2010). *Judging war, judging history, behind peace and reconciliation*. Stanford, CA: Stanford University Press.

Heideman, L. (2016). Institutional amnesia: Sustainability and peacebuilding in Croatia. *Sociological Forum, 31*(2), 377–396.

Held, D. (2002). Law of states, law of peoples: Three models of sovereignty. *Legal Theory, 8*(1), 1–44.

Helman, S. (2002). Monologic results of dialogue: Jewish–Palestinian encounter groups as sites of essentialization. *Identities, 9*(3), 327–354.

Henkin, L. (2000). Human rights: Ideology and aspiration, reality and prospect. In: S. Power & G. Allison, *Realizing human rights: Moving from inspiration to impact*. New York: St Martins' Press, pp. 3–38.

Herman, E., & Peterson, D. (2010). *The politics of genocide*. New York: Monthly Review Press.

Herman, J. (1992). *Trauma and recovery*. New York: Basic Books.

Heywood, A. (2003). *Political ideologies* (3rd ed.). New York: Palgrave Macmillan.

Hilberg, R. (1993). *Perpetrators, victims, bystanders*. New York: Harper Collins.

Hill, T. (2008). 1948 after Oslo: Truth and reconciliation in Palestinian discourse. *Mediterranean Politics, 13*(2), 151–170.

Hirsch, M. B. J. (2007). From taboo to the negotiable: The Israeli New Historians and the changing representation of the Palestinian refugee problem. *Perspectives on Politics, 5*(02), 241–258.

Hochschild, A. (2012 [1983]). *The Managed heart: Commercialization of human feeling*. Berkeley: University of California Press.

(2016). *Strangers in their own land*. New York: New Press.

Hopgood, S. (2013). *The endtimes of human rights*. Ithaca, NY: Cornell University Press.

(2018). What is the greatest challenge to the future of human rights? We the people are. *Conversations*. Retrieved 19 May 2019 from https://theconversation.com/amp/what-is-the-greatest-challenge-to-the-future-of-human-rights-we-the-people-are-105428?

Horvatinčić, S. (2017). *Spomenici iz razdoblja socijalizma u hrvatskoj – prijedlog tipologije*. PhD thesis, Sveučilište u Zagrebu.

Huber, D. (2011). *Normative power Europe? The EU's foreign policy of democracy promotion in the Palestinian Authority*. KAS Working Paper 98. Jerusalem: Konrad-Adenauer- Stiftung.

Huntington, S. (1991). *The third wave: Democratization in the late twentieth century*. Norman: University of Oklahoma Press.

Husanović, J. (2015). Economies of affect and traumatic knowledge: Lessons on violence, witnessing and resistance in Bosnia and Herzegovina. *Ethnicity Studies*, *2*, 19–35.

Hutchinson, J. (2009). Warfare and the sacralisation of nations: The meanings, rituals and politics of national remembrance. *Millennium: Journal of International Studies*, *38*(2), 401–417.

Huyssen, A. (2003). *Present pasts*. Stanford, CA: Stanford University Press.

Hyatt, J. (2000). *An introduction to the non-profit sector in the Balkans*. West Malling: Charities Aid Foundation.

Hynes, P., Lamb, M., Short, D., & Waites, M. (2010). Sociology and human rights: Confrontations, evasions and new engagements. *International Journal of Human Rights*, *14*(6), 811–832.

Impunity Watch. (2013). Policy brief: Guiding principles of memorialisation. Retrieved 28 February 2020 from https://knowledge.hivos.org/sites/default/files/publications/2013iwpolicybriefguidingprinciplesofmemorialisationenglish_0.pdf

 (2015). Asia exchange report: 'Memory for change': Memorialisation as a tool for transitional Justice. Retrieved 28 February 2020 from http://historicaldialogues.org/2015/08/20/report-on-asia-exchange-memory-for-change/

Institute for War & Peace Reporting. (2006). Martic witness details Croatian war casualties. Retrieved 20 May 2019 from https://iwpr.net/global-voices/martic-witness-details-croatian-war-casualties

International Committee of the Red Cross. (2010). Croatia/Serbia: More action needed to find missing persons. Retrieved 28 February 2020 from www.refworld.org/docid/4cd290072.html

International Criminal Tribunal for the Former Yugoslavia. (2019). Key figures of the cases. Retrieved 20 May 2019 from www.icty.org/en/cases/key-figures-cases

International Federation of Red Cross and Red Crescent Societies. (2010). Croatia/Serbia: More action needed to find missing persons. *Refworld*. Retrieved 20 May 2019 from www.refworld.org/docid/4cd290072.html

International Holocaust Remembrance Alliance. (2016). Press release: IHRA plenary meetings Bucharest. Retrieved 28 February 2020 from www.holocaustremembrance.com/sites/default/files/post-bucharest_press_release.pdf

International Justice Resource Center. (2013). UN publishes guide for measuring human rights. Retrieved 28 February 2020 from https://ijrcenter.org/2013/02/19/un-publishes-guide-for-measuring-human-rights/

IPSOS. (2011). Nation building: Serbia. Retrieved 28 February 2020 from www.hf.uio.no/ilos/forskning/prosjekter/nation-w-balkan/dokumenter/nb_serbia.pdf

James, M., Baby, S., & Kressel, D. (2019). The Spanish model and its circulation in Latin America and Central Eastern Europe. Retrieved 28 February 2020 from http://passes-present.eu/fr/criminalising-violet-pasts-multiple-roots-and-forgotten-pathways-1950s-2010s-43830

Jansen, S. (2002). The violence of memories: Local narratives of the past after ethnic cleansing in Croatia. *Rethinking History*, *6*(1), 77–93.

Joas, H. (2013). *The sacredness of the person: A new genealogy of human rights.* Washington, DC: Georgetown University Press.
Joinet, L. (1996). *The administration of justice and the human rights of detainees: Question of the impunity of perpetrators of human rights violations (civil and political): Revised final report.* United Nations Special Rapporteur on the Impunity of Perpetrators of Violations of Human Rights (Civil and Political Rights). 1996/119.
Johnstone, G., & Van Ness, D. (2007). *Handbook of restorative justice.* Devon, UK: Willan Publishing.
Jones, C. (2009). The writing on the wall: Israel, the security barrier and the future of Zionism. *Mediterranean Politics, 14*(1), 3–20.
Jović, D. (2017). *Rat i mit: Politika identiteta u suvremenoj hrvatskoj.* Zaprešić: Fraktura.
Kabasakal Arat, Z. (2008). Human rights ideology and dimensions of power: A radical approach to the state, property, and discrimination. *Human Rights Quarterly, 30*(4), 906–932.
Karačić, D. (2012). Od promoviranja zajedništva do kreiranja podjela. In: *Re: vizija prošlosti: Politike sjećanja u Bosni I Hercegovini, Hrvatskoj i Srbiji od 1990 godine.* Sarajevo: ACIPS, pp. 17–78.
Karlsson, K. G. (2010). The uses of history and the third wave of Europeanization. In: M. Pakier & B. Strath (eds.), *A European memory? Contested histories and politics of remembrance.* Berghahn Books, pp. 38–55. Retrieved 28 February 2020 from https://books.google.ie/books/about/A_European_Memory.html?id=nSuKDs8UOBsC&printsec=frontcover&source=kp_read_button&redir_esc=y#v=onepage&q&f=false
Kelbler, J., & Stančić, M. (2016). Tito u eks-ju opstaje, a sve srpsko brišu. *Novosti.* Retrieved 20 May 2019 from www.novosti.rs/vesti/naslovna/drustvo/aktuelno.290.html:586449-Tito-u-eks-ju–opstaje-a-sve–srpsko-brisu
Kennedy, D. (2002). International human rights movement: Part of the problem? *Harvard Human Rights Journal, 15,* 106–126.
(2012). International human rights movement: Still part of the problem? In: R. Dickinson, E. Katselli, C. Murrey & O. Pederson, *Examining critical perspectives in human rights.* Cambridge: Cambridge University Pres, pp. 19–34.
Khalili, L. (2005). Places of memory and mourning: Palestinian commemoration in the refugee camps of Lebanon. *Comparative Studies of South Asia, Africa and the Middle East, 25*(1), 30–45.
Khoury, N. (2016). National narratives and the Oslo peace process: How peacebuilding paradigms address conflicts over history. *Nations and Nationalism, 22*(3), 465–483.
Kidron, C. (2009). Toward an ethnography of silence: The lived presence of the past in the everyday life of Holocaust trauma survivors and their descendants in Israel. *Current Anthropology, 50*(1), 5–27. doi: 10.1086/595623
(2012). Alterity and the particular limits of universalism comparing Jewish–Israeli Holocaust and Canadian–Cambodian genocide legacies. *Current Anthropology, 53*(6), 723–754. doi: 10.1086/668449
Kimmerling, B. (1983). *Zionism and territory: The socio-territorial dimensions of Zionist politics.* Berkeley: University of California Press.

Kiza, E., Rathgeber, C., & Rohne, H. (2006). *Victims of war: Aan empirical study on war-victimization and victims' attitudes towards addressing atrocities*. Hamburg: Hamburger Edition HIS Verlagsges.

Knežević, G. (2016). Yugo-nostalgia prevails in Serbia, Bosnia. Balkans without Borders. Retrieved 27 February 2020 from www.rferl.org/a/balkans-without-borders-yugo-nostalgia-serbia-bosnia/28511123.html

Kobalek, K. (2016). What is the context of memory? In: G. Sebald & J. Wagle, *Theorizing social memories: Concepts and contexts*. New York: Routledge, pp. 171–183.

Koldas, U. (2011). The Nakba in Palestinian memory in Israel. *Middle Eastern Studies, 47*(6), 947–959.

Koo, J., & Ramirez, F. (2009). National incorporation of global human rights: Worldwide expansion of national human rights institutions, 1966–2004. *Social Forces, 87*(3), 1321–1353. doi: 10.1353/sof.0.0167

Kressel, D. (2019). Getting off the tiger: The Spanish transition to democracy in Latin America's southern cone. *Global Society 33*(3): 316–331.

Kucia, M. (2016). The Europeanization of Holocaust memory and Eastern Europe. *East European Politics & Societies, 30*(1), 97–119.

Kuljić, T. (2002). *Prevladavanje prošlosti: Uzroci i pravci promene slike istorije krajem XX veka*. Beograd: Helsinške sveske.

(2005). Monumentalizacija srpske monarhije: O suvremenim debatama oko restauracije monarhije u Srbiji. *Časopis Za Suvremenu Povijest, 37*(2), 355–370.

Kumar, K. (2006). Ideology and sociology: Reflections on Karl Mannheim's Ideology and Utopia. *Journal of Political Ideologies, 12*(2), 169–181.

Kurbjuweit, D. (2010). Let down by the US: Why Germany needs Europe. *Der Spiegel Online – International*. Retrieved 19 May 2019 from www.spiegel.de/international/europe/let-down-by-the-us-why-germany-needs-europe-a-734430.html

Kurze, A., & Vukišić, I. (2013). Afraid to cry wolf: Human rights activists' struggle of transnational accountability efforts in the Balkans. In: O. Simić & Z. Volčić, *Civil society and transitional justice in the Balkans*. New York: Springer Series in Transitional Justice, pp. 201–214.

Laitin, D. (2007). *Nations, states, and violence*. Oxford: Oxford University Press.

Laitinen, A., & Pessi, A. B. (2014). *Solidarity: Theory and practice*. Lanham, MD: Lexington Books.

Lambek, M., & P. Antze (1996). Introduction: Forecasting memory. In: P. Antze & M. Lambek (eds.), *Tense past: Cultural essays in trauma and memory*. New York: Routledge, pp. xi–xxxviii.

Landman, T. (2004). Measuring human rights: Principle, practice and policy. *Human Rights Quarterly, 26*(4), 906–931.

Langer, L. (1996). The alarmed vision: Social suffering and Holocaust atrocity. *Daedalus, 125*(1), 47–65.

Le More, A. (2004). Foreign aid strategy. In: D. P. Cobham, *The economics of Palestine*. Oxfordshire: Routledge., pp. 205–227.

(2005). Killing with kindness: Funding the demise of a Palestinian state. *International Affairs, 81*(5), 981–999.

Levy, D., & Sznaider, N. (2002). Memory unbound: The Holocaust and the formation of cosmopolitan memory. *European Journal of Social Theory*, 5(1), 87–106.
  (2006). Sovereignty transformed: A sociology of human rights. *British Journal of Sociology*, 57(4), 657–676.
  (2010). *Human rights and memory*. University Park, PA: Pennsylvania State University Press.
Lindenberg, S. M. (1997). Grounding groups in theory: Functional, cognitive, and structural interdependencies. *Advances in Group Processes*, 14, 281–331.
  (2001). Social rationality versus rational egoism. In: J. Turner (ed.), *Handbook of sociological theory*. New York: Kluwer Academic/Plenum, pp. 635–668.
Linz, J., & Stepan, A. (1996). Toward consolidated democracies. *Journal of Democracy*, 7(2), 14–33.
Loshitzky, Y. (2006). Pathologising memory. *Third Text*, 20(3–4), 327–335.
Lubej, U. (2008). Nova razstava v Dolenjskem muzeju: Cesta, ki je spremenila Dolenjsko. [The new exhibition in the Lower Carniolan Museum: The road that transformed the Lower Carniola Park.] In Slovenian.
Lukić, R. (1993). *The wars of South Slavic succession: Yugoslavia 1991–1993*. PSIS Occasional Papers 2. Geneva: Graduate Institute of International Studies.
Luthar, B., & Puznik, M. (2010). *Remembering Utopia: The culture of everyday life in socialist Yugoslavia*. Washington, DC: New Academia Publishing.
Malešević, S. (1999). Globalism and nationalism: Which one is bad? *Development in Practice*, 9(5), 579–583.
  (2006a). Debate on Michael Mann's *The Dark Side of Democracy*: Explaining ethnic cleansing. *Nations and Nationalism*, 12, 389–411.
  (2006b). *Identity as ideology: Understanding ethnicity and nationalism*. New York: Palgrave Macmillan.
  (2010). *The Sociology of War and Violence*. Cambridge: Cambridge University Press.
  (2011a). Nationalism, war and social cohesion. *Ethnic and Racial Studies*, 34(1), 142–161.
  (2011b). Ideology. In: K. Dowding, *Encyclopaedia of power*. London: Sage Publications, pp. 333–339.
  (2012a). Wars that make states and wars that make nations: Prganised violence, nationalism and state formation in the Balkans. *European Journal of Sociology*, 53(1), 31–63.
  (2012b). Did wars make nation-states in the Balkans?: Nationalisms, wars and states in the 19th and early 20th century South East Europe. *Journal of Historical Sociology*, 25(3), 299–330.
  (2013a). *Nation-states and nationalisms: Organizations, ideology, solidarity*. Cambridge: Polity Press.
  (2013b). Obliterating heterogeneity through peace: Nationalisms, states and wars in the Balkans. In: J. Hall, *Nationalism and war*. Cambridge: Cambridge University Press, pp. 255–276.
  (2013c). Is nationalism intrinsically violent? *Nationalism and Ethnic Politics*, 19(1), 12–37.

(2017). *The rise of organised brutality: A historical sociology of violence.* Cambridge: Cambridge University Press.
Malešević, S., & Ó Dochartaigh, N. (2018). Why combatants fight: The Irish Republican Army and the Bosnian Serb Army compared. *Theory and Society, 47*(3), 293–326.
Malkki, L. (1996). Speechless emissaries: Refugees, humanitarianism, and dehistoricization. *Cultural Anthropology, 11*(3), 377–404.
Mälksoo, M. (2009). The memory politics of becoming European: The East European subalterns and the collective memory of Europe. *European Journal of International Relations, 15*(4), 653–680.
Malskoo, M. (2015). 'Memory must be defended': Beyond the politics of mnemonical security. *Security Dialogue 46*(3), 221–237.
Mann, M. (2004a). *Fascists.* Cambridge: Cambridge University Press.
  (2004b). *The dark side of democracy: Explaining ethnic cleansing.* Cambridge: Cambridge University Press.
  (2012). *The sources of social power III.* Cambridge: Cambridge University Press.
  (2013). *The sources of social power IV.* Cambridge: Cambridge University Press.
Mannheim, K. (1968 [1936]). *Ideology and Utopia: An introduction to the sociology of knowledge.* London: Routledge & K. Paul.
Manojlović, B. (2016). Beyond joint narrative of the past: Segregated and integrated schools in Eastern Slavonia. *Serbian Science Today, 1*(1), 30–43.
Maoz, I. (2000). An experiment in peace: Reconciliation-aimed workshops of Jewish-Israeli and Palestinian youth. *Journal of Peace Research, 37*(6), 721–736.
  (2004). Peace building in violent conflict: Israeli–Palestinian post-Oslo people-to-people activities. *International Journal of Politics, Culture, and Society, 17*(3), 563–574.
  (2011). Does contact work in protracted asymmetrical conflict? Appraising 20 years of reconciliation-aimed encounters between Israeli Jews and Palestinians. *Journal of Peace Research, 48*(1), 115–125.
Margalit, A. (2002). *The ethics of memory.* Cambridge, MA: Harvard University Press.
Markowitz, F. (2007). Census and sensibilities in Sarajevo. *Comparative Studies in Society and History, 49*(1), 40–73.
Marrus, M. (2007). Official apologies and the quest for historical justice. *Journal of Human Rights, 6*(1), 75–105.
Marshall, S. (1947). *Men against fire: The problem of battle command.* New York: Morrow.
Masalha, N. (2003). Israel's "New Historians" and the Nakba: A critique of Zionist discourse. In: N. Masalha (ed.), *The politics of denial: Israel and the Palestinian refugee question.* London: Pluto Press, pp. 49–67.
  (2009). 60 years after the Nakba: Historical truth, collective memory and ethical obligations. *Kyoto Bulletin of Islamic Area Studies, 3*(1), 8–37.
  (2012). *The Palestine Nakba: Decolonizing history, narrating the subaltern, reclaiming memory.* London: Zed.
McFarland, S. (2015). Culture, individual differences, and support for human rights: A general review. *Peace and Conflict: Journal of Peace Psychology, 21*(1), 10–27.

McFarland, S., & Mathews, M. (2005). Who cares about human rights? *Political Psychology*, *26*(3), 365–385.

McKone, K. (2015). *Reconciliation in practice*. Washington, DC: United States Institute for Peace.

McNeely, C. (2012). World polity theory. In: G. Ritzer, *The Wiley-Blackwell encyclopaedia of globalization*. Hoboken, NJ: Blackwell. Retrieved 28 February 2020 from https://doi.org/10.1002/9780470670590.wbeog834

Medieoperatørene. (2011). *Reunion: Ten years after the war* [Video]. Norway and Serbia.

Meral, Z. (2012). A duty to remember? Politics and morality of remembering past atrocities. *International Political Anthropology*, *5*(1), 29–50.

Meyer, J. (1987). The world polity and the authority of the nation-state. In: G. Thomas, J. Meyer, F. Ramirez & J. Boli, *Institutional structure: Constituting state, society, and the individual*. Newbury Park, CA: Sage, pp. 41–70.

Meyer, J., Boli, J., Thomas, G., & Ramirez, F. (1997). World society and the nation-state. *American Journal of Sociology*, *103*(1), 144–181.

Meyer, J., & Rowan, B. (1977). Institutionalized organizations: Formal structure as myth and ceremony. *American Journal of Sociology*, *83*(2), 340–363.

Micinski, N. (2016). NGO frequent flyers: Youth organisations and the undermining of reconciliation in Bosnia and Herzegovina. *Journal of Peacebuilding & Development*, *11*(1), 99–104.

Mijatović, V. (2008). Ime promenilo 1.500 ulica. *Novosti*. Retrieved 20 May 2019 from www.novosti.rs/vesti/beograd.74.html:226317-Ime-promenilo-1500-ulica

Milanović, B. (2017). Democracy of convenience, not of choice: Why is Eastern Europe different [Blog]. Retrieved 28 February 2020 from http://glineq.blogspot.com/2017/12/democracy-of-convenience-not-of-choice.html?m=1

Milerski, B. (2010). Holocaust education in Polish public schools: Between remembrance and civic education. *Prospects*, *40*(1), 115–132.

Milošević, A. (2017). Back to the future, forward to the past: Croatian politics of memory in the European Parliament. *Nationalities Papers*, *45*(5), 893–909.

Misco, T. (2008). 'We did also save people': A study of Holocaust education in Romania after decades of historical silence. *Theory & Research in Social Education*, *36*(2), 61–94.

Misztal, B. (2003). *Theories of social remembering*. Berkshire, UK: Open University Press.

(2010). Collective memory in a global age. *Current Sociology*, *58*(1), 24–44.

Mitscherlich, A., & Mitscherlich, M. (1975 [1967]). *The inability to mourn: Principles of collective behavior*. New York: Grove Press.

Močnik, N. (2019). Collective victimhood of individual survivors: Reflecting the uses and impacts of two academic narratives two decades after the war-rapes in Bosnia-Herzegovina. *East European Politics*, *35*(4), 457–473.

Moghadam, A. (2003). Palestinian suicide terrorism in the Second Intifada: Motivations and organizational aspects. *Studies in Conflict & Terrorism*, *26*(2), 65–92.

Moghaddam, F., & Vuksanović, V. (1990). Attitudes and behavior toward human rights across different contexts the role of right-wing authoritarianism,

political ideology, and religiosity. *International Journal of Psychology*, 25(2), 455–474.
Moje Vrijeme. (2015). *Hrvatska i BiH složne: U SFRJ se živjelo bolje*. Retrieved 28 February 2020 from www.mojevrijeme.hr/magazin/2015/04/hrvatska-i-bih-slozne-u-sfrj-se-zivjelo-bolje/
Moshe Kantor Database for the Study of Contemporary Antisemitism and Racism Team. (2014). *Antisemitism worldwide*. Tel Aviv: Tel Aviv University.
Moyn, S. (2012). *The last Utopia: Human rights in history*. Cambridge, MA: Belknap Press of Harvard University Press.
 (2018). *Not enough: Human rights in an unequal world*. Cambridge, MA: Harvard University Press.
Müller, W. (2015). Germany's two processes of 'coming to terms with the past': Failures, after all? In: V. Tismaneanu & B. Iacob, *Remembrance, history, and justice coming to terms with traumatic pasts in democratic societies*. Budapest and New York: Central European University Press, pp. 213–239.
Mutua, M. (1996). The ideology of human rights. *Virginia Journal of International Law*, 36, 589–657.
 (2001). Savages, victims, saviours: The metaphor of human rights. *Harvard International Law Journal*, 42(1), 201–245.
Nagengast, C., & Turner, T. (1997). Introduction: Universal human rights versus cultural relativity. *Journal of Anthropological Research*, 53(3), 269–272.
Nagy, R. (2008). Transitional Justice as Global Project: Critical reflections. *Third World Quarterly*, 29(2), 275–289.
Nansen. (2012). *Leaving the past behind: The perceptions of youth in Bosnia and Herzegovina. Report*. Sarajevo: Nansen Dialogue Center & Saferworld. Retrieved 28 February 2020 from http://file:///C:/Users/UCD/Downloads/Leaving%20the%20past%20behind_perceptions%20of%20youth%20in%20Bosnia%20and%20Herzegovina%20(2).pdf
Neier, A. (2012). *The international human rights movement: A history*. Princeton, NJ, and Oxford: Princeton University Press.
Nets-Zehngut, R. (2015). The role of direct-experience people in promoting transitional justice: The Israeli case. In: E. Bird & F. Ottanelli (eds.), *The performance of memory as transitional justice*. Cambridge: Intersentia, pp. 115–132.
Newman, D., & Yaakobi, H. (2004). *The role of the EU in the Israel\Palestine conflict*. Working Papers Series in EU Border Conflicts Studies no. 12. Beer Sheva: EU BorederConf.
Nolan, M. (2011). Gender and Utopian visions in a post-Utopian era: Americanism, human rights, market fundamentalism. *Central European History*, 44(1), 13–36.
Nora, P. (1996). General introduction: Between memory and history. In: P. Nora (ed.), *The realms of memory*. New York: Columbia University Press, pp. 1–21.
Norwegian Directorate for Development Cooperation(NORAD). (2017). Country evaluation brief: Palestine. Retrieved 28 February 2020 from www.norad.no/om-bistand/publikasjon/2017/country-evaluation-brief-palestine/
Norwegian–Serbian Coproduction. (2011). *Reunion: Ten years after the war*. [Film].

Obradović-Wochnik, J. (2013). The 'silent dilemma' of transitional justice: Silencing and coming to terms with the past in Serbia. *International Journal of Transitional Justice*, 7(2), 328–347.
  (2014). *Ethnic conflict and war crimes in the Balkans: The narratives of denial in post-conflict Serbia*. London: I. B. Tauris.
OHCHR. (2019). The independent expert on human rights and international solidarity. Retrieved 20 May 2019 from www.ohchr.org/EN/Issues/Solidarity/Pages/IESolidarityIndex.aspx
Olesen, T. (2012). Global injustice memories: The 1994 Rwanda genocide. *International Political Sociology*, 6(4), 373–389.
Olick, J. (2007). *The politics of regret*. New York: Routledge.
Olick, J., & Levy, D. (1997). Collective memory and cultural constraint: Holocaust myth and rationality in German politics. *American Sociological Review*, 62(6), 921–936.
Omer, A. (2009). It's nothing personal: The globalisation of justice, the transferability of protest, and the case of the Palestine solidarity movement. *Studies in Ethnicity and Nationalism*, 9(3), 497–518.
Orlić, O. (2017). Intercultural dialogue among the elderly in Zadar Area, Croatia. *International Journal of Culture and History (Ejournal)*, 3(3), 167–173.
Orlović, S. (2007). Europeanization and democratization of parties and party system of Serbia. *Politics in Central Europe*, 3(1–2), 92–104.
OSCE Office for Democratic Institutions and Human Rights. (2015a). Holocaust Memorial Days: An overview of remembrance and education in the OSCE region. Retrieved 20 May 2019 from www.osce.org/hmd2015
  (2015b). Teaching about and commemorating the Roma and Sinti genocide: Practices within the OSCE area. Retrieved 20 May 2019 from www.osce.org/romasintigenocide
  (2014). Report on Bosnia and Herzegovina: Roma in the genocide. Retrieved 28 February 2020 from http://roma-genocide.org/en/map/bosnia-and-herzegovina
Özyürek, E. (2018). Rethinking empathy: Emotions triggered by the Holocaust among the Muslim-minority in Germany. *Anthropological Theory*, 18(4), 456–477.
Parents Circle – Families Forum. (2017). Dialogue meetings. Retrieved 20 May 2019 from http://theparentscircle.org/en/pcff-activities_eng/dialogue_meetings_eng/
Pavasović-Trošt, T. (2013). War crimes as political tools: Bleiburg and Jasenovac in history textbooks 1973–2012. In: V. Stančetić & S. Janković, *(Mis)Uses of history: History as a political tool in the Western Balkans*. Belgrade: CSDU, pp. 13–47.
Pellet, A. (2000). 'Human rightism' and international law. Gilberto Amado Memorial Lecture, United Nations. Retrieved 28 February 2020 from http://pellet.actu.com/wp-content/uploads/2016/02/PELLET-2000-Human-rightism-and-international-law-G.-Amado.pdf
Perugini, N., & Gordon, N. (2015). *The human right to dominate*. Oxford: Oxford University Press.

Petrović, E. (2000). Ethnonationalism and the dissolution of Yugoslavia. In: Y. Halpern & D. Kideckel (eds.), *Neighbors at war: Anthropological perspectives on Yugoslav ethnicity, culture and history*. University Park: Pennsylvania University Press, pp. 164–176.

Porat, D. (2004). From the scandal to the Holocaust in Israeli education. *Journal of Contemporary History*, *39*(4), 619–636.

Power, M. (2000). Reconciliation, restoration and guilt: The politics of apologies. *Media International Australia Incorporating Culture and Policy*, *95*(1), 191–205.

Prošić-Dvornić, M. (2000). Serbia: The inside story. In: Y. Halpern & D. Kideckel (eds.), *Neighbors at war: Anthropological perspectives on Yugoslav ethnicity, culture and history*. University Park: Pennsylvania University Press, pp. 317–338.

Prtorić, J. (2017). How socialist Yugoslavia's legacy is being removed from the landscape. *The Srpska Times*. Retrieved 20 May 2019 from http://thesrpskatimes.com/how-socialist-yugoslavias-legacy-is-being-removed-from-the-landscape/

Pugh, M. (2002). Postwar political economy in Bosnia and Herzegovina: The spoils of peace. *Global Governance: A Review of Multilateralism and International Organizations*, *8*(4), 467–482.

Pundak, R. (2001). From Oslo to Taba: What went wrong? *Survival*, *43*(3), 31–45.

Pundak, R., Ben-Nun, A., & Finkel, L. (2012). More relevant than ever: People-to-people peacebuilding efforts in Israel and Palestine. *Palestine–Israel Journal*, *18*(2–3), 46–53.

Rabinowitz, D. (2001). Natives with jackets and degrees: Othering, objectification and the role of Palestinians in the co-existence field in Israel. *Social Anthropology*, *9*(1), 65–80.

Radaelli, C. (2003). The Europeanization of public policy. In: K. Featherstone & C. Radaelli (eds.), *The politics of Europeanization*. Oxford: Oxford University Press., pp. 27–57.

Radio Free Europe. (2017). Yugo-nostalgia prevails in Serbia, Bosnia. Retrieved 20 May 2019 from www.rferl.org/a/balkans-without-borders-yugo-nostalgia-serbia-bosnia/28511123.html

Radović, B. (2004). Yugoslav wars and some of their social consequences. In: Ž. Špiric, G. Knežević, V. Jović & G. Opačić (eds.), *Torture in war: Consequences and rehabilitation of the victims: Yugoslav experience*. Belgrade: IAD, pp. 25–68.

Radović, S. (2006). Gradski prostori od mesta do nemesta, i vice versa: Slučaj beogradskog Starog Sajmišta, Spomen mesta – istorija sećanja. *Zbornik Radova Etnografskog Instituta SANU*, *26*, 145–160.

Ramet, S. (2004). Explaining the Yugoslav meltdown, 1: 'For a charm of powerful trouble, Like a hell-broth boil and bubble':1 Theories about the roots of the Yugoslav troubles. *Nationalities Papers*, *32*(4), 731–763.

Rieff, D. (2017). *In praise of forgetting: Historical memory and its ironies*. New Haven, CT: Yale University Press.

Risse, T. (1999). International norms and domestic change: Arguing and communicative behavior in the human rights area. *Politics & Society*, *27*(4), 529–559.

Ritzer, G. (1996). *The McDonaldization of society: An investigation into the changing character of contemporary social life.* Thousand Oaks, CA: Pine Forge Press.

Rivera, L. (2008). Managing 'spoiled' national identity: War, tourism, and memory in Croatia. *American Sociological Review, 73*(4), 613–634.

Roht-Arriaza, N. (2004). Reparations in the aftermath of repression and mass violence. In: E. Stover & M. Harvey (eds.), *My neighbor, my enemy: Justice and community in the aftermath of mass atrocity.* Cambridge: Cambridge University Press, pp. 121–123.

Ron, Y., Maoz, I., & Bekerman, Z. (2010). Dialogue and ideology: The effect of continuous involvement in Jewish–Arab dialogue encounters on the ideological perspectives of Israeli-Jews. *International Journal of Intercultural Relations, 34*(6), 571–579.

Rosoux, V. (2016). Negotiating friendship: Franco–German and Franco–Algerian cases. *PIN Points, 43*, 13–19.

Ross, L., & Nisbett, R. E. (1991). *The person and the situation: Perspectives of social psychology.* New York: McGraw-Hill.

Rouhana, N., & Korper, S. (1997). Power asymmetry and goals of unofficial third party intervention in protracted intergroup conflict. *Peace and Conflict: Journal of Peace Psychology, 3*(1), 1–17.

Rouhana, N., & Sabbagh-Khoury, A. (2014). Settler-colonial citizenship: Conceptualizing the relationship between Israel and its Palestinian citizens. *Settler Colonial Studies, 5*(3), 205–225.

Roy, O. (2003). *Globalized Islam: The search for a new Ummah.* New York: Columbia University Press.

Rudd, K. (2008). Apology to Australia's indigenous peoples. ParlInfo. Retrieved 25 May 2019 from http://parlinfo.aph.gov.au/parlInfo/search/display/display.w3p;query=Id%3A%22chamber%2Fhansardr%2F2008-02-13%2F0003%22

Russou, H. (2007). History of memory, politics of the past, for what? In: K. Jarausch & T. Lindenberger (eds.), *Conflicted memories: Europeanizing contemporary histories.* Oxford: Berghahn Books, pp. 23–37.

Rydgren, J. (2007). The power of the past: A contribution to a cognitive sociology of ethnic conflict. *Sociological Theory, 25*(3), 225–244.

Sa'adi, A. (2002). Catastrophe, memory and identity: Al-Nakbah as a component of Palestinian identity. *Israel Studies, 7*(2), 175–198.

Saferworld. (August 2010). The missing peace: The need for a long-term strategy in Bosnia and Herzegovina. Retrieved 28 February 2020 from www.nansen-dialogue.net/pdf/missingp.pdf

Sagy, S., Adwan, S., & Kaplan, A. (2002). Interpretations of the past and expectations for the future among Israeli and Palestinian youth. *American Journal of Orthopsychiatry, 72*(1), 26–38.

Sahlins, M. (2013). Difference. *Oceania, 83*(3), 281–294.

Said, E. (1979). *The question of Palestine.* New York: Vintage Books.

(2001). *Blaming the victims: Spurious scholarship and the Palestinian question.* London and New York: Verso.

Sanbar, E. (2001). Out of place, out of time. *Mediterranean Historical Review, 16*(1), 87–94.

Schäuble, M. (2011). How history takes place: Sacralized landscapes in the Croatian–Bosnian border region. *History and Memory*, *23*(1), 23–61.
Schimmelfenning, F., & Sedlemeier, U. (2005). *The Europeanization of Central and Eastern Europe*. Ithaca, NY: Cornell University Press.
Schull, J. (1992). What is ideology? Theoretical problems and lessons from Soviet-type societies. *Political Studies*, *40*(4), 728–741.
Schwartz, B. (1996). Memory as a cultural system: Abraham Lincoln in World War II. *American Sociological Review*, *61*(5), 908–927.
Schwartz, B., Fukuoka, K., & Takita-Ishii, S. (2005). Collective memory: Why culture matters. In: M. Jacobs & N. Weiss Hanrahan, *The Blackwell companion to the sociology of culture*. Malden, MA: Blackwell, pp. 253–271.
Scott, J. (1995). Multiculturalism and the politics of identity. In: J. Rachman (ed.), *The identity in question*. London and New York: Routledge, pp. 3–12.
Segev, T. (1993). *The seventh million*. New York: Hill and Wang.
Sekulić, D., Massey, G., & Hodson, R. (1994). Who were the Yugoslavs? Failed sources of a common identity in the former Yugoslavia. *American Sociological Review*, *59*(1), 83–97.
Seliger, M. (1976). *Ideology and politics*. London: Routledge.
Sharp, D. N. (2013). Interrogating the peripheries: The preoccupations of fourth generation transitional justice. *Harvard Human Rights Journal*, *26*, 149–178.
Shils, E., & Janowitz, M. (1948). Cohesion and disintegration in the Wehrmacht in World War II. *Public Opinion Quarterly*, *12*(2), 280–315. doi: 10.1086/265951
Shlaim, A. (1995). The debate about 1948. *International Journal of Middle East Studies*, *27*(03), 287–304.
(2000). *Israel and the Arab world*. New York: Penguin Press.
Sikkink, K. (1993). The power of principled ideas: Human rights policies in the United States and Western Europe. In: J. Goldstein & R. O. Keohane, *Ideas and foreign policy: Beliefs, institutions and political change*. Ithaca, NY: Cornell University Press, pp. 139–72.
(2011). *The justice cascade: Human rights prosecutions and world politics*. New York: W. W. Norton.
(2017). *Evidence for hope: Making human rights work in the 21st century*. Princeton, NJ: Princeton University Press.
Sikkink, K., & Smith, J. (2002). Infrastructures for change: Transnational organizations. In: S. Khagram, J. Riker & K. Sikkink, *Restructuring world politics: Transnational social movements, networks, and norms*. Minneapolis: University of Minnesota Press, pp. 22–44.
Sjoberg, G., Gill, E., & Williams, N. (2001). A sociology of human rights. *Social Problems*, *48*(1), 11–47.
Smith, A. (1981). War and ethnicity: The role of warfare in the formation, self-images and cohesion of ethnic communities. *Ethnic and Racial Studies*, *4*(4), 375–397.
Smith, C., & Sorrell, K. (2014). On social solidarity. In: V. Jeffries (ed.), *The Palgrave handbook of altruism, morality, and social solidarity: Formulating a field of study*. New York: Palgrave Macmillan, pp. 219–249.

Sorek, T. (2013). Calendars, martyrs, and Palestinian particularism under British rule. *Journal of Palestine Studies*, *43*(1), 6–23.
Spangled, E. (2015). *Understanding Israel/Palestine: Race, nation, and human rights in the conflict*. Rotterdam, Boston and Taipai: Sense Publishers.
Spini, D., & Doise, W. (1998). Organizing principles of involvement in human rights and their social anchoring in value priorities. *European Journal of Social Psychology*, *28*(4), 603–622.
Stannard, D. (1996). Uniqueness as denial: The politics of genocide scholarship. In: S. A. Rosenbaum (ed.), *Is the Holocaust unique?* Boulder, CO: Westview Press, pp. 163–208.
Starl, K., Apostolovski, V., Meier, I., Möstl, M., Vivona, M., & Kulmer, A. (2017). *Human rights indicators in the context of the European Union*. Graz: FRAME, European Commission.
Sterchele, D. (2007). The limits of inter-religious dialogue and the form of football rituals: The case of Bosnia-Herzegovina. *Social Compass*, *54*(2), 211–224.
Stetter, S. (2003). Democratization without democracy? The assistance of the European Union for democratization processes in Palestine. *Mediterranean Politics*, 8(2–3), 153–173.
Stojanović, D. (2009). Slika ratova devedesetih u srpskim udžbenicima istorije (1993–2005). In: T. Cipek & S. Bosko (eds.), *Kultura sjećanja: 1991. Povijesni lomovi i svladavanje prošlosti*. Zagreb: Disput, pp. 343–359.
Stone, D. (2006). Memory and genocide. In: D. Bloxham & D. Moses, *The Oxford handbook of genocide studies*. Oxford: Oxford University Press, pp. 1–2.
Štrbac, S. (1999). *Zločini nad Srbima na prostoru Hrvatske u periodu 90–99*. Beograd: Bilten – vanredni broj, Dokumentacioni Informacioni Centar Veritas, pp. 2–11.
Subotić, J. (2009). *Hijacked justice: Dealing with the past in the Balkans*. Ithaca, NY, and London: Cornell University Press.
 (2019). *Yellow star, red star: Holocaust remembrance after communism*. Ithaca, NY: Cornell University Press.
Swidler, A. (1986). Culture in action: Symbols and strategies. *American Sociological Review*, *51*(2), 273. doi: 10.2307/2095521
Sznaider, N. (1998). The sociology of compassion: A study in the sociology of morals. *Cultural Values*, *2*(1), 117–139.
 (2015). Compassion, cruelty, and human rights. In: R. Anderson, *World suffering and quality of life*. Dordrecht: Springer, pp. 55–65.
Talal, A. (2000). What do human rights do? An anthropological enquiry. *Theory and Event*, *4*(4), 1–16.
Tarrow, S. (1994). *Power in movement: Social movements and contentious politics*. New York: Cambridge University Press.
Teitel, R. (2003). Transitional justice genealogies. *Harvard Human Rights Journal*, *16*, 69–94.
The Srpska Times. (2017). How socialist Yugoslavia's legacy is being removed from the landscape. Retrieved 28 February 2020 from http://thesrpskatimes.com/how-socialist-yugoslavias-legacy-is-being-removed-from-the-landscape/

Thompson, J. (2002). *Taking responsibility for the past*. Cambridge: Polity Press.
(2008). Apology, justice, and respect: A critical defense of political apology. In: M. Gibney, R. Howard-Hassmann, J. Coicaud & N. Steiner, *The age of apology: Facing up to the past*. Philadelphia: University of Pennsylvania Press, pp. 31–44.
(2009). Apology, historical obligations and the ethics of memory. *Memory Studies*, 2(2), 195–210.
Todorov, T. (2003). *Hope and memory: Lessons from the twentieth century*. Princeton, NJ: Princeton University Press.
Tokača, M. (2013). *The Bosnian book of the dead*. Sarajevo and Beograd: Research and Documentation Centre (IDC) & Humanitarian Law Center of Serbia.
Tunbridge, J., & Ashworth, G. (1996). *Dissonant heritage*. Chichester: John Wiley & Sons.
Turner, B. (1993). Outline of a theory of human rights. *Sociology*, 27(3), 489–512. doi: 10.1177/0038038593027003009
(2011). The rights of age: On human vulnerability. In: J. Blau & M. Frezzo, *Sociology and human rights: A Bill of Rights for the twenty-first century*. Thousand Oaks, CA: Sage, pp. 201–222.
Turner, M. (2012). Completing the circle: Peacebuilding as colonial practice in the occupied Palestinian territory. *International Peacekeeping*, 19(4), 492–507.
United Nations Country Team. (2013). Common county assessment Bosnia Herzegovina. Retrieved 28 February 2020 from www.undp.org/content/dam/unct/bih/PDFs/Prism%20Research%20for%20UN%20RCO_Report.pdf
United Nations General Assembly. (1985). Declaration of basic principles of justice for victims of crime and abuse of power. A/RES/40/34. Retrieved 28 February 2020 from www.un.org/en/genocideprevention/documents/atrocity crimes/Doc.29_declaration%20victims%20crime%20and%20abuse%20of%20power.pdf
(2013). Report of the Special Rapporteur in the field of cultural rights. Historical and memorial narratives in divided societies: History textbooks, memorials and museums. A/68/296. Retrieved 28 February 2020 from www.ohchr.org/EN/Issues/CulturalRights/Pages/HistoricalMemorialNarratives.aspx
(2014). Report of the Special Rapporteur in the field of cultural rights, Shaheed F: Memorialization processes. A/HRC/25/49. Retrieved 28 February 2020 from https://digitallibrary.un.org/record/766862?ln=en#record-files-collapse-header
United Nations High Commissioner for Human Rights. (1985). The declaration of basic principles of justice for victims of crime and abuse of power. A/RES/40/3. Retrieved 28 February 2020 from www.ohchr.org/EN/ProfessionalInterest/Pages/VictimsOfCrimeAndAbuseOfPower.aspx
United Nations Regional Information Centre. (2014). Transitional justice. Retrieved 28 February 2020 from www.unric.org/html/english/library/backgrounders/transitionaljustice.pdf
United Nations Relief and Work Agency for Palestinian Refugees in the Near East. (n.d.). Palestine refugees. Retrieved 28 February 2020 from www.unrwa.org/palestine-refugees

United Nations Security Council. (1992). An agenda for peace: Preventive diplomacy, peace-making and peacekeeping. A/47/277 - S/24111. Retrieved 28 February 2020 from https://peaceoperationsreview.org/wp-content/uploads/2015/08/an_agenda_for_peace_1992.pdf

(1994). Final report of the United Nations Commission of Experts established pursuant to Security Council resolution 780. Retrieved 28 February 2020 from www.icty.org/x/file/About/OTP/un_commission_of_experts_report1994_en.pdf

United States Institute of Peace. (2007). The urge to remember: The role of memorials in social reconstruction and transitional justice. Stabilization and Reconstruction series no. 5. Retrieved 28 February 2020 from www.usip.org/sites/default/files/srs5.pdf

Usher, G. (2005). Unmaking Palestine: On Israel, the Palestinians, and the wall. *Journal of Palestine Studies*, 35(1), 25–43.

Van Lange, P. A. M. (2000). Beyond self-interest: A set of propositions relevant to interpersonal orientations. In: W. Stroebe & M. Hewstone (eds.), *European review of social psychology*, Vol. 11. New York: Wiley, pp. 297–331.

Van Ness, D., & Strong, H. K. (2010). *Restoring justice: An introduction to restorative justice*. 4th ed. New Province, NJ: Matthew Bender & Co.

Velikonja, M. (2008). *Titonostalgia: A study of nostalgia for Josip Broz Tito*. Ljubljana: Peace Institute.

(2009). Lost in transition: Nostalgia for socialism in post-socialist countries. *East European Politics and Societies*, 23(4), 535–551.

Veritas. (2014). *Srpske žrtve rata i poraća na području Hrvatske i bivše RSK 1990 – 1998. Godine*. Dokumentaciono Informacioni Centar Veritas. Retrieved 20 May 2019 from www.veritas.org.rs/srpske-zrtve-rata-i-poraca-na-podrucju-hrvatske-i-bivse-rsk-1990-1998-godine/

Vinitzky-Seroussi, V. (2002). Commemorating a difficult past: Yitzhak Rabin's memorials. *American Sociological Review*, 67(1): 30.

Vollhardt, J., & Bilewicz, M. (2013). After the genocide: Psychological perspectives on victim, bystander, and perpetrator groups. *Journal of Social Issues*, 69(1), 1–15.

Vukosavljević, N. (2011). *Preparing for non-violence: Experiences in the Western Balkans*. Berlin: Bergof Foundation, pp. 266–284.

Wagner-Pacifici, R., & Schwartz, B. (1991). The Vietnam Veterans Memorial: Commemorating a difficult past. *American Journal of Sociology*, 97(2), 376–420.

Wallerstein, I. (2004). *World-systems analysis: An introduction*. Durham, NC, and London: Duke University Press.

Weber, M., Henderson, A. M., & Parsons, T. (1947). *The theory of social and economic organization*. New York: Oxford University Press.

Weenink, D. (2014). Frenzied attacks: A micro-sociological analysis of the emotional dynamics of extreme youth violence. *British Journal of Sociology*, 65(3), 411–433.

Wellman, C. (2000). Solidarity, the individual and human rights. *Human Rights Quarterly*, 22(3), 639–657.

Welsh, H. (1996). Dealing with the Communist past: Central and East European experiences after 1990. *Europe–Asia Studies*, 48(3), 413–428.

Welzer, H., & Neitzel, S. (2012). *Soldaten: On fighting, killing and dying*. New York: Knopf.
White, R. (2000). Issues in the study of political violence: Understanding the motives of participants in small group political violence. *Terrorism and Political Violence, 12*(1), 95–108.
Wikan, U. (1988). Bereavement and loss in two Muslim communities: Egypt and Bali compared. *Social Science & Medicine, 27*(5), 451–460.
Winter, J. (2007). The generation of memory: Reflections on the 'memory boom'. *Contemporary Historical Studies: Canadian Military History, 10*(3), 57–66.
Women in Black. (2015). Ženski sud – feministički pristup pravdi. [Video]. Retrieved 28 February 2020 from www.zenskisud.org/filmovi.html
Woodward, A. (1995). *The harmony of illusions: Inventing post-traumatic stress disorder*. Princeton, NJ: Princeton University Press.
Woodward, S. (1995). *Socialist unemployment: The political economy of Yugoslavia, 1945–1990*. Princeton, NJ: Princeton University Press.
World Bank. (2008). Implementing the Palestinian reform and development agenda: Economic monitoring report to the Ad Hoc Liaison Committee. Retrieved 28 February 2020 from www.un.org/unispal/document/auto-insert-208572/
Yerkes, M. (2004). Facing the violent past: Discussions with Serbia's youth. *Nationalities Papers, 32*(4), 921–938.
Young, A. (1995). *The harmony of illusions: Inventing post-traumatic stress disorder*. Princeton, NJ: Princeton University Press.
Young, J. (1993). *The texture of memory: Holocaust memory and meaning*. New Haven, CT: Yale University Press.
Youth Initiative for Human Rights. (2014). Regional youth exchange program in the Western Balkans countries. Retrieved 20 May 2019 from www.yihr.rs/en/regional-youth-exchange-program-in-the-western-balkans-countries/
(2015). Outcomes to date: Youth Initiative for Human Rights – Croatia. Retrieved 27 February 2020 from http://yihr.hr/wp-content/uploads/2015/01/YIHR-Outcomes-to-date-2015-1.pdf
Zahr, H. (1990). *Changing lenses: A new focus on crime and justice*. Harrisonburg: Herald Press.
Zehfuss, M. (2006). Remembering to forget/forgetting to remember. In: D. Bell, *Memory trauma and world politics: Reflections on the relationship between past and present*. New York: Palgrave Macmillan, pp. 213–231.
Zelizer, V. (1994). *The social meaning of money*. Princeton, NJ: Princeton University Press.
Zertal, I. (2005). *Israel's Holocaust and the politics of nationhood*. Cambridge: Cambridge University Press.
Zerubavel, Y. (2002). The mythological Sabra and Jewish past: Trauma, memory, and contested identities. *Israel Studies, 7*(2), 115–144.
Žižek, S. (2005). Against human rights. *New Left Review, 34*, 115–131.
Zwierzchowski, J., & Tabeau, E. (2010). The 1992–95 war in Bosnia and Herzegovina: Census-based multiple system estimation of casualties undercount. Conference Paper for the European Population Conference, Vienna.

Index

accountability, 50, 61, 194
Adorno, Theodor, 6, 24, 56
Alexander, Jeffrey, 56, 114, 131, 173, 180
Althusser, Louis, 24
American Anthropological Association, The, 26–27
amnesia, 5, 115
Amnesty International, 3, 43, 109, 168
anti-nostalgia, 115
anti-Zionism, 92
Arendt, Hannah, 24, 31
Argentina, 17, 57, 90
Australia, 46, 193, 199
Austria, 57, 192, 197

Balfour Declaration, 76
Bauman, Zygmunt, 29
Bekerman, Zvi, 144, 148, 152, 161, 165, 167
Belgium, 63, 182, 193, 197
Bergholz, Max, 106, 137, 153, 158
BiH. *See* Bosnia and Herzegovina
Bleiburg, 115, 119
Bob, Clifford, 126, 199
Bosnia and Herzegovina, 9, 17–18, 66, 69, 95, 103, 108–109, 117–118, 121, 140, 162, 180
Boycott, Divestment and Sanctions movement, The, 84, 135, 212
Brandt, Willy, 1
brotherhood and unity, 103–106, 116, 137
Brubaker, Rogers, 38, 107, 127, 153, 181
Burma, 17
Burundi, 17

Cambodia, 17, 52
Centre for Nonviolent Action, The, 139–140, 144, 156, 158, 160, 163, 165–166, 170–171
centrifugal ideologization, 35
Chetniks, 105, 115, 119
Chile, 17, 48, 51, 58

China, 46, 90
class divisions, 15
Cold War, 205
Collins, Randall, 18, 36, 38, 126, 129, 131–132, 144, 148, 159, 162, 172, 179
colonial project. *See* colonialism
colonialism, 31, 68, 93, 184, 188, 195
Colonialism Law, The, 198
Combatants for Peace, 164
Comte, August, 128
Convention on the Prevention and Punishment of the Crime of Genocide, The, 46, 196
Croatia, 9, 15, 17, 66–67, 69, 95, 97–99, 101, 103, 107–113, 115–116, 118–121, 132, 137–138, 140, 150, 154–155, 158–159, 162, 168, 170, 178, 190, 198–199
cultural relativism, 22, 27, 30
Czech Republic, The, 197

Dayton Agreement, The, 13, 95–97, 99, 120, 138
dealing with the past. *See* facing the past, *See* facing the past
Declaration on the Homeland War, The, 198
dialogue groups, 18–19, 41, 115, 133, 135, 137–138, 140–141, 155, 189, 208
dialogue industry, 135
dogmatic power. *See* ideological power
Dokumenta, 141, 170
Donnelly, Jack, 28, 33, 35
Durkheim, Emile, 5, 26–29, 33, 36, 128–129, 131
duty to remember, 1, 6–7, 13–14, 17, 20, 41, 54, 59, 61, 64, 66, 90, 94, 114, 172, 183, 185, 189, 210

Eastern Europe, 48, 57–58, 99, 108, 121, 125, 191
Egypt, 17, 175

Index

emotional energy, 18, 131–132, 142–143, 151, 159–162, 164, 166–167, 179–180
Engels, Friedrich, 24
essentialization, 19, 148, 151, 153, 163
Estonia, 191, 195
ethnic boundaries, 97, 153, 155, 170, 181–182, 197
ethnic cleansing, 77, 87, 89, 96, 110
ethnicization, 153, 182
European Instrument for Democracy and Human Rights, The, 75
European Neighbourhood Policy, The, 74
Europeanization process, 91, 96–97, 101–103, 111, 117, 143, 190

face-to-face encounters, 11, 18, 125–126, 128, 132, 134–135, 138, 140–145, 148, 151–153, 155, 158–159, 163–165, 167–168, 171, 181–182, 210
facing the past, 1, 7, 13–15, 17, 19–20, 37, 41, 43, 52–53, 56, 59, 61–62, 64, 94, 99, 111, 114–115, 124, 132, 141, 145, 158, 170, 172–174, 181–183, 185, 189, 210
Federation of Bosnia and Herzegovina, The, 117
France, 23, 31, 46, 55, 197
Franco-German partnership, 55, 138
Frankfurt School, 24

Galtung, Johan, 71
Gaza, 71, 73, 77, 80–81, 83, 133, 137
Genocide Convention, The, 46
genocide resolutions, 67, 100
German model, 7, 61
German-Franco partnership, 137
Germany, 6, 45, 55, 59, 86, 90, 92, 121, 183, 192, 196–197, 199
Goffman, Erving, 129, 131, 145
Goodale, Mark, 27, 31, 33, 38, 47, 188
Gramsci, Antonio, 24
Greece, 195
Guatemala, 17, 48, 199

Halbwachs, Maurice, 5
Hayden, Robert, 97, 173–174
Helman, Sara, 148, 151, 153, 182
Heywood, Andrew, 23, 32
historical justice, 41, 58, 68–69, 84, 194, 199, 204, 211
historical narratives, 13, 19, 74, 89, 94, 111, 143–144, 146, 149, 153–155, 158–159, 161, 163
Historikerstreit, historian debate, 6, 56
history of mentalities, 5

Holocaust, 10, 45, 61, 63, 67, 69, 73, 76, 83–89, 91–93, 114, 120–122, 150, 152, 174, 176, 181–182, 184, 189–192, 202
Holocaust denial, 84, 197
Holocaust education, 88, 90, 121, 189–191
Holocaust remembrance, 84, 90, 121–122, 184, 190–192
Hong-Kong, 90
Hopgood, Stephen, 188, 201, 209–210
human frailty, 28
Human Rights Council, The, 37
human rights ideology, 9, 12, 15–16, 21, 33, 35–36, 39, 44, 180, 186, 199, 201, 203
human rights values, 2, 4, 8–9, 11, 15, 19–20, 39, 42, 45, 50, 64–65, 94, 103, 114, 123–124, 128, 143, 151, 166–167, 172, 181, 183, 185, 187, 192, 198, 206–207, 211
Human Rights Watch, The, 3, 183
Hutu, 14, 63, 182

ideological power, 9, 11, 13, 16, 22, 32, 34–35, 38, 40–43, 45, 54, 64, 104, 142, 166, 184, 186, 195
ideology, 23–25, 209
Impunity Watch, 17, 52, 114
Indonesia, 17
Interaction Ritual Theory, 132, 172
interaction rituals, 18, 146, 167
International Bill of Rights, The, 32, 204
international community, 1, 17–18, 50, 70, 89, 96, 99, 101, 114, 178, 189, 198
International Covenant on Civil and Political Rights, The, 45, 197
International Criminal Tribunal for Yugoslavia, The, 67, 99, 109
International Holocaust Remembrance Alliance, The, 90, 121, 184
International Sociological Association, 29
isomorphism, 1, 8, 34, 41, 68, 93, 189
Israel, 9, 13, 15, 17–18, 46, 66, 68–69, 72, 75–76, 79, 81–85, 87–89, 91–93, 97, 99, 103, 123, 132–137, 142–144, 147, 151, 154, 160, 164, 167–168, 171, 182, 184, 197–198, 206, 231
Israeli-Palestinian conflict, 67–68, 70, 75, 82, 86, 90–91, 93
Italy, 199

Japan, 46, 55, 193, 199
Jasenovac, 115, 121, 173, 184, 190
Jordan, 78, 81

justice for victims, 1, 7, 13, 17, 41, 43, 50, 52, 54, 64, 94, 121, 172, 179, 185, 189, 237

Kidron, Carol, 11, 63, 175–176
Kosovo, 17, 105, 140, 163

Latin America, 6, 29, 48, 56–57
Latvia, 191
Lebanon, 78, 81
Levy, Daniel, 34, 49, 85, 90, 92, 180, 188, 191
liberal peace, 11, 22, 56
Liechtenstein, 197
Lithuania, 191, 197

Macedonia, 103, 118, 141, 164, 191
Malešević, Siniša, 9, 11, 16, 22, 25, 35–36, 38, 106, 127, 130, 132, 153, 209–210
Mannheim, Karl, 24, 33, 36
Maoz, Ifat, 133, 165, 167–168, 172
Marx, Karl, 22–23, 26
Mauss, Marcel, 131
memorialization
    policies, 8, 51, 53, 183
memorialization laws, 189, 196
memorialization standards, 4, 43, 53–54, 62, 66
memorialization, proper, 3, 5, 61, 68
memory
    national, 2, 174
    standardization of, 12, 42
memory activism, 41
memory laws, 41, 197–198, 200
memory, Palestinian, 78
memory, securitization of, 195
micro-solidarity, 11, 36–37, 39, 67, 124–128, 131–132, 142, 151, 153, 159, 161, 165, 169, 172, 182, 187, 209
Middle East, 29, 66, 74, 77, 134
Mitscherlich, Alexander and Margarete, 56
Mogherini, Federica, 114
Moyn, Samuel, 13, 31, 35, 38, 47–48, 205, 212
museums, 2, 4, 16, 41, 51, 53, 90, 102, 104, 112, 127, 167, 189, 192, 195

Nakba, 69, 73, 76–79, 81–84, 89, 93, 150, 152, 181
Nakba Law, The, 80, 83, 198
NANSEN Dialogue Center, 138, 146, 149–150, 155, 157, 163, 168
national calendars, 16, 112, 127, 167, 195–196
nationalism, 35, 43, 78, 90, 106, 189, 192, 195, 200, 203

nationalism, ethnically-based, 4, 64, 106–107
nationalist ideology, 15, 20
Neier, Aryeh, 205
Nepal, 17
Netanyahu, Binyamin, 83–84, 133
Netherlands, The, 46, 197
nostalgia, 115, 119
Nuremberg trials, 45

Occupied Palestinian Territories, 76, 79, 137
Office of the High Representative, The, 96, 98, 100
Open Society Institute, The, 17
Organization for Security and Co-operation in Europe, The, 3, 91, 114, 120, 122
organizational power, 7, 9, 11, 13, 22, 32, 35, 37, 39, 42–43, 47, 53–54, 64, 104, 124, 126, 186
orientalization, 161
Oslo Accords, The, 13, 18, 68, 70–73, 76, 79–80, 89, 93, 97, 133

Palestine, 9, 13, 15, 17–18, 66–69, 72, 74, 76–78, 81–83, 97, 99, 103, 123, 125, 132–133, 136, 142–143, 154
Palestinian Authority, 10, 73, 75, 133
Palestinian Liberation Organization, The, 70, 78–79, 82–83, 147
Palestinian refugees, 72–74, 76–77, 79, 81, 83
Parents Circle - Families Forum, The, 135, 160, 164
Partisans, 104, 108, 115
peace industry, 64, 71, 141
peacebuilding, 3, 13, 20, 41, 50, 70, 72–73, 76, 84, 89, 97, 99–100, 111, 123, 133–134, 138–139, 159, 168, 170
Pellet, Alain, 31
Philippines, The, 46, 48
Poland, 46, 48, 57, 88, 174, 190–191, 195, 197, 199
Polish Law, The, 198
politics of regret. *See* public apologies
poverty, 37–38, 97–98, 184
psychoanalysis, 6, 25, 56, 62–63, 174
public apologies, 4, 41, 189, 192–195

racial inequality, 38
radical sociologists, 28
RECOM, 17, 141
reconciliation, 1–3, 7, 41, 48–52, 54–55, 57–59, 70–71, 73, 95, 98–99, 111–112, 114, 138–139, 145–146, 155, 158–159, 168, 170, 173–174, 204

Index

regimes, totalitarian, 3, 125
Regional Youth Cooperation Office, The, 141–142, 168, 182
remembrance
  proper way of, 1, 19, 59, 90, 138, 183
reparations, 41, 48, 51–53, 61, 102, 132, 161, 193–194, 199, 204
Republika Srpska, 95, 98–99, 110, 112–113, 117, 146, 157, 162, 170, 203
Responsibility to Protect, The, 50
restorative justice, 49–50, 59
revisionism, 61, 80, 114–115, 119, 195, 198–200
Rieff, David, 186
Romania, 46, 190, 197
Rwanda, 49, 63, 182

Second Intifada, The, 74, 135–136, 167
Separation Wall, The, 136
Serbia, 9, 15, 17, 66–67, 69, 97–99, 101, 103, 105, 107, 111–122, 132, 137–139, 141, 150, 154–155, 158–159, 162, 164, 168, 170, 176, 178–179, 190–191, 199
Sikkink, Kathryn, 34, 44, 50, 205, 207
silence, 57, 61, 63, 85–86, 115, 161, 176
Slovakia, 197
social inequality, 15, 20, 29, 37, 200–201, 203
socialism, 103–105, 119
sociology and human rights, 21, 26, 28–30, 37
South Africa, 17, 48, 55, 57, 59, 90, 193
South Korea, 192
Spain, 57, 151, 197
Spanish model, 55, 58
Srebrenica
  mass killing, 1, 67, 100, 109, 114, 140, 154, 161–162, 173, 184, 202
Sri Lanka, 17
Stanford School, The, 44
structural inequality, 134, 153
suffering, hierarchies of. *See* victimhood, hierarchies of
Switzerland, 197
Syria, 78, 81
Sznaider, Natan, 11, 30, 34, 47, 49, 58, 85, 90, 92, 180, 191

Teitel, Ruti, 33, 50
Thailand, 17
Timor Leste, 17
Tito, Josip Broz, 104, 106, 108, 116–117

transitional justice, 2–3, 17, 46, 48–52, 55–56, 60, 63–64, 67, 95, 99, 102, 111–112, 170, 176, 194, 202
Treaty of Versailles, The, 196
Treaty of Westphaliam, The, 196
Turkish Penal Code, The, 198
Turner, Bryan, 27–29, 37, 72

Ukraine, 190, 199
UN International Police Task Force, The, 96
United Nations, 3–4, 17
United Nations Office of the High Commissioner for Human Rights, The, 208
United Nations Relief and Works Agency, The, 81
United States Institute for Peace, The, 17, 51, 114
Universal Declaration of Human Rights, The, 8, 26, 43, 45, 47, 196
universalism, 22, 27–28, 30, 44, 54, 63, 175, 177
Uruguay, 48, 90
Ustaše, 105, 115–116, 119–120, 173, 190

Van Leer Institute, The, 17
victimhood, activism of, 201
victimhood, hierarchies of, 202
victimhood, Jewish, 85–86, 93
victimhood, politics of, 15, 201
violence,
  recurrence of, 43
violence, recurrence of, 2, 64
Vučić, Aleksandar, 1, 114

Walesa, Lech, 125
Weber, Max, 26, 28, 129
West Bank, The, 72–73, 77, 80–81, 83, 133, 136
Western Balkans, The, 13, 18, 66–68, 97, 101, 112, 120, 123, 133, 137, 143, 154, 179
world polity level, 2, 4, 8–9, 13, 17, 33–35, 42, 66, 90, 166

Yad Vashem, 85, 87
Youth Initiative for Human Rights, The, 140, 161–162
Yugoslav Communist Party, 105–107
Yugoslav People's Army, 104, 156
Yugoslavia, 18, 49–50, 67, 97, 103–105, 107, 110, 115–119, 137, 140, 155–156, 158, 170, 179

Zionism, 76, 80, 85, 88–89, 91

CPSIA information can be obtained
at www.ICGtesting.com
Printed in the USA
LVHW081341140622
721112LV00009B/394